IMAGINING JEWISH A

IMAGINING JEWISH AUTHENTICITY

VISION AND TEXT IN AMERICAN JEWISH THOUGHT

Ken Koltun-Fromm

Indiana University Press

Bloomington & Indianapolis

This book is a publication of

Indiana University Press
Office of Scholarly Publishing
Herman B Wells Library 350
1320 East 10th Street
Bloomington, Indiana 47405 USA

iupress.indiana.edu

Manufactured in the United States of America

Library of Congress Cataloging-in-Publication Data

Koltun-Fromm, Ken, author.
  Imagining Jewish authenticity: vision and text in
American Jewish thought / Ken Koltun-Fromm.
    pages cm
    Includes bibliographical references and index.
    ISBN 978-0-253-01570-9 (hardback : alk. paper) — ISBN 978-0-
253-01574-7 (pbk. : alk. paper) — ISBN 978-0-253-01579-2 (ebook)
1. Judaism—United States. 2. Jews—United States—Identity.
3. Jews—United States—Intellectual life. 4. Metaphor. I. Title.
  BM205.K648 2015
  296.0973—dc23
                                                      2014027403

1 2 3 4 5   20 19 18 17 16 15

For my children: Ariel, Talia, and Isaiah

Contents

Acknowledgments

It HAS BECOME an unspoken obligation among us all to sit at the kitchen table for dinner each evening, so long as we are present at our home on the Haverford College campus outside of Philadelphia. One evening our youngest son, alert to his Jewish day school upbringing, asked this question: what is the holiest thing in the world? Naomi and I knew the right answer, or the answer Isaiah imagined he was supposed to hear from us. I obliged, and told him *Torah* was the holiest thing, but Naomi said what first came to my mind: family.

I tend to see the world as ever widening circles of family: some closer, others farther away, and still others barely visible but nonetheless present. Indeed, in all honesty, I am inclined to understand my Jewish heritage and my Judaism in this way too. I also recognize my obligations to others in these terms, and I have been blessed to feel that commitment from them as well. This acknowledgment is but a small reminder that so many friends have become family, and so many of my family have become dear to me. My circle is strong because it is becoming ever so expansive.

The students at Haverford College are exceptional, and it is a distinct honor to be in the classroom with young adults who cultivate intellectual integrity and creativity. Diane Tracht is one of those students who, from her very first year here, have courageously challenged my views, and her progressive, fearless but ever compassionate voice has deeply influenced my own. Aaron Madow worked tirelessly as my student research assistant to analyze the journal *The Maccabaean* and to become an important colleague as we developed greater understanding of American Zionism. Madiha Irfan read this entire manuscript in full, and offered important critique and helpful suggestions that have found their way into this book. But far more than all her extensive work, I remember most fondly our discussions about religious practice and belief. I imagine we will continue these conversations as she becomes a colleague in religious studies. Miriam Pallant rechecked all my endnotes and quotations, itemizing numerous errors and offering sage advice about how best to correct them. She brought a sense of order, coherence, and thoughtfulness to this book and to my approach to Jewish Studies. And I am deeply appreciative for all my students from the Jewish Images class in the Fall 2012 semester. We discussed many of the issues that I have explored here in *Imagining Jewish Authenticity,* and their insightful comments have textured my own analysis. A heartfelt thank you to all.

My colleagues here and elsewhere have enlarged my familial circle in ways that I find all too humbling. Friends in the Religion Department at Haverford—

David Dawson (now President of Earlham College), Tracey Hucks, Terrence Johnson, Naomi Koltun-Fromm, Anne McGuire, Jamel Velji, and Travis Zadeh—have made this college feel like a second home to me. Their support and collegiality inspire me, and I have learned from them how to be a teacher-scholar. At various times I have ventured outside the comforting walls of my own department to discuss my work with colleagues and friends, and their voices have been strong and encouraging. I owe a special gratitude to those who participated in the Hurford Center faculty seminar with me on Material Culture—Hank Glassman, Darin Hayton, Laura McGrane, Jessie Shipley, Ruti Talmor, and Travis Zadeh—and to my colleagues in the Philadelphia Works-in-Progress group in American Judaism, especially Beth Wenger and Lila Corwin-Berman who have tirelessly coordinated our meetings. Colleagues from afar—Mara Benjamin, Zachary Braiterman, Jeremy Dauber, Nathaniel Deutsch, Arnold Eisen, Leonard V. Kaplan, Ari Y. Kelman, Akiba Lerner, Shaul Magid, Noam Pianko, and Rabbi Carnie Rose—have all listened to me criticize, expound, argue, and debate this book and more. I am truly fortunate to have colleagues like these as close friends.

Janet Rabinowitch and Dee Mortensen of Indiana University Press and copyeditor Joyce Rappaport have been remarkably supportive throughout this process, and though saddened at Janet's recent retirement, I am nonetheless grateful that Dee has taken over this project with all the graciousness that Janet has shown throughout her editorial leadership at the press. All of my authored works have been published at Indiana, and I treasure this relationship. Portions of chapter two appeared in "Vision and Authenticity in Heschel's *The Sabbath*," *Modern Judaism* 31, no. 2 (2011): 142–65, and a good deal of chapter four appeared as "Authenticity, Vision, Culture: Michael Wyschogrod's *The Body of Faith*," in *Thinking Jewish Culture in America,* ed. Ken Koltun-Fromm (Lanham: Lexington Books, 2014), 285–312. I am grateful to Oxford University Press and Lexington Books for granting me permission to reproduce the material here.

Much of what I experience and know about family has come from my spouse, Naomi Koltun-Fromm. I have learned from her what it means to be a loyal friend, a supportive partner, a compassionate listener, and a caring child to ailing parents. This book, as so much else, finds its home in our dedication and responsibility to each other.

Finally, but most decisively, I dedicate this book to our three children: Ariel, Talia, and Isaiah. As I state in the introduction to this book, I do not defend, much less construct a notion of Jewish authenticity. But if I were a bit more adventurous, and so did indeed offer a more normative approach to authentic personhood, I know it would have something to do with Ariel, Talia, and Isaiah. They embody the future I believe in, and I dedicate all that I can to them.

IMAGINING JEWISH AUTHENTICITY

Introduction

Visual Authenticity in the
American Jewish Imaginary

In THE 1960s and 1970s, the makers of Levy's Rye Bread ran their now recognizable poster campaign of Native, Chinese, Irish, Asian, and African Americans zealously devouring their leavened product. Levy's slogan—"You don't have to be Jewish to love Levy's!"—utilized the presumed knowledge that some Americans do not look Jewish. These Americans could certainly enjoy Jewish cuisine, but they could not become what they ate. Yet to Toni Eisendorf, then a young adult living in New York City, these advertisements offered a very different vision of Jewish identity. When asked to explain her attraction to Judaism after negotiating various Christian and public schools as a youth, Toni recalled the visual impact of Levy's advertisement campaign:

> The first ad I saw, in a subway station, had a little Black boy. I remember seeing this ad, and the way I interpreted it was that you don't have to be White to be Jewish. That made me feel so good for some reason. I actually felt relieved.[1]

Melanie Kaye/Kantrowitz, in her *The Colors of Jews*, retells Eisendorf's story within her own account of a multiracial Judaism.[2] For Kaye/Kantrowitz, Toni helpfully disentangles the black–white binary that too often situates black on the other side of Jewish experience, just as it presumes a white Jewish identity. But one need not read Eisendorf's story as political commentary, or even as a "feel so good" narrative of belonging to recognize the confluence of visual clues and claims to authenticity. Eisendorf sees a more genuine Jewish presence in Levy's poster campaign, and so reveals how visual authenticity works in the American Jewish imaginary.

This book tells a story about how Jews imagine authenticity by deploying images in texts, by appealing to visual metaphors, and by exploring how Jews ought to see the world, physical objects, and their bodies. I trace how American Jewish thinkers capture Jewish authenticity in and through visual discourse. But this critical project of recovery does not mean I wish to endorse any one form of authenticity, much less Jewish authenticity. This book is definitively not a normative project of that kind. It is, however, a project to retrieve the visual models deployed by some Jewish thinkers of the past one hundred years. Eisen-

Figure 0.1. Levy's Rye Bread Commercial Poster.

dorf's compelling anecdote references many of the critical motifs of this book: the subtle connections among visual expectations, cultural knowledge, racial belonging, embodied identity, and how images and texts work together. She sees Jewish in Levy's image, and that visual depiction, read together with the unstated but unconsciously absorbed poster tagline ("real Jewish Rye"), couples notions of authenticity (the "real") with visual discourse. This book expands those concerns to include reflections on the gendered body, on imagined Israel, on photographic images, and on Jewish bodies to reveal the anxiety of authentic presence. *Imagining Jewish Authenticity* suggests that Toni's story is one many like to tell, for it remains a compelling if anxious vision of Jewish belonging in America.

Even with the boy firmly in focus, Toni Eisendorf and I imagine a very different Levy's advertisement campaign.[3] As I see it, images like this one tell a complicated story: African or Native or any other kind of American may eat Jewish foods, and even enjoy them, but they remain outsiders to Jewish culture. Eisendorf's more comforting gaze, one that envisions a multiethnic Judaism, is not what I see in Levy's appeal to Jewish identity. To my mind's eye, Jewish looks white in this and other images from Levy's posters. In this vision, "real" Jewish bread, as the caption reads, identifies the border between authentic (white) Judaism and all others. But however one might locate meaning in this image/text, the poster still makes visual claims to Jewish authenticity, even if those claims are subject to the peculiarities of reader response. We do things with images, I argue in this book, and one of the things we do is visually to enact scenes of Jewish identity and belonging in America.

I am concerned with two pervasive issues in modern Jewish discourse: 1) the ways that images and texts work together to construct powerful claims to authenticity, and to restrain lingering fears of inauthenticity; and 2) how Jews deploy language in texts to materialize authenticity in Jewish, gendered, and racial bodies. The book divides along these two general lines of inquiry, with the first three chapters devoted to how images function within texts to produce nuanced modes of assertion, while the second set of three chapters focuses on the embodied language of visual authenticity. I have selected indicative texts to expose how images work with and sometimes against textual inscription (Bernard Rosenblatt's *Social Zionism*); how images reflect the tensions of textual claims (Abraham Joshua Heschel's *The Sabbath*); and how images take center stage in the performative drama of Jewish practice (Susie Fishbein's *Kosher by Design* and Betty Greenberg's and Althea Silverman's *The Jewish Home Beautiful*). Yet visual authenticity is not always presented through images; we find such discourse embodied in Jewish language as well. I turn to Michael Wyschogrod's *The Body of Faith* to explore how the language of authenticity works as embodied visual presence in the Jewish people; I examine how authenticity functions as gendered embodiment in Rachel Adler's *Engendering Judaism;* and finally I look at how visual authenticity is a racial, linguistic practice in Melanie Kaye/Kantrowitz's *The Colors of Jews*. There are, to be sure, many other texts that expose the various workings of authenticity in American Jewish thought, as there are other ways that images function with texts. But the works discussed here illustrate key rhetorical features, in word and image, of imagining Jewish authenticity in America.

The term *authenticity* is a contentious one, often associated with ideas about the "really real" out there in the world, or a true state of being located somewhere within the self. Charles Lindholm defines authenticity as "the leading member of a set of values that includes sincere, essential, natural, original, and real": "Persons are authentic," he argues further, "if they are true to their roots or if their lives are a direct and immediate expression of their essence."[4] Authenticity is also a peculiarly modern anxiety reflecting fears of inauthentic or fake appearance—an unease suggesting that what we see is not what we get. One can speak of authentic works of art, but when thinking about authentic selves persons often appeal to a sensibility or a mode of engaging the world. There are a number of ways to define authenticity, and I want to consider some of them in this introduction. I also wish to explore how *visual* authenticity draws from but also complicates these interpretive models. In each of the six main chapters of this book, authenticity looks a particular way, and each chapter notes rival accounts of Jewish authenticity. Again, I wish neither to condone nor attack these visions. But I do believe they reveal a strong desire for presence and acceptance. In the American Jewish imaginary, authenticity has proven to be an intoxicating visual sign of belonging.

Perhaps no philosopher has thought as deeply and so cogently about the nature of authenticity than Charles Taylor. But Taylor's influential short book, *The Ethics of Authenticity* (1991),[5] readily admits the influence of an earlier treatise on the subject, one that still underlies a good deal of contemporary discussions on the self. Lionel Trilling's *Sincerity and Authenticity* (1972)[6] is a collection of his lectures offered at Harvard University in 1970, and in those addresses Trilling takes on a grand sweep of literary and philosophical texts to reveal the theoretical divide between sincere and authentic selves. From Shakespeare in the sixteenth century through Diderot, Hegel, Marx, Rousseau, Wilde, and Freud in the twentieth (and that really is to name but a few), Trilling tracks the move from a notion of sincerity concerned with "the simplicity of the honest soul" that others recognize and find noble, to the modern appeal to the authentic self who "is understood to exist wholly by the laws of its own being."[7] This historical shift harbors a deep philosophical one as well, for Trilling positions sincerity as the foil to authenticity. The more insular, or inner-directed claim to authentic personhood raises the anxiety of inauthenticity, for one could readily fail to become the person one ought to be. If sincere persons could deform into dishonest ones, authentic selves could become inhuman: "Through the nineteenth century runs the thread of anxiety that man may not be man, that his relation to the world may cease to be a human one."[8] The stakes are obviously higher in the demand for authentic personhood, and so too the costs. Sincerity requires "the avoidance of being false to any man through being true to one's own self."[9] But more than an honest self, authenticity demands that the self *itself* must be true. It is not just that I need to be true to that self (being sincere); I need to ensure that the self to which I am true is itself a fully human one (being authentic).

So when Taylor appropriates Trilling's term *authenticity* to describe modern ideals, he speaks of a "higher mode of life" or a standard to which modern selves aspire. The "moral force of the ideal of authenticity" is that sense of a calling to a higher, and so more human form of life:

> It's not just that people sacrifice their love relationships, and the care of their children, to pursue their careers. Something like this has perhaps always existed. The point is that today many people feel *called* to do this, feel they ought to do this, feel their lives would be somehow wasted or unfulfilled if they didn't do it.[10]

Another way of translating Trilling into Taylor's idiom would be to understand sincerity as being true to who you are, but authenticity as becoming who you ought to be. But this calling is a deeply personal one, and spatially we imagine it as within the self. Taylor describes this variously as "a voice within," or as "inner depths," and even as a "new form of inwardness."[11] But whatever it is, it lies within the self. A good deal of Taylor's project recovers the various communal, historical, and cultural relations that offer intelligibility to this inner voice. He situates the self within a broader, communal landscape because he fears a self-absorbed atomism in which persons merely look inward, and so forget their moral and cultural ties to others. Corey Anton's work, *Selfhood and Authenticity* (2001), expands Taylor's project into a phenomenological account of a socially embodied self. For Taylor, as for Anton, authenticity as "a quest for self-fulfillment" requires social and moral resources communally shared and embodied.[12]

Taylor holds a mediating position between the "boosters" who relish this individual search for authentic personhood and the "knockers" who deride this solipsist turn to the self.[13] One recent work on ritual performance stands with those "knockers" who believe authentic selves manifest only insular forms of sincerity. Indeed, the very title of this coauthored book, *Ritual and Its Consequences: An Essay on the Limits of Sincerity* (2008), already suggests how current models of ritual practice focus almost entirely on sincere modes of behavior, but at the very real cost of daily acts of "world construction."[14] For Seligman and his coauthors, ritual is "one crucial mode of framing activities" as a form of the subjunctive: "the creation of an order *as if* it were truly the case." This tragic view, one that recognizes the world as inherently "fractured and fragmented," contrasts sharply with a sincere one: "sincere views are focused not on the creation of an 'as if' or a shared subjunctive universe of human being in the world. Instead, they project an 'as is' vision of what often becomes a totalistic, unambiguous vision of reality 'as it *really* is.'"[15] Where the one is "shared" and communal, the other is "permanent, pure, and singular."[16] For the authors of *Ritual and Its Consequences*, sincerity is "the belief that truth resides within the authentic self, that it is coherent, and that incoherence and fragmentation are therefore themselves signs of insincerity." The search for authenticity is a sincere, utopian impulse for undifferentiated wholeness.[17] For these "knockers" of authenticity, "the self *who does ritual* is very different from the self *who is sincere*."[18] They seek to rebalance the modern slide to sincerity/authenticity with greater appreciation for the social meaning-making of ritual.

Seligman and his coauthors are surely right to highlight this modern turn to authenticity. All of the texts discussed in this book support their view that the search for authenticity is a peculiarly recent one.[19] But *Ritual and Its Consequences* derides only one feature of authenticity—an insularity bordering on complete isolation—yet fails to engage a more complicated history. The easy slippage between authenticity and sincerity is one indication of this reductive account. But so too is their relatively little interest in more uplifting and compelling versions of authentic quests. Though Taylor shares many of their concerns about community and social worlds, he rightly insists that "knockers" fail to engage the moral urgency of an authentic calling that actually moves beyond the self. The search for some coherent account of the self belies a yearning for a more fulfilling life, for a touchstone to live well by, for a welcome sense of belonging in the world and among others.

And this movement beyond the insular self is precisely what I wish to track in *Imagining Jewish Authenticity*. Sincerity and authenticity are not just "inner states" but public displays and visual performances: they are implemented and achieved before others. In the texts discussed in this book, American Jews cannot just be authentic: they have to appear, embody, be seen, or look in ways that are, so they claim, visually authentic modes of being Jewish in America. Taylor's notion of authentic calling becomes in this book a *rhetorical technique* to see *how* authenticity emerges in texts and images, and *how* authenticity inhabits Jewish bodies. When texts link authenticity to visual discourse, Jewish identity as an inner state of being traverses into the public realm of display, and this more "shared" space then redoubles back to inform the meaning of authentic personhood. Visual authenticity situates "what it is to be ourselves"[20] in image, in image–text relations, in gendered and racial bodies, and in the act of looking and being seen. It is not a form of expression in which we articulate or reveal that which lies within—as if the image or body exposes an internal state of awareness.

Authenticity is not merely internal, nor is it just social; it is also visual. This book traces those visual features in and through Jewish texts that are firmly embedded within Trilling's culture of authenticity. Visual authenticity, as I employ this term of art, is a *rhetorical activity*—it is a mode of argument and persuasion—in which visual discourse, images, and bodies critically inform and anxiously produce the authentic self. Jewish authenticity as a rhetorical device—as a mode of argumentative persuasion—cultivates Jewish bodies, texts, images, and faces.

American Jewish claims to authenticity traffic within and among visual cultures. Informing Eisendorf's reading of Levy's poster advertisement is her educational upbringing, the multicultural vibrancy of New York City, and her own ethnic search for identity. Born in Italy, Eisendorf at age four moved to New York and experienced the "hodge-podge of religious and cultural exposures" of a city that, as she tells it, still embodies an underlying Jewish character: "as Lenny Bruce said, anybody who grows up in New York is a little bit Jewish."[21] She is already conditioned to see Jewish when gazing at that Levy's poster. Her visual and ethnic culture informs her mode of seeing. A good many theoretical works have analyzed the cultural power of images and the role they play in shaping identity. David Freedberg's *The Power of Images* (1989) offers a particularly trenchant study of "what images appear to do," or how viewers invest images with presence and power.[22] Images do not come on the scene as blank slates, nor do viewers meet them as objective gazers. As David Morgan rightly notes when referring to the sacred gaze, a "particular configuration of ideas, attitudes, and customs" informs our acts of seeing "within a given cultural and historical setting."[23] Rachel Neis argues this same point when studying Jewish rabbinic visual models through "the cultural and historical forces that shape the range of phenomena known as seeing." For Neis, "there is a story to be told about what seeing has meant and how it has functioned across a variety of registers (from society to sociality, from race to gender to class) in different times and places."[24] Following Neis, I want to tell a story about one particular cultural register: how visual authenticity, as a rhetorical technique, shapes "what seeing has meant" for American Jewish thinkers.

For Freedberg, Morgan, and Neis, viewers confer upon visual objects a set of cultural expectations that resonate with personal experiences and values. And they are not alone in establishing a field of visual studies that locates modes of seeing within culture, religion, philosophy, class, gender, and race.[25] Certainly W. J. T. Mitchell's work on the image/text has profoundly influenced many areas of visual studies, as it does this book, especially in my analysis of Bernard Rosenblatt's vision of Israel in chapter one.[26] Theorists such as James Elkins, Martin Jay, Morgan, Freedberg, and Neis explore how viewers work with visual objects[27] in order to do things with them.

With these theoretical concerns ever present in the background, I want to focus on David Morgan's account of "the sacred gaze" because it has critically shaped my own thinking of visual studies and the methodological direction of this book. Morgan believes that religions help to construct and order reality "for the purpose of living better, longer, more meaningfully, or with less hazard." By "authorizing order," religions confer "compelling and enduring power" to it.[28] It is important to note that, even if I find Morgan compelling about the cultural production of the gaze, I do not share his concern with the "salutary effect"[29] of images to calm an anxious viewer. But this sense of religious calm pervades Morgan's account of visual culture, for here too he emphasizes how images construct and maintain "a sense of order in a particular place and time."[30] Referring to Harry Anderson's painting *God's Two Books* (1968)—an image of a young woman gazing at a figure of Jesus within nature—Morgan suggests how religious images, to be counted *as* religious, must project coherence, security, and uniformity:

> If the image is to be a medium of communication and visual proclamation of God's revelation in nature as harmonious with his revelation in the Bible, the image can hardly function reliably if it is taken at once to convey contradictory meanings. Anderson conceived of "nature as undomesticated" in a polarized pairing with its opposite. His picture mediates the opposition.[31]

A sacred gaze enacts this harmony in the cultural act of looking: it "is a term that designates the particular configuration of ideas, attitudes, and customs that informs a religious act of seeing as it occurs within a given cultural and historical setting." Such a gaze is not a glance or a quick shift in perspective; a sacred gaze requires attention, engagement, and conditioned expectations. This "visual network," to adopt Morgan's term, establishes a field of inquiry such that researchers can now distinguish a critical object, and construct theories to understand it. The "social act of looking"[32] establishes the scholarly gaze of analysis.

For Morgan, the scholarly research question is clear: "how do images participate in the social construction of reality?" I want to revise this focus to attend to another prominent feature of the sacred gaze: how do images rhetorically function in the construction of authenticity? Here, I side with Morgan by moving away from the author's intended meaning, and focus instead on "the use to which images are put by those who are not their makers." Like Neis, I too "am less interested in *what* they saw and far more in *how* they saw."[33] Images do things because viewers put them to use. On this point, Morgan's theoretical commitments underlie the project of this book: "the study of visual culture scrutinizes not only images but also the practices that put images to use."[34] I analyze those practices in American Jewish texts that appropriate images to support claims to Jewish authenticity. Yet often this appropriation yields more disharmony than coherence, more religious anxiety than security. Unlike Morgan, I will not confine religious imagery to clear exposures of coherent meaning. I also wish to expand the sacred gaze to include visual language, and so assess how texts embody the visual in modes of speaking and writing about authenticity.

Morgan lists seven ways that religious images work for those who use them. This is not an exhaustive inventory, but a heuristic guide to what religious images do:

1. order space and time
2. imagine community
3. communicate with the divine or transcendent
4. embody forms of communion with the divine
5. collaborate with other forms of representation
6. influence thought and behavior by persuasion or magic
7. displace rival images and ideologies[35]

Religious images, in Morgan's taxonomy, help maintain a recognizable and coherent order. But in this book on Jewish visual authenticity, we will discover images that destabilize that order, and raise the specter of the inauthentic, the hybrid other, and the fear of alienation. Sometimes images protest too much, and so expose a more disturbing unease. This book takes up Morgan's fifth item—the ways that images collaborate with other forms of representation—to discuss two modes of religious exposure. Part one explores *how* images work with and at times against texts in staking claims to Jewish authenticity; part two discusses *how* visual language is encoded and recognized in Jewish, gendered, and racial bodies. Together, these two parts examine the rhetorical techniques deployed by Jewish thinkers to construct visual authenticity in America.

Yet these constructed notions of identity often disclose the anxiety of inauthenticity in their very claims to authentic belonging. Morgan's appeal to religious harmony and security belies a more complex unease: a fear of an unseen authentic presence, or a disturbing absence rather than a calming appearance. It is the anxiety that were a viewer to look away but for an instant, Jesus would no longer appear in nature as the serene mediator of opposites ("His picture [of Jesus in nature] mediates the opposition").[36] Visual authenticity is an anxious form of desire and practice to see order within recognizable chaos. It is a yearning for greater presence and belonging. This is what Seligman and his coauthors call ritual and its consequences, and it is the subject of this book.

My argument is that modern Jewish texts deploy visual discourse to substantiate, complicate, and authorize Jewish authenticity in America. This is a rhetorical claim and argument rather than a normative practice. I for one do not believe we can affirm, much less confirm notions of authenticity. But it is a consistent argumentative practice in American Jewish thought, and I seek to recover that rhetorical line of inquiry here. In that critical recovery, we discover how writers ineluctably raise the fear of inauthenticity as the very real underside and possible consequence of authentic exposures. The anxiety of inauthenticity is the inescapable companion to these arguments for visual authenticity in America, especially in those texts that deploy visual images. Now it is certainly not the case that all or even the majority of modern Jewish thinkers, however one might construct this rubric, link modes of seeing to authenticity. I do not wish to claim ownership to a master narrative, and so constrict the multiplicity of Jewish discourses. But I do want to recover a significant and revealing undercurrent that I argue travels broadly and pervasively throughout twentieth-century Jewish thought in America.

This book is a work in recovery of a rarely glimpsed narrative of visual authenticity, one that weaves a sweeping path through modes of seeing Israel, material objects, Jewish food, embodied Jews, gendered practices, and racial bodies in America. My point is not to exhaust a field of inquiry but rather to bring it to light—to expose the modes of seeing authenticity in American Jewish thought.

But then have I not opened the rubric of modern Jewish thought in ways so disparate, so meandering, so embracing that, much like the critique of my previous work on material identity, anything really goes or "counts" as Jewish thought? How can I include, in one and the same volume, a chapter on Abraham Joshua Heschel together with a focused study on Susie Fishbein's *Kosher by Design*? In what sense can we think of Fishbein's cookbook as a text in the study of Jewish thought? The rubric "Jewish thought" already expands upon the more limited category of "Jewish philosophy" to include texts usually on the outside of an accepted canon.[37] There is certainly a turf war here, in which some protect a rubric and canon to safeguard against noisy insurgents. But there is also a serious concern about method and access: how do we best articulate the boundaries between thought and culture, and the methods by and through which we access those domains? Those borders, I honestly admit, are rarely clear to me. Yet when classifying a text as Jewish thought, or as the object of study for Jewish thought, I pose these two questions: 1) does the author direct his/her work to a Jewish audience or write from within a Jewish community; and 2) does this text move me to think well, or think deeply, or even just to think differently about how to live a Jewish life? Jewish cultural texts, to my mind, show me that kind of life from within; texts in, or the subject of, Jewish thought reveal how to think well about Jewish life and experience. To my mind, Heschel's *The Sabbath* is a text in Jewish thought, and Fishbein's *Kosher by Design* is a fitting object of study for Jewish thought. But I cannot, a priori, defend my decision to include Fishbein's *Kosher by Design* or even Kaye/Kantrowitz's *The Colors of Jews* in a study of American Jewish thought, although both authors self-consciously write from within and for a Jewish community. I can only ask you as readers, upon reviewing my analysis of these texts, whether they have moved you to think well about the Jewish rhetoric of visual authenticity. They have certainly worked in this way upon me, as have the many other texts discussed in this book, and so, in my view, deserve their place as legitimate objects of study for Jewish thought. Torah, after all, is not only the first five books of the Hebrew Bible; it may very well include other texts and practices that expand our notions of Jewish experience. But which texts, images, or text-images actually prove effective in this way can only be gleaned after our exposures to them. This is not an essentialist concern but a pragmatic one: the critical question is whether these texts work well. To be sure, this question is ongoing: I do not seek to redefine a canon, but rather wish to open it up for continual debate for and by Jewish communities. I am suggesting that what "counts" as the subject of modern Jewish thought is more or less a crowd-sourcing problem. And as with all functional claims like this one, the interpretive concern is to show *how* they work well as texts in Jewish thought. In this sense, the category of "Jewish thought" is a constructed one *after the fact,* because what "counts," in the end, is what moves us to think well about Jewish life and practice. This book claims that *Kosher by Design, The Colors of Jews,* and the other texts discovered herein show us *how* to think well about visual authenticity as a Jewish rhetorical practice.

I have divided the book into two parts, with each in roughly chronological order. The first part turns to the image–text relation and the anxiety of (in)authenticity, while the second attends to the embodied language of authenticity in Jewish, gendered, and racial selves. Collectively, these two parts argue that visual authenticity is a pictorial and linguistic practice in the American Jewish imaginary. The three chapters comprising each of these sections are in total six focused studies of individual works in modern American Jewish thought that reveal the substantive themes of the book. I could have chosen other texts than Rosenblatt's *Social Zionism,* for example, to illustrate how images and texts function together to envision Israel. Scholarly work from Naomi Cohen, Mark Raider,[38] and many others demonstrate just how widespread this practice is in American Jewish thought. But Rosenblatt's work usefully reveals how the text–image functions, sometimes against each other, to visually engage Jewish authenticity. His is not the only book to do so, yet it is one of the most instructive examples of this practice. This could be said as well for the other texts discussed in this book.

The three chapters in part one argue that images work against texts to construct a more compelling rhetorical argument (chapter one), that images reproduce textual dynamics and anxieties (chapter two), and that images appeal to staged performances of Jewish authenticity (chapter three). I do not mean to imply that images can *only* function in these ways, but these are three compelling rhetorical techniques deployed in modern Jewish thought.

The opening chapter on Rosenblatt's *Social Zionism* (1919) reveals how images of Palestine substantiate and at times complicate arguments for Jewish authenticity in America. Rosenblatt (1886–1969) held important leadership positions in the early American Zionist movement, and published articles in *The Maccabaean*—a leading Zionist journal before and after the First World War. *Social Zionism* is a collection of essays, some dating back to 1910 and many appearing in *The Maccabaean,* and it showcases fanciful images of Palestine. These sketches of desert wastelands, wandering Bedouins, and Jewish farmers were common portrayals and tropes of an uninhabited land awaiting Jewish conquest. In Rosenblatt's own times, his call for "self-realization" mirrored pervasive Zionist ideology. In many ways, there is nothing new in Rosenblatt, and his argument for Jewish renewal and social regeneration, not in America but in an unencumbered, untrammeled territory, is by now worn and, in some circles, decidedly belligerent and destructive. But my interest is not in *what* Rosenblatt argues but in *how* he argues it. I explore *how* images work rhetorically with texts to expose, and sometimes undermine, Rosenblatt's narrative of Jewish authenticity. Here we can *see* authenticity in sketches that capture Rosenblatt's appeal to cultivate the self through cultivating the land. Yet these images fail as proof texts to confirm textual arguments. Instead, they work alongside texts in less linear and sometimes more combative modes to generate distinctive claims and anxieties. We must attend to texts differently than images, but also see how they powerfully work together to produce a more robust argument than any one text or image could do so on its own. This is what the rhetoric of authenticity looks like for American Jews gazing beyond their national borders.

For Rosenblatt, American Jews should recover a lost authenticity beyond America in a new land. But for Abraham Joshua Heschel, such authentic roots can be rediscovered at home if one learns how to see things in space as conduits to a spiritual reality in time. In chapter two I portray Heschel's *The Sabbath* (1951) as a call for authentic Jewish experience as protection against the captivating enchantments of American capitalism. American Jews must reenvision space, and the things within it, as transformative mirrors to spiritual wonder. To Heschel, Jewish seeing converts material objects into spiritual icons of the eternal in time. Authentic Jewish existence is possible in America only when Jews learn to see material things in this way. For Heschel, the Sabbath day facilitates this phenomenological mode of visual piety. The Sabbath educates Jews how to see eternity in time, and enables that very form of seeing—or so Heschel argues throughout his text. But Heschel's work also includes woodcut engravings from his friend Ilya Schor. *The Sabbath* is, like Rosenblatt's *Social Zionism,* an image/text, but one that mirrors Heschel's own concern with representation: iconic things can function as conduits to the eternal, but they can also fail as signifiers to the holy, and so enrapture viewers within material things. Where images often function in Rosenblatt's text to articulate a claim unannounced in the text itself, here in *The Sabbath* Schor's engravings visually mimic Heschel's textual anxiety that spatial objects might captivate the self rather than motivate experiences of spiritual wonder. This fear of the inauthentic—in both text and image—reveals a shift in the rhetorical exposures of visual authenticity. Images can make extra-linguistic claims, as they do in Rosenblatt's *Social Zionism,* but they can also reproduce the very anxieties of textual discourse, as they do here in Heschel's *The Sabbath.*

The concluding chapter to this first part examines the display of Jewish cuisine in two cookbooks: *The Jewish Home Beautiful* (1941) and *Kosher by Design* (2003). Both texts, though published some sixty years apart, have broadly influenced Jewish culinary and display practices in America. My hope is that they become equally influential for modern Jewish thought, for they reveal how images present and perform authenticity. These cookbooks—the one published by the National Women's League of the United Synagogue of America (a league associated with the Conservative movement), and the other distributed by ArtScroll, an Orthodox press—are really instruction manuals for authentic Jewish life in America. Their authors continually provide homespun advice about festival decorations, table décor, proper dispositions, and food habits to coopt traditional practice within Jewish aesthetic taste. Betty Greenberg and Althea Silverman of *The Jewish Home Beautiful,* and Susie Fishbein for *Kosher by Design,* each make claims about tradition, practice, and law in and through their discussions of Jewish cuisine. Yet each text includes photographs and stylistic images to authorize innovations and to defend them against claims to inauthenticity. To modulate their anxiety that innovation leads only to inauthentic novelty rather than to a resurgence of traditional piety, Greenberg and Silverman deploy images as *performative* works to strengthen their apologetic narrative of Jewish continuity. Images do important labor in their text, as they do in Fishbein's *Kosher by Design.* Fishbein, too, worries that her elegant aesthetic might appear as ornamental flourish rather than substantive elegance to enrich traditional practice. So her professionally designed food stagings reveal traditional authority within a modern, tasteful sensibility. Rather than the heavy kugels and cholents of *The Jewish Home Beautiful,* Fishbein displays the far lighter, and certainly healthier tricolor gefilte fish and the sweet-pea kreplach. These foods deliver tradition and Jewish continuity as performance and designed stagings; here we see the drama of Jewish visual authenticity in America.

In the second part of *Imagining Jewish Authenticity,* I explore how Jewish thinkers embody the language of visual authenticity in people (chapter four), in gender (chapter five), and in race (chapter six). No thinker to my mind has engaged the theological import of the Jewish body as forcefully as Michael Wyschogrod, whose book *The Body of Faith* (1983) occupies my attention in chapter four. The printing of the second edition (1989) embraces a new subtitle—God in the People Israel—and this change from the original subtitle (Judaism as Corporeal Election) fittingly describes Wyschogrod's central preoccupation: God's dwelling in material Jewish bodies. This is no metaphor, for the body of faith is for Wyschogrod a visual, material body that we can see in the people Israel. While all live in God's image, only embodied Israel enjoys God's presence, and so only Israel remains God's chosen community. This embodied triumphalism is visual authenticity as material body and visible marking. Wyschogrod's unapologetic theology of the Jewish body witnesses to God's indwelling as authentic visual exposure. But such a singular focus on embodiment leaves Wyschogrod vulnerable to a perplexing but not altogether infrequent occurrence: the conversion of non-Jews, and so non-Jewish bodies, into Jewish ones. How does the Jewish God dwell within what once had been foreign material? For Wyschogrod, as I make clear in my analysis, this is a visual problem: he cannot see God in those converted bodies, even though he knows God dwells within them as part of the people Israel. But recognizing conversion *as* a problem reveals just how indebted Wyschogrod is to an embodied account of visual authenticity.

An embodied Israel comprises particular bodies, and those bodies are gendered. In chapter five, I read Rachel Adler's *Engendering Judaism* (1998) as strong critique of Wyschogrod's visual certainty in the (mostly male) Jewish form, and as a progressive call for new modes of interactive, engendered engagement with other bodies. Adler wishes to tell and read traditional stories to yield a more inclusive, pluralistic, and embodied Judaism. But her sense of embodiment is certainly not Wyschogrod's: she imagines a "polymorphous experience of sexuality" in which the erotic covers "the entire surface of the body."[39] Gazes that once reified the other into a sexualized body transform into an engendering vision of the play, sensuality, and materiality of embodied persons. Adler argues that we make God present when we see others as embodied, gendered, and passionate beings who seek authentic experiences through communal solidarity. Polymorphous, erotic bodies are authentic ones, so Adler believes, and we should recognize them through an engendering gaze in order to build just communities together. Engendering Judaism is, for Adler, the embodied, gendered practice of visual authenticity.

From engendered bodies I move to racialized ones through a close reading of Melanie Kaye/Kantrowitz's *The Colors of Jews* (2007). This is an overtly political text, one that argues for a "radical diasporism" (as the subtitle has it) in which actors move among multiple identities, encounters, and places. Kaye/Kantrowitz's displacement of the center still harbors a progressive vision for a multiracial politics, but I focus my reading on her interviews of "colored" Jews: a term Kaye/Kantrowitz employs to undermine the black–white binary in both African and Jewish American communities. Though Kaye/Kantrowitz situates these interviews within her narrative of diasporic politics, the interviewees themselves are far more conflicted and trapped within a racial vision of Jewish identity. I want to explore how these interviewees articulate notions of race in ways that Kaye/Kantrowitz obscures as she directs them toward her radical politics. To be clear, this is not a discussion of race and Judaism, nor is it a broader intervention into notions of race and religion. My very narrow concern here is to uncover the rhetorical moves of Kaye/Kantrowitz's interviewees in order to recover the language of authenticity as racialized discourse. Though sympathetic to her call for a broader, more nuanced, and multifaceted account of racial vision, I seek to retrieve how Navonah, Yavilah McCoy, and Toni Eisendorf (to name a few of her interviewees) articulate race, and how their language of authenticity ties bodies to visual display.

I conclude this narrative of the Jewish imaginary with a look at one popular image/text. The Passover story in American *Haggadoth*—the stories recalling the exodus from Egypt that Jews tell every spring—commands an imaginative leap of solidarity: "In every generation, a person is obligated to view himself as if he were the one who went out from Egypt."[40] Images often accompany this *Haggadah* text, and I explore, by way of revisioning the previous six chapters, *how* visual authenticity works within this particular image/text. One of these *Haggadoth* contains only text, yet suggests readers produce their own vision:

> He should picture himself as a slave who has been freed. How he would con-template the greatness of his Liberator! How he would sacrifice all he pos-sessed—and himself—for Him! By imagining such a picture of the mind, he will be impressed by the miracles and he will see that the world has a Creator and Governor, Whom we should fear and serve.[41]

This text suggests that if we cannot see authentic images, then we should at least create them for ourselves. Envisioning oneself as a slave in Egypt enlivens the ex-perience and, as this *Haggadah* would have it, deepens spiritual contemplation. Seeing, in this sense, really is believing. Yet it is a belief that we partially con-struct through the sacred gaze. Visual authenticity is not something we encoun-ter so much as advance and deploy; it is a rhetorical strategy of belonging. This is an anxious homecoming, and one that this book seeks to recover as a compelling undercurrent in American Jewish thought. But this act of critical recovery is it-self a claim to visual authenticity, for it elevates these subterranean influences in order to render them visible. Visual authenticity is, finally, not a story to tell but one we need actively to see.

Section I.
The Anxiety of Authenticity in Image and Text

1 Seeing Israel in Bernard Rosenblatt's *Social Zionism*

It is conceivable that one could view the Zionists' deliberate mediation of the
Jewish experience in Palestine as manipulation, or worse, exploitation. But
that would misrepresent their deep-seated quest for, and sincere belief in, the
authenticity of their claims. This was, in the Zionist imagination, one of the
chief means of national liberation for the Jews: they had to be able to see their
potential as a people and a nation, quite literally, before their eyes—preferably
in the best possible light, as a blossoming flower—in order to perceive themselves as fully human.

—Michael Berkowitz, *Western Jewry and the Zionist Project, 1914–1933*

In an essay discussing Israel in American Jewish education, Walter Ackerman (1925–2003) recalls how every American kid attending Jewish schools of his
generation, at one time or another, went to see the film *A House in the Desert*
(1948). This now classic Zionist promotional film tells the story of the *ḥalutzim*—
those vanguards of a rejuvenated Jewish people in the land of Israel whom Arthur Goren and Mark Raider have explored in some detail.[1] Building a kibbutz in
the desert region known in Israel as the Arava, the *ḥalutzim* produced their first
crops and made the desert bloom. Ackerman acknowledges the heavy romantic
propaganda, yet still recalls its visual impact: "But I have never forgotten the last
frame of that movie—a fragile sliver of white bud bursting through the dry and
dusty brown of desert waste." That frame holds its power for Ackerman in ways
that Jewish education, focused on "the reliance on *telling*,"[2] can rarely capture
with the same urgency and vitality. Images captivate the senses in ways such that
even the most romantic of pictures seems right and fitting. *A House in the Desert* deploys images to make arguments—a visual form of *telling* that travels very
deeply into historical memory.

Bernard Rosenblatt's *Social Zionism* (1919) is also a form of visual telling,
with engravings of Palestine on every one of its pages. Originally from Poland
but raised in the United States, Rosenblatt (1886–1969) was a leader in the American Zionist movement, at one time sat on the editorial board of the American
Zionist journal *The Maccabaean*, and held the post of honorary secretary of the
Federation of American Zionists (FAZ).[3] His *Social Zionism* is a collection of

earlier essays, some dating back to 1910, mostly from *The Maccabaean*. Rosenblatt has much in common with other American Zionists, especially Horace Kallen and Louis Brandeis, who each appropriated the ideals of the American progressive movement for the "upbuilding" of Palestine.[4] This progressive agenda infused what came to be known as the Pittsburgh Program (1918), a document with six planks that Kallen drafted and Brandeis, among others, later modified.[5] Although Rosenblatt characterizes his book as "an introduction to the study of certain planks in the Pittsburgh Program," it represents far more his vision of a Jewish state that promotes social justice, economic fairness, and agricultural independence.[6] Working the land and making the desert bloom—the *ḥalutz* ideal pictured in *A House in the Desert* and in Rosenblatt's text—revitalized the Jew to become, as Jeffrey Shandler and Beth Wenger describe this imaginary, "proud, athletic, activist, visionary."[7] In Palestine a Jew could achieve "self-realization" (what in Hebrew was called *hagshamah atzmit*), and so transform himself, in what was mostly a male discourse, from the weak, Diaspora traveler to the authentic, muscular *ḥalutz*.[8]

These were widespread claims, and one finds them throughout early American and European Zionist depictions of the new Jew in Palestine. Indeed, much of Rosenblatt's political and social rhetoric fits well within what historian Anita Shapira labels as the "defensive ethos" of Zionist discourse: "The Jews have no aspirations to rule in Palestine—they are coming to colonize the wilderness and to develop regions that to date have gone unploughed. They bring tidings of progress and development to the land, for the benefit of all its inhabitants."[9] To be sure, those other "inhabitants" are rarely acknowledged; Rosenblatt, like many of his contemporaries, imagines a land without a people—a land empty, barren ("the wilderness"), and awaiting its developers. Zionists like Rosenblatt never intended to colonize a people because they never fully recognized the existence of others on the land.

But Rosenblatt certainly desired to colonize the American Jewish self, and this because American Jews could only achieve authentic personhood through cultivating the barren land. The *ḥalutz* ideal witnesses to Rosenblatt's anxious meditations on (in)authenticity: his fear that residing in America will emasculate Jewish vitality and creativity. Jews must travel to Palestine to find themselves, to become who they really are, and so prevent the inevitable weakening of American Jewish identity. Appeals to Jewish authenticity travel together with fears of inauthenticity, and tracking the one inevitably means to cross paths with the other.

Here too, appeals to authenticity and their related fears are common motifs in early Zionist literature. Rosenblatt is not alone, and not even distinctive in many of his claims for a new, American self. Yet I am not concerned about *what* Rosenblatt argues but rather about *how* he argues it. This chapter focuses on the multiple ways that images interact with texts to produce a more nuanced, rhetorical argument for authentic personhood. In *Social Zionism* we can actually see how these claims to authenticity work with images, for Rosenblatt ties progressive calls to social justice and the authentic self to what Jonathan Sarna describes, somewhat mutedly, as "romantic sketches of Holy Land scenes."[10] These images make arguments and interweave with Rosenblatt's written text to produce the kind of lasting "frame" that so captivated Walter Ackerman, even as they remain part of a rich history of the Zionist adoption of "Jewish art" and the "symbolic return to Jewish selfhood and authenticity."[11] The sketches reshape, alter, and expand Rosenblatt's arguments concerning Zionism and the authentic Jewish self. This blending of text and image constructs Palestine as an empty wasteland (like Ackerman's "desert waste") inhabited by wandering, primitive Bedouins. It is a land waiting for Jewish colonization and the rebirth of Jewish authenticity.[12] But it is also the American frontier—one that underlies the American dream of ever expansive space to begin again, once more. A new, authentic self beckons to replace the old. This is a visual authenticity in the making, and we can see it in the ways that images complicate, and sometimes even contradict, textual claims.

Rosenblatt's Social Zionism

The romantic sketches in *Social Zionism* reveal how images function with textual claims to produce the rhetoric of visual authenticity. I follow David Morgan's suggestion "to explain what the picture does,"[13] but Zionist images too often become examples of textual arguments rather than (in my analysis) features of those arguments. Note, for instance, the excellent work by Mark Raider in his *The Emergence of American Zionism* (1998), in which he includes compelling images of the *ḥalutz* ideal. Raider discusses one striking set of images that grace the cover of the Hebrew journal *Shaharut* (Youth)—one scene from 1918, the other from 1920.[14] For two years *Shaharut* displayed the image of three youths in a small boat "rowing toward the Palestinian shore." Raider describes this image as a "straightforward nationalist message," but *Shaharut* displaced this message with another in 1920 to contrast Pharaoh with Moses: the one symbolizing enslavement, the other freedom and redemption. For Raider, this new image "represents a return to more traditional forms of Zionist mythologization." The Zionist reading of this exodus story is clear, for "behind Moses, a winding path leads toward a Palestinian landscape and a radiant sun."[15] Both images for Raider represent ideas or claims, for each "synthesizes the ideas of homecoming and a new beginning," or "implicitly reflects the impact of 'Ahad Haamism' in the American context." They are mere "expressions of Zionist mythology," or "reflect vastly different approaches to the concept of Zionist self-realization."[16] These Zionist representations indicate or represent, but they do not actively make claims. They are examples of Zionist discourse rather than producers of it.

But to see these images as active producers of knowledge, as I hope to do for Rosenblatt's *Social Zionism,* we must recognize how written texts and visual images work together to construct, maintain, and sometimes complicate arguments. Images are more than "expressions of" something; they do things—as they certainly did for Ackerman's memory of *A House in the Desert*—and we do things with them. We should not read texts first, and *then* turn to images as "proof" or "evidence" of those written arguments.[17] Images and texts work together as creative forms of production to offer combative, less linear, and more nuanced modes of argumentation. Black-and-white sketches function with written inscriptions in Rosenblatt's *Social Zionism* to become constructed narratives, and so operate within registers beyond mere supplemental visual evidence.

By recognizing images as constitutive features of arguments, the notion of a "text" expands to include visual acts of persuasion.[18] My focus on what we do with images, rather than what they merely reflect, parallels a growing trend in literary studies to read texts as political actors. Poetry, for instance, does not reflect the dilemmas of an age so much as it helps constitute and configure them. Eric Zakim's critique of Anita Shapira's political history elucidates this stance well. In his literary history of the Zionist slogan, "To Build and Be Built," Zakim focuses on Shapira's tendency to read poetry as a representative source of political events. Although Zakim justly praises Shapira's *Land and Power: The Zionist Resort to Force 1881–1948,* he finds that she chooses "only those literary texts that explicitly thematize conflict and what she calls a 'defensive ethos.'" Shapira limits her perspective "to a thematic reflection of conflict," and this, according to Zakim, brands poetry "as reflective proof of the ethos Shapira describes." Zionist poetry never emerges within this methodological view as "constitutive of the history Shapira is describing."[19] And it is this sense of constitution—the active creation of an ethos rather than a reflective description of it—that Zakim wants to trace in poetic works, and I discover in Rosenblatt's *Social Zionism.*

In a book of some one-hundred-and-fifty-one pages, *Social Zionism* contains a bit more than thirty sketches. Since each page displays one image, many of these scenes repeat in patterned sequences. There are four sketches in *Social Zionism* that originally appeared in *The Maccabaean* during the years 1918–1919,[20] but a number of images maintain striking similarities.[21] Yet the function of these sketches differs significantly in the two published venues. In *The Maccabaean,* images appear as decorative appendages to articles, surfacing as fillers at the end of a page to offer an aesthetic accessory to the article's content. Images in *Social Zionism,* however, function as constitutive features of Rosenblatt's arguments in ways that move beyond their aesthetic value in *The Maccabaean,* and perhaps even beyond Rosenblatt's own intentions. In this sense, the sketches in *Social Zionism* are different *kinds* of images than those found in *The Maccabaean,* even if they are artistically comparable. The context within which these images appear decidedly informs the work they do. In *The Maccabaean*, they show elegant taste; in *Social Zionism*, they make claims about Jewish authenticity.

Within the argumentative structure of Rosenblatt's *Social Zionism*, images make claims about personal identity in ways that constitute authenticity as a visual practice. We can see what authenticity looks like in and through the juxtaposition of writing and image in Rosenblatt's text. Again I want to emphasize that many, if not all, of his ideas became common currency in early progressive visions of Zion, and one can readily glean from his later biographical work, *Two Generations of Zionism* (1967), just how much he follows the intellectual and administrative efforts from Brandeis and others. Yet Rosenblatt produces a uniquely *visual* account of social Zionism and Jewish authenticity, and so his text helps us to see how images rhetorically work with and against texts. His narrative interweaves romantic sketches with his own prose to perform the kind of compelling account that so moved Walter Ackerman in his viewing of *A House in the Desert*. This visual–textual focus appears on the very first page of his book, and continues unabated throughout.

Social Zionism is an extended argument in support of the Pittsburgh Program as the natural heir to the First Zionist Congress in Basel in 1897. If Herzl had won the day with his political Zionism, then Rosenblatt seeks to do the same for his American brand of social Zionism. The Basel Platform declared political independence for the "Jewish race who had determined to build a Jewish state." Herzl informed the world about the Zionist political agenda; the Pittsburgh Program, by enunciating how "social justice" underwrites this agenda, "gives us a picture of the *kind* of state for which the Zionists are striving."[22] From the outset, Rosenblatt locates the Pittsburgh Program as the necessary progressive model to enact Herzl's political vision.[23] *Social Zionism* as visual text seeks to reduce the tension between political and practical Zionism, as they were often labeled, through a developmental process from a state directive to a "picture of the *kind* of state."[24] Rosenblatt turns from Herzl's visionary rhetoric to the actual vision of a national homeland.

Yet this notion of a movement's natural evolution concedes too much. Later in his book, Rosenblatt fuses his social Zionism with Herzl's political campaign, situating his account of social justice at the very heart of Zionist discourse:

> Herzl, however, was not a crafty politician, but a social prophet, and it is high time that we begin to appreciate the "Social Zionism" of the author of the Judenstatt and Altneuland. Social Zionism comprehends both Practical and Political Zionism, and supplements the two by the concept of a Jewish Commonwealth in Zion which would serve as a model for the nations in the agelong battle for social justice.[25]

As Zionists often quoted the biblical prophets, especially Isaiah, to ground the legitimacy of their movement in biblical origins, so too Rosenblatt appeals to

Herzl to establish authentic roots for American Zionism. Still, the anxiety of the inauthentic lingers dangerously in the background. Rosenblatt feels compelled to ground his social Zionism in the original architect. He seeks a foundation upon which to root his progressive vision. This move to origins belies his own anxiety that his socialist program might not seem genuine, or might perhaps appear too progressive. Where Zionist history recovered biblical foundations, traversing and thereby silencing the intermittent two thousand years of Jewish heritage, Rosenblatt also links foundations with progressive visions, fashioning the "age-long battle for social justice" as the authentic source for the Jewish Commonwealth in Zion. His social Zionism *is* authentic Zionism. It is a claim borne out of an anxiety of inauthenticity.

This anxiety exposes both Rosenblatt's rhetoric of legitimacy and his theory of colonization. To justify a Jewish political community in Palestine, Rosenblatt envisions it as a "model for the nations." The Pittsburgh Program expresses far more than the particular strivings of the Jewish people: it serves a world in need of a living example. In this updated, socialist account of the chosen people, Rosenblatt offers the Jews as a living model for a redeemed world:

> The Pittsburgh Program, indeed, has world wide significance. Its result may prove to be of benefit not to ourselves alone, but to all the world. In making Palestine a laboratory for momentous experiments in the quest for social justice, we are dedicating the future Jewish State to a world purpose, even as Moses transformed our ancestors into a "chosen people," who, from the vantage ground of the Holy Land, were to bring the message of divine justice to the world. . . . Can there be a higher or nobler mission?[26]

The notion that Palestine could become a "laboratory" for social experiments had a wide following in the American Zionist movement, especially from progressive thinkers like Rosenblatt, Kallen, and Brandeis.[27] Jonathan Sarna notes, as well, that the major aim of Rosenblatt's *Social Zionism* was "to promote the creation of 'a model community [in Palestine] based on Social Justice.'"[28] That model simulates Moses' own creative moments when he fashions, apparently without divine assistance, his own "chosen people" to carry the progressive message to all. Social Zionism is not only about Jewish authenticity and power; for Rosenblatt, it is a humanitarian movement for universal justice, but one evidently chosen only for a few.

Shapira notes this sense of moral integrity that suffused early Zionist discourse, even if now such intentions appear far less honorable. She also concedes how this ethical stance tended to focus on the cultivation of an uninhabited land. The slogan "A land without a people for a people without a land" suggested a willful blindness to the Arab and Bedouin populations actually living in Palestine.[29] As Michael Berkowitz reveals, these claims also appeared in visual representations of Palestine: "As often as possible, Arab towns and dwellings were shown unpopulated, or with very few inhabitants."[30] For his part, Herzl rarely concerned himself with the native inhabitants of Palestine, but believed in the Jewish colonizing mission, both to improve the native Arab population and to help the world's "wretched and poor."[31] Rosenblatt adopts this view as well, and like many of his contemporaries understands the Zionist movement as good for both Jews and Arabs, even if he rarely envisions Arabs productively living on the land. This was part of Zionism's "higher or nobler mission," and like Herzl before him, Rosenblatt extends this ethical humanitarianism beyond those living in Palestine. The land becomes an experimental laboratory for social justice. Rosenblatt as scientist conducts social experiments that, in principle, could be recreated and tested elsewhere. The Pittsburgh Program, in his view, is really a social scientific program to test and observe voluntary subjects in the quest for communal harmony. If the experiment works in Palestine, then it could be duplicated in other "laboratories" as well. To be "chosen" is to be an experimental subject for social justice. Rosenblatt adopts the scientific method as his own, and in his "social scientific turn"[32] has channeled the Jewish mission to the world. Palestine becomes a "Holy Land" for all, even if Rosenblatt envisions it only for some. The rhetorical force of this text lies squarely on Rosenblatt's appeal to social justice.

Imagining Wasteland and Colonization

The images in *Social Zionism* reveal a land and a people in need of such redemptive work. The sketch on the first page of Rosenblatt's "Introduction" conjures up a lone Bedouin on a camel, traversing a landscape barren but for an ancient village along the horizon (this image was originally published in *The Maccabaean*). There is only one tree planted within the town, and ominous clouds loom beyond it. The round, clay roofs of the buildings (quite typical for this imagined architecture) mold effortlessly into the landscape, summoning that timeless sense of the "Holy Land" that Jeffrey Shandler and Beth Wenger claim has "remained frozen in time since antiquity." The Bedouin traveler, of course, also fits the scene as that imagined "primitive" who, like the very land he inhabits, is a timeless icon of the "picturesque."[33] Rafael Medoff argues that early Zionists often imagined Palestinian Arabs as wandering Bedouins, and did so in ways that exhibited "relatively little interest in the Palestinian Arabs."[34] Zionists with various motivations often juxtaposed this natural scene to the modernized representations of Zionist settlements. Yael Zerubavel recognizes how images of the desert and settlement are "oppositional symbolic landspaces": the one empty, unproductive, barren, uncivilized, and effeminate, the other fertile, cultivated, cultured, and masculine.[35] The Bedouin desert, as an "empty" and "unmarked" space,[36] is a deprived land in need of redemption. This lack also signifies those living on that land; Zerubavel, Shapira, and Berkowitz demonstrate how Arabs and Bedouins appear as natural features of a barren landscape.[37] Both the land and people require the missionary work of Rosenblatt's social Zionism.

Figure 1.1. Bedouin on Camel. Bernard Rosenblatt, *Social Zionism* (1919).

The implications of such depictions, as both Shandler and Wenger note, have certainly been momentous for contemporary Middle East politics.[38] But if such fantasies endure to inform visions of Palestine, they also have an important purpose for Rosenblatt's American Zionists of the 1920s. For, as with all other depictions in this text, the Bedouin on the first page of *Social Zionism* travels alone. He gazes upon a village emptied of inhabitants, of commercial life, of anything that might signify or suggest a living, thriving community of inhabitants. The stark buildings melt into the desolate topography. With a single palm tree providing little shade or comfort before the ominous cloud on the horizon, this town could be anywhere, or nowhere. This is not a community, nor is it property; this is the primitive in its natural condition. If the text argues for social justice, the image raises the possibility that justice does not apply to nature, or to those who live there.

As the primitive wasteland, the sketch presents the need and readiness for the Zionist experimental laboratory, even if these experiments may not be applicable to native inhabitants. For as Rosenblatt will argue some pages later, that land is empty of both structure and society. According to Zerubavel, views like Rosenblatt's were quite common among early Zionist leaders:

> Zionist settlers characterized the Arab settlement by disorder, filth, and neglect. The Arab village represented a total disregard for the social distinctions that informed the European notion of order: inside and outside, hygiene and dirt, human beings and animals.... The Zionist settlement, in contrast, introduced order into the chaotic local landscape, thereby transforming the desert into a civilized space.[39]

The lone Bedouin rider in *Social Zionism* is merely an onlooker to a blank slate. Rosenblatt sees only an empty wasteland: "it was necessary that the land should lie fallow, so that when we begin to build the structure of the Jewish Commonwealth we can be free to fit the stones of the House of Israel with Justice and Righteousness."[40] In this colonization project, there remains nothing to overcome, subdue, or to conquer. This is colonization by settlement but not by force, one that models the European colonization of "vast and uninhabited territory."[41] To be sure, as scholars have often remarked, Zionism harbored no "mother country," and so differed in significant ways from other colonizing efforts.[42] And Rosenblatt, like many of his contemporaries, distinguished between colonization and colonial exploitation: "We are laboring to rejuvenate a nation, not to rule over subject races."[43] But Rosenblatt could defend this contrast only by denying a visual presence to those other races in the land. Palestine appears as an empty slate awaiting the colonization of a vast empty space—as if Rosenblatt views colonization in the beginning as a Genesis creation narrative. My point is that the land, but not its inhabitants, requires a form of justice. So while Rosenblatt's text argues for justice on a universal scale, the images restrict it to property. This is the rhetorical work performed by the images in *Social Zionism*.

The sketch of the traveling Bedouin presents an argument for colonization of a land but not a people. He travels not *to* the buildings but alongside them, passing them by as he would any other object along his path. The village holds little interest or concern for a wandering traveler. The image provokes Rosenblatt's desire to transform a natural primitive state into a progressive laboratory for social justice. This sense of the innocent primitive—where neither architecture nor society emerge as recognizable features of the social landscape—means that another, more visible, people must inhabit the land to better transform it into a just one. The principles of justice and righteousness, as Rosenblatt imagines them, demand a settling and settled people. This the lone Bedouin cannot become, and as W. J. T. Mitchell observes, cannot plausibly be as the imagined primitive:

> The primitive or aboriginal dweller on the land (the "pagan" or "rustic" villager) is seen as part of the landscape, not as a self-consciously detached viewer who sees nature for its own sake as the Western observer does. In addition, the native dweller is seen as someone who fails to see the material wealth and value of the land, a value that is obvious to the Western observer.

The Bedouin lives off the land as a natural inhabitant, but he does not use the land to build a community of social justice. This failure of exploitation is *his* failure, and one that confers "a presumptive right of conquest and colonization on the Western observer, who comes armed both with weapons and arguments to underwrite the legitimacy of his appropriation of the land."[44] The desolate land functions as visual proof that Bedouins cannot become legitimate owners; its lack is theirs as well.[45] The emptiness of the land, then, reflects the shallowness of the self. The Bedouin is not a member of a chosen people armed with an experimental laboratory to make the desert bloom. Images like this one empty Palestine of authentic selves, and as Edward Said suggests, turn "its landscape instead into an empty space."[46]

Mitchell claims that as a category, landscape can serve "as an aesthetic alibi for conquest, a way of naturalizing imperial expansion."[47] This is, to my mind, only part of the work performed by this and other images in *Social Zionism*. We see how images work against the text to limit the expanse of social justice.

Only unmarked territory requires justice; after all, the project here is to make the desert bloom. But native inhabitants remain adrift in this scene. The Bedouin is out of place; he wanders without a goal, always appearing on-the-way—making a profoundly homeless journey of sterile wanderings. The sketch transforms this empty space into rightful place; social Zionism becomes authentic presence. And the image offers one more argument that directly contradicts the textual call for social justice: it effectively transfers the American Jewish anxiety of belonging onto the imagined Bedouin as inauthentic traveler. Jews *belong* here, in this transformed land. It is their rightful inheritance and mission. But if one belongs, then the other becomes homeless. This Bedouin, however foreign and exotic, absorbs the American Jewish fear of alienation in these pictorial landscapes.

The images in *Social Zionism* have turned native inhabitants into wandering Jews—a reference to the popular myth, beginning in the seventeenth century (although with roots much earlier), that described a ghostly wanderer who, without home or settlement, travels aimlessly from land to land. Todd Presner argues that nearly all of the cultural representations of this type "emphasize the fact that the Jew is wandering—by foot—across the world." He is neither an explorer nor a pioneer, but only "a spectator on the world: he never creates anything, he never changes anything, and he never leaves anything behind."[48] Rosenblatt's chosen people become the bearers of social justice by displacing the wandering Bedouin and marking him as the wandering Jew. Though not on foot, the camel-riding Bedouin projects a traveling, rootless indifference. He wanders in a barren land alone, living neither in any recognizable space nor striving to be in one. This Bedouin is merely "passing through the space, walking or riding idly."[49] But American Jews do not see these wandering Bedouins as part of their own future. Instead, they envision modern social scientists who colonize space in order to cultivate the self. Rather than primitive gazers who traverse a land, they discover and build an authentic place. Rosenblatt pictures the inauthentic other as traveling Bedouin for all the Jews to see. The images conjure the space of social justice against the dislocated wanderings of native Bedouins.

The Bedouin image captures Palestine as the ideal land upon which to establish a scientific laboratory for social justice. Though the sketch of modern landworkers will not appear until some four pages later, where they harvest wheat and cultivate their own "self-realization of the individual,"[50] Rosenblatt already "places" them in his introductory remarks. The words on the page alongside the Bedouin image conjure up a "Jewish race," not a lone traveler, and "a Jewish State," but not a village dissolving into a barren landscape. If Zerubavel is right that notions of the desert and settlement continually announce the presence (or absence) of the other, then the lone Bedouin wandering in the desert asserts its opposite: the modern Jewish community of Zionist settlers. The coupling of word and image assert what is not seen: the replacement of the inauthentic with Jewish

Figure 1.2. Bedouin Observing Western Ship. Bernard Rosenblatt, *Social Zionism* (1919).

presence. The image awaits the text to be fully whole and present, and so wasteland calls out to its other: it is a landless people in waiting for Jewish settlement.

Presner notes how images of wandering Jews never reveal them traveling by ship, and so they cannot be European conquerors nor a truly political nation.[51] A good number of Zionist works attempt to counter that depiction, and in *Social Zionism* there is one exceptionally powerful image of this kind. The sketch accompanying Rosenblatt's discussion of "the new Jewish state" and the "Jewish Industrial Army," wherein citizens might enlist as "'soldiers in industry,'"[52] reveals the possible destination of the Bedouin traversing a barren landscape. An enormous ship (perhaps even two ships, although it is difficult to know for certain), carrying the "Jewish Industrial Army" has arrived to create the Jewish state for the Bedouins on land, who await its arrival. It magnificently dwarfs the tiny sailboat along the shore, a weighty reminder to the ship's symbolic import in Western culture. Such vessels, according to Todd Presner, signified Western "knowledge, education, heroism, bravery, freedom, and statehood."[53] For literary scholar Hannan Hever, the cultural logic of the sea-crossing vessel implicates an Ashkenazi Zionist discourse, "the customary sea crossing that constantly appears in the hegemonic Ashkenazi Zionist description, the symbolic and normative crossing of the same Mediterranean Sea that laps the shores of both Alexandria and Tel Aviv."[54] These powerful images and associations surface as well throughout Rachel Arbel's collection of Zionist visual depictions between 1897 and 1947, revealing massive ships arriving to colonize and settle the land.[55]

The vessel in Rosenblatt's text carries all the authority of Western modernity, technology, navigation, and largesse. It maps terrain, while others traverse, or in this scene, merely accede to the ship's authoritative power. Though the sailboat and the Bedouin onlookers remain passive gazers, the ship does not overrun what lies before it. The vessel simply reduces all before its path in size and stature. Berkowitz is right to argue that "Arabs were not completely written out of the presentation of Palestine to European Jewry, but they were accessory, at best, to the grand project of the Jews rebuilding their land."[56] The sailboat just happens to be in the way—a mere insignificance before a much grandeur project. And so, too, the Bedouin observers are merely witnesses to this social engineering. The

American Zionists have not come to colonize a people, or even to bring social justice to them; rather, they arrive to cultivate a land, and in doing so liberate themselves.[57] As spectators to this self-realization, the inhabitants may also gain some dignity and liberty. But they remain out of focus: they are bystanders to these "soldiers of industry" mapping "the road to 'Social Justice.'"[58] Images make this argument against the textual appeals to Zionism's "world purpose." But together, text and image project the colonizing work of that "grand project of the Jews rebuilding their land."

The ship has arrived as metaphor for the militant power of the state and the Industrial Army. Rosenblatt employs managerial language to convey a sense of mastery: "we shall establish," "we shall be able to regulate," and all this control "will guide us along." Yet the passive Bedouin onlookers articulate but another feature of this scene: there is nothing and no one to dominate—the land and its people lie dormant and wait as passive witnesses to the building of "an industrial democracy in the Holy Land."[59] Indeed, that very image of "the Holy Land" is a land "frozen in time since antiquity."[60] It draws from that romantic landscape associated with the pristine desert that Zerubavel tracked during the pre-State *Yishuv* years. The Holy Land recovers its ancient roots by yielding fertile pastures that reveal the land's latent productivity.

Only the Zionist settler draws forth this untapped resource. Like many of his colleagues, Rosenblatt appeals to the prophet Isaiah to articulate that Zionist sense of "upbuilding" the land. Here the Isaiah text *as image* informs his claims to self-realization. Rosenblatt inscribes text into image, grounding biblical prophecy in landscape. But he also inserts image into text, creating a rooted vision of Isaiah's call to build for one's own. This settler belongs to a biblical heritage, and though represented alone, stands together with Isaiah's "Mine elect."[61] This is a chosen people, and this is their land.

The image portrays a large sun in the distance, together with the Zionist worker who sprinkles seeds upon the plowed land. The straight lines of the field confirm that Western technology has traveled from ship to land, where tilling the land creates that "muscle Jew" who, as Presner nicely puts it, "through his discipline, adaptability, and strength" cultivates a "rootedness that is tied to the fertility of the ground."[62] The text from Isaiah authorizes the ship's arrival to colonize the land (to build houses, to inhabit them, to plant vineyards); the "final Jewish state" brings to fruition this biblical injunction for it.[63] Native inhabitants disappear in this scene; only "Mine elect shall long enjoy the work of their hands."[64] Here is the authentic, masculine self rooted in the redeemed, colonized, and feminized land. He is alone, to be sure, but is not lonely, for the village lies at the edge of the plowed field (just above his left shoulder). Rosenblatt calls this "true liberty":[65] an image of authentic (masculine) self and landscape. Even the absent others remain stubbornly present, alluded to in Isaiah's warning that "they shall

"And they shall build houses, and inhabit them;

"And they shall plant vineyards, and eat the fruit of them.

"They shall not build, and another inhabit,

"They shall not plant, and another eat;

"For as the days of a tree shall be the days of My people,

"And Mine elect shall long enjoy the work of their hands."—

(ISAIAH, Chapter 65—Verses 21, 22)

Figure 1.3. Isaiah Biblical Text with Image. Bernard Rosenblatt, *Social Zionism* (1919).

not build, and another inhabit." The native Bedouins fail to establish, regulate, control, or guide, and so must stand to the side and become small before the Jewish state. Authentic beings require a holy land to cultivate, and so become the true natives to this biblical property. As Daniel Boyarin suggests, "the Jews, as Zionists, constitute themselves both as natives and as colonizers."[66]

Images in *Social Zionism* turn colonizers into natives. The Bedouins wander and traverse a land they barely inhabit—though in 1917 Arabs comprised more than 80 percent of the Palestinian population. The Zionist pioneers cultivate a land and set up shop.[67] They plant trees and firmly root themselves in the land; large vessels anchor in the harbor, as settled as Rosenblatt's Jewish Industrial Army. So even if these Zionist settlers arrive in modern ships, through their labor and cultivation they become natives and proper inhabitants of the land. The Bedouins, by contrast, become the inauthentic foreigners to a land they neither

Figure 1.4. Desert Wasteland. Bernard Rosenblatt, *Social Zionism* (1919).

develop nor inhabit. This is a recurrent theme in Zionist discourse, and Rosenblatt appears to appropriate it without much reflection. Again, I want to emphasize that much of what we find in Rosenblatt we also discover elsewhere in texts of this period. But *Social Zionism* illustrates how images produce extra-linguistic arguments that nonetheless work with texts to construct powerful Zionist rhetoric. The land belongs to those who cultivate it, and the Bedouins and Arabs reveal their foreignness by allowing it to lie fallow. Although Rosenblatt's text does not argue this, his images do.

This incongruous binary between those who appear as natives (but are really wanderers along a wasteland) and those who emerge as settlers (but are truly autochthonous) is visually manifest in two paired images.[68] The first pictures a sparse, arid land with a scattering of small trees and a herd of sheep grazing behind a wooden fence. This land is entirely uninhabited, and yet the fence and collection of animals suggest the work and presence of herders. The lines are scattered and wavy, signifying lack of control and direction. This peaceful, nomadic landscape recalls the eternal "Holy Land" of ancient shepherds who wandered the biblical terrain. But a very different image appears in concert with this passive territory, one that suggests a modern, cultivated environment. Note the grazing field marked by horizontal straight lines—a clear sign that fallow land has been transformed into agricultural plenty. The Zionist laborer continues to work the land, harnessing animal power to cultivate a latent fecundity. Masculine labor transforms a barren desert into blossoming splendor—a vision of gendered spaces and heteronormativity. The absent Bedouin ought not appear here, for he remains the weak male who fails to cultivate the feminine land; this land has only one expectant suitor. The visual claim for a more natural union between Holy Land and Zionist colonizer bears additional fruit: small buildings arise among the trees, and the hills become the backdrop to what was formally nomadic space. One could view these two images discussed here as one (leaving to the side, for the moment, the depiction of the town on the right), with the artist now taking a broader, more sweeping view of the terrain. Where the focus had once been the grazing sheep on the hillside, now those hills form the background to agricultural production. The pioneer worker arrives to create something out of nothing.

Figure 1.5. Plowing Fields and City on a Hill. Bernard Rosenblatt, *Social Zionism* (1919).

The land is a blank slate: "Where others have had to destroy and rebuild, we shall have only to build."[69] The Bedouins are no longer in view, becoming the feminized other to the masculine strength of the muscular Jew.

Within this visual claim to masculinity appears a flowing river separating the farm from the bustling city on the hill, together with a sharp, thin line running on a slight angle from one side of the river to the other (from the sun's rays on the upper left toward the city). The sun enlightens the city dwellers too, and these angular buildings contrast sharply with the rounded, out-of-focus structures of desert dwellings. There are, to be sure, many possible interpretive readings for this juxtaposition between town and country, but one thing seems clear: this environment is altogether different from the one depicting the roaming fields with the herd of sheep. The sharp lines, in both field and town, protect the settlement from desert encroachment. Marking a space is more than an act of transformation; it is also an act of defense against chaos. This is a masculine branding, and it deflects the classic antisemitic smears of Jewish femininity. This is a cultivated, gendered authenticity of the male Jewish imaginary.

There are really two kinds of natives to this land, and the one supersedes the other. The Bedouin shepherd lives in accordance with, but does not maintain a direct and flourishing relation to, the environment, simply accepting the landscape as it is. But the Zionist colonist who now cultivates the land and builds a nation creates an environment that mirrors his own sense of authentic self. The one passively reflects his own femininity in the feminine landscape; the other actively cultivates his own masculinity by transforming the feminine land into a fertile presence. The Zionist colonizer has gone native.

Seeing Authenticity in Zion

Recall the image of the desert wasteland, with the solitary Bedouin traversing an ancient village as backdrop (Figure 1.1). *Social Zionism* follows that image with a wide-angle view of the village, with small sailboats in the harbor, and the Bedouin as he passes by the village. Perhaps the large vessel carrying Rosenblatt's Industrial Army lies just out of view to the right of the sailboats. But readers would have to construct that larger panorama and splice together scenes between the margins, as viewers often do in graphic novels.[70] Here the cloud still looms on

Figure 1.6. Bedouin next to Shore. Bernard Rosenblatt, *Social Zionism* (1919).

the horizon, even as the sun beats down upon the village rooftops (the shading in both images suggests how the sun lies almost directly above the buildings). There are more trees, although they grow quite distant from the town. But now we understand why people live here: the village borders a large body of water. Villagers have access both to and from the community—a point made visually secure by the presence of either one or two sailboats. This is a soothing, tranquil vision, one that suggests a cool breeze as the boats either sail by or dock effortlessly in the shallow water. It depicts another powerful image of the desert as original nature, a form of purity that "withstood the pressure of history and modernity and preserved its primal beauty and integrity."[71] The sailboats appear less as seafaring cruisers and more like recreational vessels for short excursions. One could imagine a pleasant daytime sail and a ride along the shore. The prospect suggests a remoteness and a quiet peacefulness—a scenic and charming rural vision. No industry, sweatshops, or other city ugliness can be found here. The vision recalls the state of nature before prophetic missions and chosen people, before seafaring cruisers and the Zionist Industrial Army, and certainly prior to any yearning or pressing need for social justice.

The image presents the passive other to the more progressive, vigorous challenge of social Zionism. For Rosenblatt, only in "concrete experience" and in a "final Jewish state we shall develop a model community based on Social Justice."[72] But we do not see this in the sketch: neither state, community, nor concrete experience lead to justice for all. The image depicts the inauthentic other to Rosenblatt's textual argument; it is a world-in-waiting for a Jewish commonwealth in Palestine—an innocent state of nature anticipating a progressive model for social justice. Such a yearning for colonization exposes the inauthentic as that which lurks behind all authentic visions: sterility, compliancy, and wandering existence persist as the backdrop to the active, textual reclaiming of social justice and scientific progress. In image, mindless wandering enables more authentic, textual visions.

The state of nature depicted in this image refers to both land and a people. In Rosenblatt's text, people are intimately tied to land, such that land both reflects and sustains personal identity and self-realization (*hagshamah atzmit*).

1. Political and civil equality irrespective of race, sex, or faith of all the inhabitants of the land.

2. To insure in the Jewish national home in Palestine equality of opportunity, we favor a policy which, with due regard to existing rights, shall tend to establish the ownership and control of the land and of all natural resources, and of all public utilities by the whole people.

3. All land, owned or controlled by the whole people, should be leased on such condi-

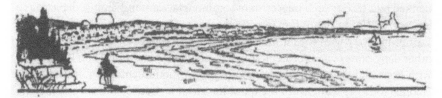

Figure 1.7. Text with Shore. Bernard Rosenblatt, *Social Zionism* (1919).

The land looks barren because the people are too. With the peaceful landscape come untroubled souls without yearnings for a better life. The Bedouin lives an inauthentic life upon illegitimate land; but even more, he never really aspires to an authentic mode of existence—it never becomes a worthy goal or noble pursuit. This form of innocence without "concrete experience" witnesses to a mode of being-in-the-world that remains passive, at ease, sterile, and inauthentic. All this contrasts sharply with the seven articles of the Pittsburgh Program listed on these pages. The first three articles appear with the image, the latter four on the next page, but they all read "as a prophecy of the future Commonwealth in Zion" designed to replace the barren stagnation depicted in the desert scenes. The list also reads as a Zionist progressive call for social justice:

1. political and civil equality
2. ownership of land and natural resources by "the whole people"
3. land leases to insure "continuity of possession"

4. the establishment of cooperatives

5. protection from land speculation [this article was eventually removed from the published document in Pittsburgh]

6. free public education

7. the establishment of Hebrew as "the national language of the Jewish people"[73]

It remains unclear whether the appeal to "the whole people" and the application of safeguards to protect the "continuity of possession" apply to non-Jews as well. The image on the page, however, suggests they need not, for it depicts only a lone figure traversing the land rather than a "whole people" possessing it. This mirrors what Arthur Goren discovers in Zionist films, in which one notices "the stark contrast between the 'primitive' peasant Arabs and the energetic, progressive *halutzim*."[74] In *Social Zionism*, the *text* allows us to read about the just *halutzim*, but the primitive Arabs appear only in images.

Yet a new day arises, and we see it in the image accompanying the latter four articles of the Pittsburgh Program. Here, the *halutz* ideal visually displaces the stance of the wandering Bedouin. A bright, massive sun emerges on the horizon, flanked by a forest. Such images were commonplace among Zionist depictions of a new era. We see them in many of Ephraim Moses Lilien's works that contrast European Jewry with the far more muscular, progressive Zionist pioneer, and in other depictions of a reborn Palestine.[75] Something new appears on the horizon, with hope and vision for a redeemed future. A monumental sun, heralding the "momentous experiments in the quest for social justice,"[76] now dwarfs the once ominous clouds.

The sun reappears two pages later, together with two farmers working the land. This image marks the first appearance of figures harnessing animals to cultivate the land. The rising (or setting) sun, now reduced in size compared to the human figures in the foreground, gently reminds us of human labor: these workers have been tilling the soil for some time, perhaps even from before dawn. One of them bends over as he harvests the wheat fields; the other, wearing a rancher-style hat for protection against the sun, holds what looks like a scythe in his right hand while his left grasps either a wheelbarrow or a tiller tied to two oxen. Neither dresses remotely like the camel-riding Bedouin. Michael Berkowitz claims that similar scenes, showing Jewish farmers working under the sun, "were a conspicuous attempt to parry the stereotype of Jews as an innately urban people, averse to nature and agricultural pursuits."[77] But the text suggests another concern with individual freedom and state interference. Rosenblatt defends a form of state involvement that still guarantees and protects individual liberty. For persons to flourish, state government cannot just "let-well-enough-alone," and must be involved in civil life. But that does not only mean enforcing legal rulings. Governments can surely burden communities, but they can also enable

INTRODUCTION 11

tions as will insure the fullest opportunity
for development and continuity of possession.

4. The co-operative principle should be applied as far as feasible in the organization
of all agricultural, industrial, commercial,
and financial undertakings.

5. The fiscal policy shall be framed so as to
protect the people from the evils of land
speculation and from every other form of
financial oppression.

6. The system of free public instruction
which is to be established, should embrace
all grades and departments of education.

7. The medium of public instruction shall be
Hebrew, the national language of the
Jewish people.

The second, third and fourth principles comprise a declaration of Social Zionism, as a complement to the Political Zionism of the older days.

The Pittsburgh Program is the excuse as well
as the justification for this little volume. The author
first used the phrase "Social Zionism" in an article
appearing in the "Collegiate Zionist" in July, 1910.
Since that day such phrases as the "Zion Commonwealth," "Jewish Industrial Army," and many other

Figure 1.8. Pittsburgh Program with Sunrise. Bernard Rosenblatt, *Social Zionism* (1919).

Figure 1.9. Farmers Plowing Field. Bernard Rosenblatt, *Social Zionism* (1919).

human flourishing. Social Zionists recognize that "the state can be utilized as a power for the self-development of society as well as for the self-realization of the individual." In this way, Rosenblatt and others create more than a Jewish state; they are "determined to build a model state in the Holy Land—freed from the economic wrongs, the social injustices and the greed of modern-day industrialism."[78] The image accompanying these words shows precisely how the Zionist creates a model state that enables individual liberty without overwhelming it with state interference.

With a focus on labor, the image also depicts how the model state cultivates the self. Here too the land mirrors personal fulfillment; the bounty of the land—situated far from urban grime, unemployment, and poverty—enables a heightened sense of personal achievement and "self-realization." Cultivation leads individuals to become more complete, modern, and authentic. This is classic labor Zionist rhetoric and a core image related to the figure of the *ḥalutz*. It also draws heavily from the charismatic Zionist ideologue A. D. Gordon (1856–1922), who at the age of forty-eight settled in Palestine to restore his self by working the land:

> It is life we want, no more and no less than that, our own life feeding on our own vital sources, in the fields and under the skies of our Homeland, a life based on our own physical and mental labors; we want vital energy and spiritual richness from this living source. We come to our Homeland in order to be planted in our natural soil from which we have been uprooted, to strike our roots deep into its life-giving substances, and to stretch out our branches in the sustaining and creating air and sunlight of the Homeland.[79]

This new, wholesome man flourishes in nature's image. Like nature itself he can be planted, rooted, and when given life, can stretch out his branches. And as Presner, Boyarin, and others point out, this "we" in Zionist discourse most often refers to a male tiller of the feminine land as the creator of the new state.[80] Rosenblatt certainly appeals to male individuals who cultivate authentic relations to the land.[81] It is, after all, the male workers in the image who help build the state. And this socialist state, Rosenblatt argues, enables rather than hinders individual liberty. In the context of this textual argument, the image of the field workers gives weight to Rosenblatt's discussion of a socialist state. We do not see the state anywhere; like Gordon, viewers gaze, instead, straight into nature and see men cultivating themselves by impregnating the land ("to strike our roots deep into its life-giving substances"). The masculine self is productive because the state is present but invisible. The visual image shows us that Rosenblatt's claims are realistic and just.

This sketch rhetorically functions alongside written texts and other visual imagery to produce a more robust vision of social Zionism. It integrates with previous (and subsequent) sketches to distinguish a landscape of nostalgic innocence from the progressive "upbuilding" of the self in making the desert bloom. The Bedouin figure roams over impoverished terrain; the Zionist worker cultivates a land eager to be fertile. That sense of eagerness, perhaps even accompanied by the memory of a distant and forgotten wealth, suggests a return to authentic presence. The sun continually arises and sets on the horizon, but now it has social Zionists to help prepare the land. These Jewish workers return to their authentic, wholesome selves in working a land that needs them. *"Anu banu artza livnot u'lehibanot ba"*—these are the words from the popular folk song that conveys the *ḥalutz* ideal: "We have come to the land to build it and to rebuild ourselves in the process."[82] Zakim describes this political slogan as "a construction of a Jewish subject in the land that hungrily strives to control the landscape in order to construct itself."[83] I find this formulation invitingly obscure, for who is it that "hungrily strives," the Jewish subject or the land? But that, indeed, is the point: the two have become so intertwined that each hungers for the other. In building a model state, these social Zionists also build model selves. And the land as feminine "other" desires to be cultivated and renewed. The images in *Social Zionism* do not accompany the text, nor do they merely confirm it. Instead, they help constitute Rosenblatt's claim to authentic "self-realization" in the working of an expectant land. Like Walter Ackerman's viewing of *A House in the Desert*, these images make authenticity visible, even as they make the anxiety of inauthenticity recognizable as the impotent, Bedouin other.

Envisioning America in Zion

Rosenblatt's *Social Zionism* interweaves visual images and written texts to produce an American Zionist depiction of the authentic self. As Ilan Troen points out, there are competing American and Zionist frontier myths. For the Zionist, "the pioneer cannot be a solitary person acting alone and for self-interest. The idea of mission on behalf of the nation is the most common and strongest association with *halutziut*." But the American ideal offers another vision altogether: "pioneers and pioneering in the United States have been traditionally viewed as sources of a form of individualism that is rooted in the realization of self-interest."[84] Though Troen's distinction seems a bit overwrought, it nonetheless locates Rosenblatt's text within both the "Zionist" sense of pioneering when he discusses the Pittsburgh Program, and in "American" ideals in claims such as this: "Men know now that the state can be utilized as a power for the self-development of society as well as for the self-realization of the individual."[85] We can see this American sensibility in Rosenblatt's discussion of state meddling and the accompanying sketch of the two workers. The image offers the "self-realization of the individual" but not of society: these laborers work alone with their oxen. According to Troen, such images suggest an American "little house on the prairie" far removed from the "concrete experience" in the land:

> The crucial distinction is that Zionist colonization was a highly centralized and directed experience that often supported socialist and communist forms of settlement. It encouraged individual and collective self-sacrifice rather than "individual self-betterment," which was the guiding ethos and purpose of the American pattern.[86]

The rhetoric in Rosenblatt's text appeals to both these collective and individual accounts of settlement, but the images project an American concern for the authentic individual. Troen believes this kind of visual exposure yields a distinctively American-type account of the frontier, in which strong and self-made individuals conquer the Western countryside. Rosenblatt's *Social Zionism* shows us how this American version of Zionism appears: an image of two male laborers, separated from their communal homes, who cultivate themselves and the land alone. This is the American dream of individual achievement through singular effort, rather than, for example, the German fantasy of a more integrated and wholesome "Mediterranean man."[87] Authenticity lies within the self and the agricultural land that makes self-realization possible. The laboratory in Zion cultivates American roots.

When Rosenblatt appeals to the Zionist sense of "centralized and directed experience," he tends to focus on the nature of the state rather than on the functioning of a social community. States protect and enable individual rights, and this, too, according to Troen, is a common American vision of liberal society. *Social Zionism* shows us neither *kibbutzim* (collective settlements) nor *moshavim* (cooperative settlements), but only individual workers supported by an abstract state as custodian and protector of liberty. Perhaps this mirrors the American concern for economic efficiency that many found lacking in such collective enterprises.[88] But Rosenblatt worries that poverty and unemployment produce "conditions that are unfavorable to the physical development of man," and so the state must intervene "for the protection of our economic life." Destitution, inactivity, and poor working conditions are the true "forces of coercion that set bounds to the self-development of the individual."[89] A "dweller of a city slum" or a "frugal and industrious employee in the sweatshop . . . is not legally a slave," but "he is not free—he is the slave of the Social System of his day."[90] The state can help remove these impediments to freedom; modern workers in the field enact individual liberty far removed from the industrious city and its slave inhabitants.

Figure 1.10. Patterned Fields. Bernard Rosenblatt, *Social Zionism* (1919).

The desert conceals poverty and unemployment. In this way, images evoke a quite distant state that protects from afar. The state's very absence nonetheless betrays a real presence: individual liberties are still in force and well-protected. In fact, a model state prevents "forces of coercion" from limiting "true liberty." The state ensures a level playing field, as it were, so that individuals flourish as distinct selves without social pressures to conform: "Only after we have removed the despotism of physical needs can we succeed in building a higher self, a better and nobler type of man."[91] The visual absence of the state enables another kind of visual presence: these field workers function like Americans yearning for individual liberty. Yet these Americans are more authentic and more true to themselves because they cultivate a land as their laboratory for individual self-realization.

This is an American vision of "self-realization" and the *ḥalutz* ideal. Rosenblatt ties self-realization directly to the land, such that the American Zionist cultivates Palestine in order to cultivate the self. Note the image following the two farm workers: it depicts the results of their labors. We see an expansive field of wheat, now bundled into bushels—a harvest of bounty. In the distance lies the village, with the same rooftops by which the Bedouin passed and looked away. But this village resembles a community now, with a forest beyond it, and a more welcoming cloud provides appropriate shade. We even glimpse a second forest, and perhaps another dwelling site, as the field stretches to the top right corner of the sketch. Take note of the straight lines dissecting the landscape. Zerubavel suggests how this vertical pattern imposes Western rationality on a chaotic landscape:

> One of the most prominent features of the Jewish settlement was the introduction of straight lines in the landscape, which gave it a modern character. The imposition of the grid system on a natural landscape represents a western view associated with rationality and technological progress and contrasts with the narrow, curved streets of the old towns and villages.[92]

This is how the desert blooms; the image shows us what modern technology achieves, both for the once fallow land and for the persons who cultivate it. The houses still dissolve softly into a landscape, but the scene is no longer isolated and

Figure 1.11. Roaming Bedouins on Camels. Bernard Rosenblatt, *Social Zionism* (1919).

shallow. Instead, the village echoes the profound transformation of the fields. These dwellings belong to and fit organically within the modernized landscape. In this image, we see the fruits of labor: the workers' absence maintains a firm presence in agricultural and communal fullness. Gordon's vision of the self reflected in nature appears here as well: one gazes in satisfaction at the wonderful bounty of the land and with pride at the strength of those persons elevated by it. The self is firmly rooted and planted, such that nature and man are one. The visual image encourages us to see authentic selves *in* the land even when they are not visually present.

Rosenblatt argues that these are the images of land and self that one expects from a socialist state. When the state encourages true liberty, it also curtails those physical "forces of coercion" that bind persons to a primitive existence. The images of bountiful fields and muscular workers suggest a modern, "simple program" of voluntary institutions. Rosenblatt distinguishes this socialist agenda from "the philosophy of Anarchism" that compels communal membership without personal consent.[93] The picture of the fertile harvest reveals what a social Zionism can produce. But anarchy prevails when Bedouins simply roam across a barren field, as they do in the image of Bedouins traversing an arid landscape with two pyramids in the background. The figures remain nondescript, and but for the hunched human in the foreground, all are darkened and traveling . . . nowhere. The lines are incongruous and sporadic, suggesting a wandering that never ends. This is what visual inauthenticity looks like, and it exposes Rosenblatt's profound fear of a sterile American Judaism. The disorder produced by these juxtaposed images—the one with a worked field, bountiful harvest, and hospitable village, the other with traveling Bedouins—reveals the rhetorical force of visual images. They inform Zerubavel's insight that "Bedouins passing through the space, walking or riding idly are juxtaposed with Zionist pioneers rigorously engaged in working their land."[94] The Zionist pioneers are rooted; the Bedouin travelers are unmoored. The images, and not Rosenblatt's written text, transform the wandering Jew into the rambling Bedouin. Again, images do not reflect the written argument so much as constitute it. The state protects individual self-realization; without it, all we have is a wasteland of individual wanderings. The image of the wandering Bedouin makes that point visually explicit.

Figure 1.12. The American Cowboy in Zion. Bernard Rosenblatt, *Social Zionism* (1919).

These sketches embrace an American Zionist image of the *ḥalutz* as Western cowboy, even as the text situates him within a community of voluntary state institutions. This Zionist cowboy is alone *in image,* but not far from the civilizing presence of the state *in text.*[95] He resembles depictions of the *shomer* (the guardian) who protected outlying villages, but he lacks the Bedouin garb often worn in these pictures.[96] Safeguarding his individual freedom, the cowboy-turned-Zionist rides into the sunset, but not with lawless abandon. The state remains in force, but the image reassures us that a socialist form of Zionism need not undermine individual liberty. The Bedouins, in contrast, exist as lone travelers or group vagabonds without social structure or state intervention. In these depictions of the archaic other, *Social Zionism* presents the absence of state institutions as contributing to a life of anarchy, sterile wanderings, and primitive, inauthentic existence. Juxtaposed, these images and texts construct social Zionism as fulfilling American individual liberty and the Western frontier myth, even as they make visible a decaying life of isolated captivity. *Social Zionism* reveals, even as it anticipates, an authentic awakening. Jews must travel to Zion to become truly American Jews.

Race and Environment

American individualism transforms a wasteland into an authentic home for Jewish self-cultivation. Rosenblatt simply refuses to accept the land as barren, or the inauthentic as autochthonous, and so he proposes a distinction between primary and secondary environments. In Rosenblatt's taxonomy, the primary environment simulates a state of nature that "imposes" itself upon the "various races." White people, for example, cannot thrive in the tropics, just as Eskimos "perish in the mild and inviting climate of California." This racial geography, one that appropriates a polygenesis discourse of race relations,[97] yields important lessons for colonizing civilizations, for the British will never "inherit the riches of India," and though the Americans have conquered the Philippines, they will never live and prosper there.[98] The Jewish Zionist, then, cannot plausibly thrive in a primary environment of barren hillsides. He must transform the primary landscape and "impose" his will upon it; in this he becomes the masculine heir to a feminine land awaiting a strong hand. Certainly the primary environment suits

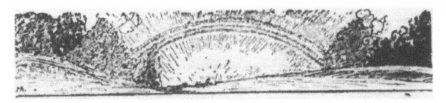

Figure 1.13. Sunrise. Bernard Rosenblatt, *Social Zionism* (1919).

the effeminate Bedouin herder who acquiesces to nature's will. But Rosenblatt believes such passive acceptance never rises to the level of nation building, for only a secondary environment turns a people into a nation:

> In short, while humanity is limited by a primary environment consisting of soil, climate and physical situation, man is ever evolving a secondary environment consisting of past experiences, present conditions and ideals, and aspirations for the future, which tend to differentiate one group of people from another. . . . History, when read aright, stands as an ever willing witness to sanctify this secondary man-created environment.[99]

The images in *Social Zionism* give the lie to Rosenblatt's assertion that "man is ever evolving a secondary environment." Not true: only the Zionist laborer does so here. The Bedouin, who fails even to appear in a "man-created" landscape, exists within and is limited to the primary environment. Without an active political history, he produces neither a culture nor a nation (he is, Rosenblatt tells us here, merely a member of a race). The Jews, however, began as a nation, became a race, and are now recovering their national "inheritance." The land is theirs by birthright, so Rosenblatt argues, and they recover it by returning to authentic sources. Rosenblatt can speak of a Jewish genius because the Jew has "preserved a unity of type"[100] that can now be recreated in the secondary environment. The Zionists thereby reenact the biblical transformation of a tribe into a nation, reestablishing Moses as the original father who molded them into a nation and brought them to this land. Just as Moses transformed a race into a nation (according to Rosenblatt's biblical history), so too will social Zionists develop a primary, racial landscape into a secondary, national one.

An emerging nation never arises out of a restricted primary environment. It must, instead, be brought forth and imposed by historical actors willing to labor for personal and cultural renewal. The images in Rosenblatt's *Social Zionism* have advanced this claim throughout, but now they do so explicitly. Recall the images, like this one, of the rising/setting sun, in which a new creative beginning sets forth over a once barren land. Aspirations of the future await on the horizon—a secondary environment in the making. Those ideals and possibilities materialize

Figure 1.14. The Star of David. Bernard Rosenblatt, *Social Zionism* (1919).

as a state-in-the-making as that sun becomes the dawn of a recovered nation. This sketch, appearing within Rosenblatt's argument for Jewish "distinct inheritance," resonates in symbolic imagery, with the Star of David now in the position of the sun, and the two olive urns replacing the forestry. It also reproduces common tropes in the Zionist catalogue of visual images.[101] Here, the produce of a nation replaces the natural splendor of the environment. But that environment is no longer the primary one of the Bedouin herder and his sheep. One creates a nation out of the imposed secondary environment, an "environment of Israel with its priests, prophets and warrior kings."[102] As Rosenblatt tells it, history (and by this he means national history) is an "ever willing witness" to this nation building. But the images, too, work on their viewers to make them visual accomplices to this act, motivating viewers to recognize how a secondary environment "forms the basis for nationality."[103] As Presner points out, the Jews (unlike European colonists) sought an "ethnic-national connection to the land."[104] For Rosenblatt, this racial tie confers a right and duty to transform natural terrain into colonized land. The images work to subdue ethical concerns and to make this question a rhetorical one: "is it right, is it good, that nationalism should have triumphed and should continue to triumph over the dreams of Universal Brotherhood?"[105] Of course, because "we Internationalists have the vision of a great United States of the World, in which every State . . . would unite with all others in the ever-lasting war for righteousness and social justice."[106] Zionists turn Palestine into one of those great states of the world, and they transform the primary environment of the Bedouin into a secondary environment modeled on America. It is right and good because the land has been made holy, and the true inhabitants have returned to their authentic selves. With the dawn of "the New Jerusalem" comes the "self-realization of Israel" as a state, people, and land.[107]

This self-realization can be helped along by a biological science that shapes personal character in much the same way as Zionists impose their will on the primary environment. Rosenblatt includes a section called "Eugenics and Zionism" in his second chapter, and returns to these motifs later in his book as well. He does filter out more disturbing sections from his original *Maccabaean* article, including discussions about the fitness of Russian Jews to emigrate to Palestine, and about a possible fund to support fertile couples; this fund "might be utilized with beneficial results for a scheme of Eugenics."[108] Like many of his generation, Rosenblatt associated races with mental traits and believed that science could strengthen the Jewish genius now rooted "on his own soil":

> Morality is the keynote to the Hebraic character, and history has shown that this national genius of the Jew can be evolved only on his own soil. The Land of Israel and the Children of Israel seem to be the only elements of a wonderful compound.[109]

This type of alchemy can sound ominous, especially as it becomes active in Rosenblatt's messianic fervor. It was, however, a popular topic for discussion among the middle and upper-middle classes in America both before and after the First World War, and was common currency in Zionist conversations during the early part of the twentieth century.[110] Rosenblatt draws upon an established lineage of European race science broadly accepted within "bourgeois notions of morality." Concerns about racial fitness and the promotion of "healthy sexual practices" were part of that discourse.[111] Here too, Rosenblatt appropriates far more than he reveals.

Still, it is striking how Rosenblatt unites land, character, and race. Torn from his soil, the Jew "has been denied the full expression of his genius," but in Palestine Jews can "live the life of super-men."[112] Rosenblatt wants to turn "natural evolution" into one more directed and "purposive"[113]—a move that mirrors the creation of a secondary landscape out of a primary environment. The social Zionist should adopt eugenics as an intentional program "to plan his own evolution and to be the master-builder of future generations,"[114] and so shall become, in Mitchell Hart's helpful phrase, "a potential healer, a mediator between the 'unhealthy' Jewish present and a regenerated future."[115] In this, Rosenblatt follows Max Nordau and Felix Theilhaber by placing his own "hopes for the regeneration of Jewish racial strength in a Zionist form of eugenics."[116] Race science arrives to overcome American Jewish inauthenticity, and cultivates in its place a more authentic breed of social Zionists.

Rosenblatt's scientific racist engineering imagines the Holy Land as a controlled laboratory to manipulate and design. He proposes that a newly established American Palestine Company should "have the power and discretion of selecting the residents to be settled upon its lands, and it should utilize this selective process with a definite end in view and for a specific purpose." In this way, Zionists could redeem themselves and the land by promoting "a nobler type of man and a more efficient society, by eliminating the weak and the vicious, the feeble and the criminal, as factors in the propagation of mankind."[117] Rosenblatt offers a labor-saving view of both the active colonizer who enriches the self and the passive witness who accepts his own sterility. If the American Palestine Company could supplement "the process of 'natural selection' by a scientific selection," then eugenics truly offers "an opportunity of establishing in the Chosen Land a cho-sen people."[118] This is "self-realization" by scientific selection "on the principle of mental and moral fitness."[119] It is an authenticity gained by manipulation.

But the images accompanying Rosenblatt's defense of Zionist eugenics have so little in common with that discourse. The sketches recycle motifs articulated earlier in *Social Zionism* that produce a far different account of "self-realization." If eugenics might engineer a chosen people, then these images reveal how one cultivates the self by working the land. Authenticity is not a biological achieve-ment but a process of self-cultivation. Rosenblatt's textual appeal to eugenics diverges from the visual imagery, and so readers must negotiate between the contrasting arguments of written word and visual inscription. But in appealing to scientific racism, Rosenblatt exposes his fear that self-cultivation might not en-sure authentic renewal. American individualism alone might fail, and so appeals to biology help fortify self-realization. Rosenblatt's scientific racism, I suggest, betrays the textual anxiety of inauthenticity that shadows the visual desire for authentic presence.

The sketches throughout *Social Zionism* display how textual claims to au-thenticity work with and sometimes against visual images to envision a waste-land, to see American Jews in Zion, and to justify the colonization of a land. But these images also reveal the inauthentic other as foreign traveler, and so display that peculiar anxiety of (in)authenticity that again and again haunts Rosenblatt's text. The images in *Social Zionism* make authenticity visible by anxiously root-ing the self in a landscape beckoning its arrival, but they do so in ways that ex-pand, support, and even contradict Rosenblatt's textual claims. This rhetorical device, in which images and texts provide competing modes of persuasion, does not fracture the text as a whole, but instead offers a more robust account of visual authenticity. The Jewish Zionists depicted in Rosenblatt's written text recover themselves by returning to the image of land desirous of their labor. The culti-vated straight lines of the fields, the angular buildings arising in the towns, and the cowboy surveying the land of his creation all outwardly manifest an inward authentic turn. This authentic pose contrasts with the sterile, passive existence of the Bedouin traveler who replaces the unsettled wandering Jew as the unwanted interloper. But the straight lines must be hard, secured, and rooted to prevent a relapse to wasteland. And biological science prevents such backsliding. These protections, I have suggested, come with the territory: the anxiety of inauthen-ticity is an uneasy but characteristic feature of strong claims to authenticity. The images in *Social Zionism* depict this dynamic by initially presenting the native Bedouin as intruder to the Zionist inheritance, but then ultimately erasing him as inauthentic self. When we see the American Zionist tilling the land, we wit-ness his return home—not figuratively, but physically, to the place that cultivates his own authentic growth. The Jew becomes the man he ought to be when he colonizes the feminine place where he belongs. This is the heteronormative marriage made not in heaven but in the empowering dialogue between texts and images in Rosenblatt's *Social Zionism*.

That dialogue is more than a Zionist defense of colonization. Technology manipulates nature to yield fruits of human labor, and the effect is astounding: Jewish settlers transfigure the state of nature before our eyes. The sketches in *Social Zionism* transform the "natural" desert landscape into fertile soil, and thereby constitute the vertical lines of the field as the most natural of exposures. These images establish what nature *ought* to look like, and so propose what it really does look like. Inauthenticity has been wiped clean. We see authenticity regained as an awakening of the true self in its cultivated but always natural environment. Yael Zerubavel articulates well how this arrival is "constructed as *The Place*, the territory that was marked, named, and historicized, and hence became the national space."[120] The Jewish self, too, is marked, named, and constituted as the national space for authentic being, and we can see this in Bernard Rosenblatt's *Social Zionism*. In this work, images and texts conspire to mark a land and self as inescapably Jewish, and authentically so.

2 Seeing Things in Abraham Joshua Heschel's *The Sabbath*

> Most of us seem to labor for the sake of things of space. As a result we suffer from a deeply rooted dread of time and stand aghast when compelled to look into its face.
>
> —Abraham Joshua Heschel, *The Sabbath*

When Abraham Joshua Heschel (1907–1972), perhaps the most recognized American Jewish thinker of his generation, published *The Sabbath* (1951),[1] Jews were facing a new reality in America: their lifestyles were far more suburban than urban; there was less antisemitism in the wake of the Holocaust; and yet people were still driven by consumerist pressures and technological advances. Jews were wealthier too, and were living alongside their Christian neighbors, with middle-class choices open to them. With greater acceptance and visibility, American Jews could see a different, more enticing future filled with luxury goods, seductive comforts, safe homes, honest work, and caring families. Though Rosenblatt feared such a home precisely because of those enticements, a good many American Jews sought a calming presence after the horrors of the previous decade. The then popular television series *The Goldbergs*[2] offered homespun advice for common, familial tensions, but those conflicts were often resolved, muted, and visually displaced to allow a more cohesive, accommodating picture. Jews could visualize themselves as the Americans they wanted to be, and yearned for the security of home so often denied them elsewhere. Rosenblatt's social laboratory was too far away, both geographically and psychologically, from the accommodating charm of American culture.

Heschel's *The Sabbath* sought to challenge this comforting image of American Jewish experience. He appeals to the grandeur of time in contrast to the entrapments of space, advancing a phenomenology of being to help deflect the technology of acquisition. Jews could certainly enjoy the fruits of American capitalism, democracy, and geographical security, but were to live amid this material wealth while searching for spiritual meaning in time. Heschel seeks to deflect an "enslavement to things"[3] that seduces Jews into desiring only physical delights—delights that blind them to the ineffable splendors of spiritual moments. Even as

America beckoned in the accommodating episodes of *The Goldbergs,* Heschel's *The Sabbath* partitioned the material goods from the spiritual, and in doing so, summoned American Jews to covet things in time as well as in space.

For Heschel, America is both a land of opportunity and a threat to Jewish religious experience and authenticity. To subvert material enticements, *The Sabbath* sets out to educate Jews about spiritual values that lie beyond America's borders, even if those borders are still on this side of the Atlantic. He would not seek to transport the American frontier to the barren landscape in Palestine; instead, Heschel sought to reposition Jews within America. Authentic Jewish experience, Heschel argues, involves a release from material luxury and an awakening to spiritual wonder. The claim running throughout *The Sabbath* is clear: these ineffable moments of experience enable Jews to recognize holiness in time as a spiritual sense of being in accord with a reality beyond material goods.

Heschel ties that spiritual sensibility to Jewish vision and authenticity. Jewish authenticity requires a visual capacity to see beyond material things to their spiritual wonder. For Rosenblatt, a seeing beyond could only mean a geographical displacement of bodies to a distant land. Only there, in *that* land, could American Jews cultivate and grow their authentic selves. But for Heschel, Jewish visual awareness makes possible an authentic life in America. To be sure, in *The Sabbath* Heschel writes far more about Jewish experience than about Jewish seeing. But when the text calls for an experiential commitment to wonder, and a reawakening to spiritual plenty in everyday life, it also demands a new mode of seeing that transforms material sight into spiritual perception. Indeed, Heschel argues that Jews must envision time rather than gaze at things in space. In his view, envisioning spiritual things rather than material objects facilitates authentic Jewish experience in America.

Heschel grounds Jewish authenticity in visual models of phenomenological experience. His portrayal of sabbatical time as a revelatory moment of the ineffable requires a visual practice in which Jews unlearn consumerist forms of gazing at objects in space. To experience the Sabbath as authentically Jewish, Heschel argues, Jews must see things differently. In this sense, authenticity is a practice furthered by visual knowledge. In *The Sabbath,* Jewish authenticity is a mode of perceiving spiritual objects as windows to eternity, and a comportment to those objects in ways that manifest this spiritual awareness. This interplay between authenticity and vision situates Jews within but not of the American landscape. Looking beyond (American) things toward their spiritual meaning uproots Jews from a homeland that Heschel fears will blind them to spiritual realities. For Heschel, Jewish authenticity demands a more distant relation to America, but not one that requires complete abandonment of it. Certainly Rosenblatt shares Heschel's anxiety about American capitalism, but he also yearns for roots. Yet Rosenblatt couples land with authentic selves in ways that Heschel finds spiritually tenuous, for grounding identity in the land can too easily cause one to slide into idolatrous homage. Jews can find their place within American borders, Heschel believes, yet still remain a people apart. *The Sabbath* seeks to enact this separation by enabling a sight beyond American materialism and technology, evoking a "scopic mentality" that Elliot Wolfson calls an "iconic visualization."[4] In Heschel's schema, Americans gaze *at* things, but Jews look *through* them to the holy.

This fear of the inauthentic haunts Heschel's prose, as it does the many engravings included in *The Sabbath* by Ilya Schor. These images reproduce the very argumentative tension we find so pervasive in Heschel's text: the appeal to seeing *beyond* even as viewers gaze *at* material splendor. This anxious rhetoric of (in)authenticity reveals how images function as mirrors to textual dilemmas and claims. I explore this dynamic by marking three distinct movements of vision and authenticity in *The Sabbath:* 1) authentic Jewish vision as a mode of seeing *through* rather than looking *at* objects; 2) authentic sight as privileged vision of a chosen people; and 3) modes of authenticity and vision as enacted by Schor's engravings in *The Sabbath.* Jean-Luc Marion's analysis of the icon as a mode of being seen by an other, together with his critique of the idol as capturing the other within my gaze, helps to elucidate how Heschel and Schor fashion Jewish vision as authentic sight. Marion too promotes a form of physical unseeing, for he, much like Heschel, fears the seductive allure of material objects—a Western ocular anxiety so well documented in Martin Jay's *Downcast Eyes,* and one that, as Asher Biemann and Rachel Neis argue, has deep historical roots in the Jewish tradition as well.[5] This anxiety appears in *The Sabbath* as a fear of the inauthentic gaze that Heschel associates with American technical civilization. Heschel develops his alternative spiritual focus through a gendered account of the Sabbath queen. Though he draws upon traditional imagery of the Sabbath as Israel's bride, Heschel nonetheless reinstates the male fantasy of ever present female desire for the male gaze. In this account of the Sabbath, Jewish sight becomes authentic vision: a mode of seeing that grounds Jewish perception as chosen. Jews who see time by gazing through objects are themselves always seen[6] and desired by the Sabbath queen, and so are protected from the anxiety of (in)authenticity. This positionality heightens the status of Jewish sight over and against technical modes of gazing at and acquiring material objects. Authentic Jewish vision establishes Jews as the chosen people in America.

This chosen people becomes a people apart in the American landscape. Heschel appeals to a quiet stillness to protect Jews against the whirling circulation of consumer goods; he hears musical notes to hush the noise of technical civilization; and he betrays a nostalgia for Eastern European culture to better resist the pressures of suburban conformity. All this is meant to insulate Jews from the allure of American culture. But Jews need not travel to a distant land to build and to be built. They may live in America, even if they remain foreigners at home. Ilya Schor's engravings, appearing before each chapter in *The Sabbath,* capture this sense of a home beyond the American shores. Here my concern is neither Schor's intentions nor the social reception of his images, but rather how his art replicates Heschel's spiritual vision of authenticity liberated from material entrapments. Schor's images direct a viewer's gaze toward a nostalgic sense of holiness and authentic culture, beyond American technical civilization. But his works do not escape the anxious equivocation inherent in Heschel's prose, for his images might fail as iconic signifiers to the holy. Instead, Schor's engravings may captivate and seduce in the very ways that material things do in Heschel's text. Schor's engravings powerfully exhibit the very anxiety that haunts Heschel's claims to authenticity; images and texts encourage an iconic mode of seeing the holy, but they also risk the failure of signification. In *The Sabbath,* text and image echo both the appeal and fear of a visual authenticity intent on seeing Jews within, but not of, America.

Seeing through to the Beyond

A few years after writing *The Sabbath,* Heschel alluded to this religious practice as "the reference to the transcendent in our own existence, the direction of the Here toward the Beyond."[7] Though Heschel does not refer to vision, he nonetheless evokes a mode of seeing through material things in order to experience biblical notions of the holy—a divine spiritual presence that Heschel labels the ineffable. Seeing *through,* rather than gazing *at,* physical objects limits the seductive allure of what Heschel calls "technical civilization."[8] He worries that material achievements will seduce Jews into seeing only physical splendor, and so lead them to an inauthentic mode of existence. To prevent this visual tendency, Heschel grounds Jewish authenticity in an alternative visual practice. *The Sabbath* exchanges representations of technology and economic abundance for iconic images of sabbatical time.

Heschel is a categorical, dualistic thinker, even as he recognizes the subtle variations and slippages between terms. In *The Sabbath* he sharply distinguishes the good (and the beautiful) from the holy. God created a good world, but the seventh day is holy, and distinctively so. For six days "we live under the tyranny of things," even good things, but "on the Sabbath we try to become attuned to *holiness in time.*"[9] Visual images and physical things reside in space, and as Wolfson notes, Heschel equates "time with godliness in a manner that is unthinkable with respect to space."[10] The "primitive mind," as Heschel calls it, is preoccupied and moved by these spatial objects, too often drawn to their beauty and visual allure. This pagan mind worships deities tied to a particular land, or those found, and so venerated, in "mountains, forests, trees or stones."[11] Primitives see and thus honor God as material presence. Einat Ramon persuasively argues that Heschel is obsessed with paganism and idol worship throughout his writings, and he often associates modern technical culture with ancient pagan worship.[12] All this reveals a kind of inauthentic focus on the material object as sacred thing. Heschel's fear of visual idolatry surfaces throughout *The Sabbath*, and as Ramon suggests, he ties it closely to technical culture, but with historically strong Jewish anxieties as well.[13] Just as Heschel's primitives worship the physical world, so too technical civilization "is man's conquest of space." Idolatry arises from seeing divinity in physical things. The primitive gaze, as a mode of gaining technical control of space, stops at the object, as it were, and discovers God therein. The eyes adore nature, "as if He were a thing, not a spirit."[14] Heschel seeks to displace this inauthentic visual mode of technical acquisition of the sacred by appealing to a Jewish sight that moves beyond the things themselves. Such a seeing *through* rather than looking *at* physical objects,[15] Heschel contends, restrains both idolatrous worship and the conquest of space.

To see through things—to become Jewish seers rather than primitive, American gazers—we must protect our eyes from visual seductions. Heschel's primitives are really boorish idol worshipers, in his view. They reside in America, but not only there:

> The reverence for the sacred image, for the sacred monument or place, is not only indigenous to most religions, it has even been retained by men of all ages, all nations, pious, superstitious or even antireligious; they all continue to pay homage to banners and flags, to national shrines, to monuments erected to kings or heroes.[16]

Memorials deflect attention from truly sacred images, Heschel implies here, for the material signifiers fail to indicate appropriate, religious meanings. Even more, such primitives cannot "realize an idea"[17] without a visual aid to see and revere. In this sense, the very need for a "sacred monument or place" demonstrates a failure of spiritual perception. Heschel's analysis of primitive visuality suggests a profound distrust of physical sight, a "suspicion of vision"[18] directed at material form. But it also belies the anxiety of (in)authenticity—that perhaps one could always misperceive and misdirect the gaze to find God in material space. For Heschel, material vision reveals a sensual, perhaps even a good world of "thinginess,"[19] but not a spiritual world of holiness. The sense of the ineffable that Heschel seeks to evoke in *The Sabbath* requires a form of unseeing the world as primitive holiness in space.

Heschel's primitive visuality acquires the object as its very own. This vision is a controlling sight, one that subdues and gains "power in the realm of space."[20] Such a covetous gaze is monolithic: every thing comes under its purview. But such a dominant vision could never acquire time, so argues Heschel. Technology offers abundant riches and rewards for exploiting nature and enhancing human life. Yet Heschel protects holiness from an acquiring vision that locates, defines, analyzes, possesses, and discards things in space. If technical vision seeks to gain power over time, then this gaze simply transforms time into a spatial thing. But time as a moment of eternity, as a mode of holiness, remains unseen. Heschel establishes strong borders to distinguish technical acquisition from experiential religious wonder. He fears boundary crossings. To access the spiritual world of the ineffable, one cannot simply transpose a visual practice in space to one in time. Instead, he seeks a "spiritual eye"[21] that opens a world of holy presence.

When technical vision attempts to control time, it transforms holiness into a "treacherous monster with a jaw like a furnace incinerating every moment of our lives."[22] Here the anxiety of (in)authenticity terrorizes with these "Frankensteins of spatial things" that become "forgeries of happiness,"[23] threatening persons with their freakish appearance. According to Heschel, we conjure up these monstrous hybrids because we do not know how to see time: "Most of us seem to labor for the sake of things of space. As a result we suffer from a deeply rooted dread of time and stand aghast when compelled to look into its face." To look into the face of time requires presence rather than control: a temporality that inhibits the acquisition of spatial objects. To see time's face entails a slowing down, a kind of submission to the ineffable presence of the holy. To experience holiness in time also necessitates a second sight that refuses to gaze at and control beautiful objects. Persons must glimpse away from the world of spatial things in order "to face sacred moments."[24]

Monstrosities as inappropriate mixtures and deformed hybrids frustrate well-defined categories. They cross borders, and so appear foreign and dangerous.[25] Monstrosities are also visual spectacles. They capture and captivate the holy in space. In his appeal to freaks and monsters, Heschel belies his protective strategy to safeguard holiness in time from inauthentic modes of seeing. Holiness looks monstrous, so Heschel contends, because it has inappropriately crossed over to space from its proper home in time. Locality informs authentic presence, for true holiness resides only in one realm. No longer residing where it belongs, holiness becomes a visual monstrosity and so an inauthentic thing. Instead of dragging holiness into space, Heschel locates it within the visual presence of time.

Wolfson alerts us to the phenomenological modes of perception in which vision accesses holiness in time. According to him, medieval Jewish mystics were experiential seers of God:

> The mystical vision, and not merely the postexperiential account or description of it, is at the core metaphorical or analogical, for it seeks to make the spiritual world "perceptible" to the material by relating an object from the latter to the former. The symbolic vision bridges the gap between the invisible and the visible, the spiritual and the corporeal, by lending approximate expression to the transcendental truth.[26]

These Jewish mystics recognize material things as conduits to a spiritual world. Their vision is analogical because they associate spatial things with spiritual realities. According to Wolfson, vision "bridges the gap": new visual registers open a visible world to the invisible. The mystical gaze approaches the invisible, but does not possess and control it within the material world. Objects retain what David Morgan helpfully describes as an "*iconic* status" in which "seeing them means encountering their referents in a powerful way."[27] Heschel wants American Jews to see the world in this way.

This mystic gaze approaches a world rich with spiritual traces, and it is one that Jean-Luc Marion has sought to uncover through his phenomenological account of the icon. Marion continually warns his readers that "the manner of seeing decides what can be seen" and that two "modes of apprehension" configure an image either as icon or idol.[28] Vision originates with a subject seeing an object and gazing upon it. A gaze constructs an object as idol by taking hold of it and establishing residency there. The idol, in turn, enraptures the gaze such that the idol fills its entire visual spectrum: "the idol fascinates and captivates the gaze precisely because everything in it must expose itself to the gaze, attract, fill, and hold it." Idolatrous worship is a form of physical seduction by a fabricated idol that "dazzles with visibility." As the passive "landing place" and "mirror" to the human gaze, the idol conforms to the seer's fantasies of expectation and desire.[29] The idol entraps the viewer within the visible.

The icon reverses the gaze, for it "does not result from a vision but provokes one." In Marion's account, the icon "is not seen, but appears."[30] Envisioning an icon really consists of an unseeing of the idolatrous gaze that Heschel associates with primitive sight and possessive, technical culture. This new, iconic vision is a mode of experiential presence that allows the invisible to appear, paradoxically, as the most visible. But to enact this visionary experience, persons must gaze through the icon to reveal a depth beyond the material thing. Rather than gaze *at* the icon, the spectator, according to Marion, transgresses vision to discover (in clear echoes of Levinas) a sacred face:

> Instead of the invisible mirror, which sent the human gaze back to itself alone and censured the *invisable,* the icon opens in a face that gazes at our gazes in order to summon them to its depth. . . . The icon alone offers an open face, because it opens in itself the visible onto the invisible, by offering its spectacle to be transgressed—not to be seen, but to be venerated.

Before an idol, vision stops at and succumbs to the object as spectacle, but the icon "summons one to travel through the (invisible) mirror, and to enter, so to speak, into the eyes of the icon."[31] Iconic vision moves toward the spectator who becomes someone "to be perceived" rather than a viewer who gazes.[32] In this phenomenological account, we recognize not only Levinas's influence on Marion, but also Marion's own fear of physical vision that Martin Jay traced in contemporary French thought. For I do not gaze at the icon; instead, the icon sees me: "I look, with my invisible gaze, upon a gaze that envisages me; in the icon, in effect, it is a matter not so much of seeing a spectacle as of seeing another gaze that sustains mine, confronts it, and eventually overwhelms it."[33] This is seeing as unseeing—far less a vision than a relational experience of the Levinasian Other as face. Robyn Horner describes this encounter in the appropriate passive voice: "what is made visible in the icon is the gaze of the invisible other." Iconic seeing really is being seen by an Other, or as Rachel Neis phrases it, "this is the dream of the (divine) image that looks back at its viewers."[34] For Horner, "what is important is not our experience of God, but God's experience of us."[35] Seeing through objects as iconic images positions the seer as a chosen subject of God's vision.

Heschel adopts a similar posture in situating Israel at the center of God's visual desires. Like Marion, he endeavors to link iconic vision with chosenness. But here I want to stress how Heschel associates primitive sight with a form of Marion's idolatrous vision, and how a gaze beyond those things—Jewish seeing—opens up Marion's icons. Heschel seeks to transform material idols into spiritual icons by redirecting sight beyond technical civilization. The one and the same object can function both as idol or icon, depending on the posture taken by the seer. Heschel's primitive gazers see only idols, and fashion time as an inauthentic presence of holiness. In order to move beyond this idolatrous worship, Heschel appropriates a phenomenological account of iconic vision in which viewers search through the object to an invisible Other who, paradoxically, gazes back as authentic holiness in time. On this side of the temporal divide, Heschel's God returns the gaze; but from the other side of eternity, Heschel's God has always been searching for a Jewish seer who moves beyond technical civilization.

These senses of visuality inform Heschel's allegorical reading of Shimeon ben Yoḥai's challenge to the Roman Empire and its great works.[36] In Heschel's retelling of this Talmudic story, three rabbis sit together in Palestine in the year 130 CE to discuss political power.[37] Rabbi Judah ben Ilai admires the Roman roads, market places, bridges, and bathhouses. Rabbi Jose remains silent, but Rabbi Shimeon is far more critical: "All that they made they made for themselves. They made roads and market places to put harlots there; they built bridges to levy tolls for them; they erected bathhouses to delight their bodies." Upon receiving word of this argument, the Romans exalted Rabbi Judah, exiled Rabbi Jose, but put to death Rabbi Shimeon "who reviled our work."[38] To escape his punishment, Rabbi Shimeon made off with his son Rabbi Eleazar, lived out of sight in a cave, and for twelve years studied Torah. When informed of the emperor's death and the annulment of his decree, Shimeon and Eleazar finally emerged from the cave. But upon seeing laborers plowing fields, they exclaimed: "These people forsake eternal life and are engaged in temporary life!" Whatever they gazed upon was consumed by fire, and a "voice from heaven" responded: "Have ye emerged to destroy My world? Return to your cave!"[39] After twelve more months underground, Rabbi Shimeon and his son arose to see "an old man carrying two bundles of myrtle in his hand." When asked about the significance of the herbs, the old man replied, "they are in honor of the Sabbath." "At that moment," the story concludes, "both found tranquility of soul."[40]

Heschel argues that Rabbi Shimeon "fled from the world where *eternity was the attribute of a city* and went to the cave where he found a way to endow life with a quality of eternity."[41] Urban politics and labor succumb to false idol worship, and so both the rabbi and his son despaired of this world—their vision engulfing in flames all that their eyes capture. According to Neis, stories of destructive rabbinic gazes can be found in both Palestinian and Babylonian texts.[42] Though Heschel fails to emphasize this visual destruction, the text highlights it. For if, after twelve years of Torah study and prayer, Rabbi Shimeon and Eleazar still despaired of "temporary life," they only emerged from the cave to undermine God's creation through a consuming vision. But some twelve months later, as they resurfaced a second time from the cave, they did not see a man dedicated to the labor of everyday life but an old man honoring the Sabbath. Rather than plowing the fields, the man endowed life with "a quality of eternity." These rabbis now *saw* eternity in time; they recognized a physical act not as a mere attribute of everyday, urban life, but as a conduit to holiness. Both rabbis now recognized an idolatrous act ("these people forsake eternal life and are engaged in temporary life!") as an iconic turning of everyday life into moments of eternity. Their new vision yielded tranquility rather than destruction, a quietude in the midst of urban chaos. Shimeon and Eleazar did not see a laborer so much as spiritual, iconic presence. Here authentic acts reveal eternity in time. This is a physical unseeing of the material idol, and an iconic witness to the visual apparatus of Jewish authenticity.

The Authenticity of Visual Presence

Drawing from ancient rabbinic sources, Heschel depicts Israel's destiny "to be the groom of the sacred day." This longing for a mate, however, originates with the Sabbath's quest for companionship, for "the seventh day stands in need of man." Israel's need now becomes the Sabbath's longing, and Heschel locates Israel as the privileged actor in this religious drama. The purpose of this gendered relation is to establish Israel as the chosen suitor. The Sabbath engenders the feminine allure of the *Shekinah* as she manifests God's presence. Israel willingly accepts her advance, becoming "engaged to holiness, to eternity."[43] Much of this language echoes Jewish midrashic lore, and mirrors Heschel's theological claims about a God who searches and yearns for human contact. But note how Heschel situates Israel's vision of holiness. Engaged to eternity, Israel plays a chosen role in the holy drama of God's manifested presence in time. Israel is now *seen* and longed for, and thereby recaptures its rightful place as conduit to the holy. This male positionality, as I read it in *The Sabbath,* is the allure of authenticity as essential visual presence.

Heschel welcomes competing images of the Sabbath so that no single representation becomes "crystallized as a definite concept." Such a "mental image" would enrapture the primitive mind that would personify the image and, so Heschel fears, worship it.[44] Yet even as Heschel defends this plurality—noting how Rabbi Hanina, for example, would celebrate the Sabbath as queen and at other times as king[45]—the Sabbath as spiritual bride to the male Israel remains the dominant metaphor in *The Sabbath:* she is the true queen who "comes to Israel lovely and perfumed."[46] Heschel's prose is both metaphoric fancy and gendered desire: the male body remains the focused center of this divine movement. At the heart of this romantic courtship is a male centrality that provokes the female advance. So we read this tale of cosmic union:

> After the work of creation was completed, the Seventh Day pleaded: Master of the universe, all that Thou hast created is in couples; to every day of the week Thou gavest a mate; only I was left alone. And God answered: The Community of Israel will be your *mate.*[47]

The Sabbath once again approaches, and God responds to her craving for a partner. Her solitude indicates a problematic status. As the story continues, God reminds Israel of a prior commitment: "When the people of Israel stood before the mountain of Sinai, the Lord said to them: 'Remember that I said to the Sabbath: The Community of Israel is your mate.' Hence: *Remember* the Sabbath day to sanctify it."[48] In Heschel's narrative, Israel must be commanded to remember the Sabbath's rightful claim for a companion. She desires, and he accepts her advances.

Though God plays matchmaker, and the Sabbath pleads for a mate, it is still Israel who remains the focus of this religious narrative. Heschel establishes Israel's chosenness as privileged sight. According to Jacques Lacan, looking is desire, both for the object of my gaze, and for the gaze of that other who longs for me. But looking is also a trap, for we are "caught, manipulated, captured, in the field of vision."[49] In Heschel's narrative, Israel desires this entrapment, awaiting to be enraptured by the seventh day. The Sabbath confers privileged access to authentic presence. But Heschel presents this desire for companionship as if it were the Sabbath's own. It is the Sabbath, and not Israel, who initially yearns for a mate. In this, the Sabbath mimics God's search for a seer beyond technical, American civilization. Israel, as the male bearer of this approach, rushes out "in a dance" and exclaims, "Come, let us go out to welcome the *Queen Sabbath.*"[50] In Heschel's view, when celebrating the Sabbath, "we adore precisely something we do not see."[51] Israel does not see because he is already captured in the field of vision, and is chosen as the one who is seen and desired. Neis has described the predicament "to be seen but not to see" as the rabbinic understanding of Jewish existence after the destruction of the Second Temple.[52] God still favors Israel even after historical catastrophe. Though he does not mention the Holocaust, Heschel nonetheless wishes to recapture that sense of favored partnership unchanged by tragedy. Here within the visionary field of the Sabbath, chosenness still appears as natural and authentic.

Heschel seeks to deflect this reading of bride and groom as privileged narrative by noting the metaphorical character of the language. Recognizing that images of bride and queen might lead to idolatrous worship, Heschel suggests how the Sabbath only hints at God's need for Israel. To call her queen or bride is "merely to allude" to a spiritual reality rather than to "represent a substance."[53] Such claims energize Edward Kaplan's defense of Heschel's metaphorical prose and the safe distance it maintains between "substance" and spiritual reality. Kaplan artfully defends Heschel, suggesting how the Sabbath queen imagery is a "vehicle" that merely "illustrates" a feature of God. Such an image "does not touch God's substance in itself but evokes only that sanctity accessible to intuition."[54] In somewhat apologetic prose, Heschel defends rabbinic notions of the Sabbath queen against idolatrous images of the divine:

> It would be an oversimplification to assume that the ancient rabbis were trying to personify the Sabbath, to express an image which was in their minds. . . . The rabbis did not believe that the seventh day was endowed with human features, with a figure or a face; their ideas did not result in either visible or verbal iconography. They rarely went beyond the venture of cherishing the endearing terms of queen or bride. This was not because of a dearth in imaginative power but because what they were eager to convey was more than what minds could visualize or words could say.[55]

In overcoming vision, both physical and one directed by the "mind's eye,"[56] the rabbis only refer to a presence rather than seek a chosen status. In Heschel's phenomenological approach, Israel retreats from visual engagement with the holy.

But even this unseeing marks Israel's vision as privileged sight. The Sabbath invites Israel to experience divine presence. Israel gazes upon the Sabbath, yearning both to gaze *at* and *beyond* her—reflecting precisely the phenomenological move at the heart of Heschel's visual iconography. This male look seeks to be caught and to move beyond the field of vision, and it is this privileged exposure that situates Israel at the heart of the divine drama. For Heschel, to see "*within* the Sabbath" means that she "surrounds us like spring which spreads over the land without our aid or notice."[57] Israel has become a chosen "us" with special access to the divine. The Sabbath binds and envelops, advances and "spreads" without Israel's notice or assistance.

As the Sabbath advances, she also protects Israel from the noisy bustle of American technical culture. If "technical civilization" seeks to dominate space, then Israel finds refuge in "a world of spirit":

> To set apart one day a week for freedom . . . a day of detachment from the vulgar, of independence of external obligations, a day on which we stop worshipping the idols of technical civilization, a day on which we use no money, a day of armistice in the economic struggle . . . is there any institution that holds out a greater hope for man's progress than the Sabbath?[58]

To Heschel's ears, technology is all noise, the "clattering commerce" of the capitalist engine as ever new products arise and disappear, and desire is once again manipulated and controlled. Yet the seventh day "has blown the market place away," and replaces noisy chatter with "a song in the wind." This is quiet, serene music—a "song in the silence of the night"[59]—that creates "islands of stillness" as bulwarks against a raging and forceful economy. On the Sabbath, so Heschel insists, we live *"independent of technical civilization."*[60] Israel, for at least a day, removes himself from the clamor of American capitalism and returns to the quiet, protective home of Sabbath tranquility. The seventh day disengages Israel from American culture, technology, and consumerism, and protects her chosen community to pursue "the greater hope for man's progress."

Jonathan Crary has defined modernization as "a process by which capitalism uproots and makes mobile that which is grounded, clears away or obliterates that which impedes circulation, and makes exchangeable what is singular."[61] Crary's is but one of what must be hundreds of competing accounts of modernity, but I find his analysis useful for understanding Heschel's fear of technology's global sweep and the inauthentic gaze. Heschel wants to escape from the field of technical vision and the spectacle of monstrous objects. This is less an unseeing, or even a seeing through, and far more a desire not to see at all: to be still, quiet, unprovoked, desensitized. Heschel's seeing through to the beyond has generated a longing not to see, but also provokes a yearning for a grounding, healing presence. If looking is desire, then Heschel's Sabbath music renounces ocular, possessive cravings. It is a plea not to gaze at a thing but instead to look beyond to the ineffable. Looking "at" leads only to idolatry and to "the tyranny of things."[62] When the Sabbath spreads her wings without Israel's notice, she numbs his senses to things in space, protects him from the anxiety of (in)authenticity, and draws him into the quiet song of time. She must save Israel from America's desirous, consuming gaze. Heschel thus describes the Sabbath as a "day on which we learn the art of *surpassing* civilization."[63] In musical tones that silence noise, Heschel's seventh day teaches Israel how not to look at, and so not to desire, America's technology and culture.

This blindness[64] exposes Heschel's modernist anxiety before excess, where the material fecundity of things overwhelms the senses. Better to live on "islands of stillness," where the ground is firm and quiet, than within urban dissonance, so Heschel warns. In the 1950s, many Jews listened well, and rushed to the suburbs to recover a protective silence. Yet Heschel fears that urban sounds travel far, and so his Sabbath protects Israel from material contamination. Now "*within the Sabbath*" and her soundproof barriers, Israel can pursue its privileged access to the divine and see through material things to the beyond of the holy: beyond civilization, beyond technology, beyond materiality as spatial thing, beyond America. Israel sees in this way because he has been chosen to do so. In Heschel's narrative of visual presence, Israel has been given a day as bride, and she enables a vision beyond the idol to iconic holiness. This is the privileged sight/site of Jewish authenticity.

Representing Authentic Presence in Schor's Engravings

With all of Heschel's distrust of vision fixating upon spatial objects, *The Sabbath* still includes a good number of material images. Ilya Schor's engravings depict objects in space, even things that many Jews worship in space. They accompany each chapter of Heschel's text, and seek to induce spiritual wonder through the representation of evocative things. Schor's art elicits the visual mode of seeing time that Heschel portrays in *The Sabbath,* and mirrors Heschel's own anxiety that things can seduce the self into a cold individualism, even as they can also reawaken spiritual wonder. Like Wolfson's Jewish mystics who re-experienced divine revelation at Sinai through the hermeneutical act of reading,[65] Schor's engravings confront readers as visual markers of the ineffable. They evoke a world beyond technical culture and commerce, and consider looking through to the beyond to be an authentic vision. Schor's images are persistently nostalgic of an Eastern European Jewish heritage, and move a viewer's gaze away from American civilization toward a more ethereal, Edenic past. Here, in Schor's woodcut engravings, vision and authenticity converge to magnify Heschel's account of the Sabbath as "a palace in time."[66] *The Sabbath* is a visual text in which word and image blend to reproduce the anxiety of (in)authenticity.

Schor's engravings induce a vision that searches beyond and through the image to the ineffable. But his images could also fail as iconic representation: even as they appeal to a world beyond, viewers might very well stay put and gaze resolutely at the things themselves. Again here, the very search for authenticity elicits the anxiety that it might not be found. Heschel faced this dilemma in his own writing, and it lies at the heart of iconic images as possible candidates for material idols. *The Sabbath* seeks to move readers from the seductions of space to the splendors of time, from the ownership of things to the holy presence of the ineffable, and finally from the gaze at idolatrous things to a spiritual being in accord with iconic images. These active states are ever present possibilities rather than historical moments. They are phenomenological modes of experiencing the world. But as aesthetic objects, Schor's works could just as easily ensnare readers within the sensual image as they could ignite an iconic vision of the authentic beyond. This too is characteristic of Heschel's prose: however much he pits beauty against holiness, or displaces physical sensations for spiritual wonder, he continually reasserts a more complex, textured, and dynamic interplay between material pleasures and spiritual pursuits. Like Schor's images, Heschel's language could entertain with aesthetic delight while also be witness to an ineffable holiness. This mirrored interplay between text and image provokes a more common, and far more anxious, drama between material pleasure and spiritual awareness.

So despite Heschel's account of the Sabbath as holiness in time, representations of the seventh day function as both icon and idol. Images might entice a vision to the beyond, or ensnare it within the physical beauty of the spectacle. Heschel often distinguishes between two kinds of things: those physical objects that point to a world of mystery and grandeur, and those fallen materials that seduce visual senses, and thereby excite desires to control the divine rather than *to be* in the presence of God. For Heschel, physical objects as mere things damage spiritual selves—and so one must see them differently through a "spiritual eye" unmoved by their seductive allure. Schor's engravings appeal to this form of spiritual vision, even as they tempt a more aesthetic enjoyment in representational art. Ira Eisenstein, in his book review of *The Sabbath,* noted how Schor's illustrated woodcuts evoke a "semi-mystical quality" that "preserve the flavor of old-world Jewry."[67] But Nahum Glatzer recognized the material pleasures of Schor's work and their vexed place within the book as a whole. Though his engravings "add much to the beauty of the book," Glatzer believed Schor's images fit uneasily with Heschel's prose: "they might very easily serve to distract the reader from the acuteness and immense actuality of the text."[68] Glatzer warns us that images and the written word comprise a larger "text" that may complicate Heschel's inscription. Yet Heschel's prose also conveys a "beauty" that might distract readers from the acute "actuality" of textual reasoning. Both text and image risk this distraction. As seekers of refined taste, readers may opt for more aesthetic modes of textual and visual pleasure. Heschel's text and Schor's images tempt readers in this way. Perhaps the taste of "old-world Jewry" is not precisely the flavor readers seek to consume, nor the vision they desire to evoke. Icons could always become idols.

In Heschel's *The Earth Is the Lord's*—a text published a year earlier (1950) but one that often appears together with *The Sabbath*[69]—Schor produced idealized images of *shtetl* life in Eastern Europe, evoking a "romanticized folk-past."[70] When Henry Schuman published *The Earth Is the Lord's,* he hired Schor to help create an aesthetic product, one that would both recall Eastern European Jewry and be marketable to an American audience.[71] But even as aesthetic accessories, these images remain central to the work as a whole, as Glatzer's comment suggests about *The Sabbath.* They now become part of a larger textual argument about vision and authenticity. Schor's images offer a nostalgic return to an Eastern European community of unity and wholeness that was altogether lost after the Holocaust. They recall a lost world to Jewish Americans, a world utterly destroyed but one that still resonated with authority. Schor's engravings sought to re-enliven culture through nostalgia, recalling and thereby revivifying the Eastern European heritage of American Jewry. Many of his images in *The Sabbath* do this kind of rhetorical work, drawing the reader back to a simpler, wholesome past. Schor's woodcut engravings render Eastern European culture as authentic heritage.

Schor believes Jewish art functions as visual windows to an authentic past. In an essay translated from his native Yiddish, and published after his death in 1961, Schor sets out to define Jewish artistic style.[72] He includes the typical lament (Jews possess little if any style) and so too the culprits—the biblical commandment against graven images, and Jewish assimilationist strategies. Either Jews lacked creativity or they appropriated it from their neighbors.[73] But Eastern European Jews escaped this double bind, and produced a unique and vibrant artistic culture:

> The daily physical life of the people assumed an obvious Jewish character. It developed a folk feeling peculiar to this branch of world Jewry. This feeling was cemented with the traditional religious spirit and resulted in the emergence of a uniquely Jewish style or way of life.... Whatever Jews did in Eastern Europe was distinct and unique to its own community. It usually differed in every form and fashion from their surrounding gentile neighbors, and in time this folk feeling led to the appearance of original creations in the arts.[74]

This "unique expression" also captured the essence of Jewish life: in Eastern Europe one could discover, and portray the authentic Jewish type "naturally." Schor understands his own images as mere artistic replications of an organic Judaism. He brings to America what had been destroyed, but he does so faithfully: "the model posed, the canvas stood ready, and on the palette were arrayed many hues and colors; all awaited the hand of the artist."[75] Jewish art is Eastern European Jewry reproduced on canvas; the artist's hand merely replicates what lies before him. Only this artistic style remains "true to the Jewish *shtetel* [sic],to the Jewish way of life." This is pure representation as authentic reproduction; it is a claim to unmediated, immediate experience. This appeal to *mimesis* stands against a good deal of Jewish reflection on art as nonrepresentational; but Schor's return to nature reflects the mid-century Jewish reclamation of Jewish "national" art.[76] Schor's convenient slip from a notion of community (*shtetel*) to "the Jewish style or way of life" nicely illustrates the point: authentic Judaism *is* the *shtetl* Judaism of Eastern Europe. It is a "natural platform" and "source" that has always inspired Jewish art. Not even the Holocaust can uproot this organic source, even if it can no longer be seen and touched.[77]

Schor returns to the only authentic roots he knows, and creates artistic works to reveal a reality now visibly displaced by the "experimental" modernism popular in 1950s America. To Schor, modernist architecture is "cold, strange and stiff," and Jews have too easily adopted this foreign style—imitating the assimilatory practices that Schor believes is so pronounced in, and lethal to, Jewish artistic creativity. Since contemporary Jewish art "bears little relationship to Judaism," Schor's works must "become the link which would unite that which is gone with that which has remained, the past with the present."[78] Americans have forgotten their heritage; by contrast, Ilya Schor recalls an Eastern European past as authentic religious source.

Heschel appropriates the same tropes, images, and nostalgia that Schor himself used in his essay on Jewish style. In a brief tribute to his friend in the wake of his death,[79] Heschel writes of the "sober intoxication with truth [that] dominated the life and art of Ilya Schor." And like his friend, Heschel too associates authentic Judaism with "the inwardness and piety of our people of Eastern Europe." Schor resurrected "the warmth, the intimacy, the joy" of *shtetl* Judaism, and "deposited for posterity the spirit of a world that is no more." His artistic magic lies precisely in this mode of revivification wherein Schor's works restore a forgotten heritage. Schor exposes Eastern European inwardness and piety as authentic Judaism. Heschel accordingly concludes that Schor's works "create the whole atmosphere of the Sabbath" and make it "easier for us to adore, to be astonished."[80]

But in Heschel's taxonomy, adoration leads to idol worship, whereas astonishment induces iconic visions. This is the inescapable, anxious tension within Schor's representational art (as both Eisenstein's and Glatzer's reviews make clear), as it is within Heschel's own prose. These images and texts make claims about authenticity and vision, but they cannot enforce them. They might transport American Jews back to an authentic past now imagined as whole, earthy, and organic; or they might captivate them, and so induce delight in artistic sentimentality. We would only know for certain if we followed a reception history of the work as a whole, and recovered how readers actually appropriated Heschel's book (we hear some of this in Eisenstein's and Glatzer's reviews, but certainly not enough to make broader historical and interpretive claims). But even if such retrieval were possible, we can still examine how Schor's woodcut engravings interact with Heschel's prose in ways that mimic the tensions and movements of iconic vision. Examining Schor's engravings in *The Sabbath* reveals how his images mirror Heschel's agitated claims to visual authenticity.

In the prologue to *The Sabbath* (and for some editions, in the title cover as well), viewers encounter Schor's engraving of a cathedral in time, with an inscription from Exodus 20:8—"Remember the Sabbath day, to keep it holy." Above the cathedral stands a bearded Jew with prayer shawl (*tallit*) draped delicately over his head and shoulders. He stands beside the Sabbath table, lights kindled,

Figure 2.1. A Cathedral in Time. Wood Engravings by Ilya Schor from THE SABBATH: ITS MEANING FOR MODERN MAN by Abraham Joshua Heschel. Copyright © 1951 by Ilya Schor. Reprinted by permission of Farrar, Straus and Giroux, LLC.

with a raised cup to recite the blessing over the wine. Schor decorates the cathedral with a number of beautiful ornaments associated with Jewish ritual holidays: a *shofar* (Rosh Hashanah), *lulav* and *etrog* (Sukkot), two tablets representing the Ten Commandments (Shavuot), and so on. The clouds, stars, and sun surrounding the cathedral draw the reader's gaze up toward this "old-world" Jew. He stands alone, gazing upward still. Here in the prologue we discover inscription (the biblical text) and image collapsed together, and so too a gaze that looks at and beyond. Indeed, the bearded Jew trades in cultural codes associated with authentic Jewry, and Heschel himself grew a beard to represent the prophetic voice of Jewish America.[81] That sense of prophetic gaze and voice materializes as the eyes read, or merely recognize the Hebrew, and move steadily upward to the cathedral and Sabbath table, following the flowing lines of the clouds. The engraving appears as if it, too, were moving upward, beyond the canvas and border of the physical text. Indeed, *all* images found in *The Sabbath* produce this directionality, where spiritual vision moves upward toward the Beyond, and material civilization inevitably chains one down below. Schor's woodcut induces a dual movement: one directed *at* the material wealth and harmony of Jewish ritual traditions, and a gaze *beyond* things to a reality they serve or signify. The bearded, pious Jew at the engraving's upper surface looks directly out and away from the commotion below. He meditates in the presence of awe, reverence, and silence. This Jew appears—now inscribed as authentic prophetic presence—little concerned with material splendor, and looks beyond it to see holiness. The invisible realm of the ineffable seems quite distant from the material world below.

A similar movement, although one far more ambivalent, opens for the viewer of this engraving. Schor's image provokes a look at the representational objects, but it also entices a view *beyond* them, doubling the gaze of the bearded figure at the very top. But is this *beyond* achieved by leaving the Hebrew text and ritual items behind, mired as they are in physical space and aesthetic beauty? Might the image fail to evoke a visuality of looking *through* things to their spiritual sources? For Heschel, material things seduce and captivate the senses, but they also open a window to a reality of silence, wonder, and amazement. A thing either functions as an idolatrous commodity enslaving the self, or it acts as a religious icon revealing the holy. Schor's prologue engraving displays this dangerous tension within iconographic representation. As seductive image, the cathedral in time, situated in the middle of the prologue woodcut, suggests a nostalgia for lost wholeness and a yearning for authentic heritage. But as conduit to the holy, the Jew engraved at the apex of the picture elicits a movement beyond things. Wholeness is not present; it exists on the far side of the cathedral toward the beyond. Even more, the clouds travel from the ground upward, suggesting a look away from rather than through the material thing as icon to the holy. The nostalgic modes conjured by Schor's *shtetl* imaginary yield an authenticity beyond this world; his

Figure 2.2. Beyond Civilization. Wood Engravings by Ilya Schor from THE SABBATH: ITS MEANING FOR MODERN MAN by Abraham Joshua Heschel. Copyright © 1951 by Ilya Schor. Reprinted by permission of Farrar, Straus and Giroux, LLC.

woodcut heightens both the nostalgia for presence and the dilemma of representing it. As Heschel continually asserts in *The Sabbath*, persons can always fail to see through, and instead either gaze at or move beyond the material world. This is the anxiety of visual authenticity. Schor's engraving motivates a gaze at, through, and beyond material things toward authentic presence. It reproduces the thematic concerns and anxieties discovered in Heschel's labored prose.

Many of Schor's engravings in *The Sabbath* retain the conflicting sensibilities in Heschel's writings. The sketch introducing the chapter "Beyond Civilization" offers a vivid example of such visual unease (see figure 2.2). This is one of Schor's darker, more disturbing images, as it evokes a yearning for release from the chains of culture. We see a figure tethered to a bustling world of roads, buildings, trees, and community: a world, in short, of communal obligations and material seductions. This figure looks above to an imagined, liberating image of Adam and Eve in Eden. There they stand together, Eve with the seductive fruit in one hand, Adam's arm in the other, as they draw the figure's gaze upward toward the brilliant sun. This prelapsarian vision "beyond civilization" is certainly not the Eastern European *shtetl*, but still reproduces its seductive allure: a serene, picturesque, organic community of authentic purpose. Much like the prologue image, this engraving of the chained figure stimulates an upward gaze that follows the trajectory and movement of the woodcut. Everything flows from the broken and fragmented world that enslaves the figure to the full, rounded vision of Eden that liberates her. This is a seeing beyond as emancipatory vision—a liberating gaze of unseeing the world in order to conjure up the prelapsarian fantasy of wholesome desire. Beyond civilization, vision ultimately searches for an Edenic time of authentic presence.

Schor's image for "Beyond Civilization" prepares a reader for Heschel's argument that "on the Sabbath we live, as it were, *independent of technical civilization.*"[82] This "as it were" hints at Heschel's equivocal stance on how one *really* lives in sabbatical time. But it also reveals the equally ambiguous meanings lurking in Schor's engraving. Again, this is not merely an issue of reception history or theory. I take this to be the anxiety of iconic representation as such.

Schor invites this representative challenge when he mirrors Heschel's own struggles with material splendor and spiritual awareness. Witness his engraving that introduces Part I (of three parts) of *The Sabbath*. Here, Schor depicts the *shtetl* imaginary: son and daughter, together with their devout mother, welcoming the husband/father to the Sabbath table. With candles alighted to commence the Sabbath day (it is already dark outside the window behind the candlesticks), and with the kiddush cup prepared for the father's blessing (and challah, too, lies between the cup and candles), all is set to transform the everyday into holy time. The father—who apparently has completed his work at synagogue as his family has done theirs at home—is flanked by two angelic (perhaps even ghostly) fig-

Figure 2.3. Welcoming the Sabbath. Wood Engravings by Ilya Schor from THE SAB-BATH: ITS MEANING FOR MODERN MAN by Abraham Joshua Heschel. Copyright © 1951 by Ilya Schor. Reprinted by permission of Farrar, Straus and Giroux, LLC.

ures, with the one responding to or eliciting the open arms of the young daughter by the table. Schor decorates this scene under a wedding canopy (*ḥuppah*), and so reproduces Heschel's image of the Sabbath bride. The Sabbath awaits her bridegroom, and he enters the serene quiet of the Jewish home. On the decorative covering high above the table lies a small, white bird gazing upward, and on the other side of this covering we find a raised cup. The entire *ḥuppah,* together with its wedding motifs, frame the movement from the good six days of the week to the holy seventh day of Sabbath time.

Even as the girl's arms reach out, the boy stands back, and the father appears steady and deliberate as he ascends the stairs with his two escorts. The children and mother stand expectant, but still must wait patiently. In this transition from the rush of everyday life to the quiet stillness of sabbatical time lies the representative challenge of Schor's woodcut engraving. How long will it take the father to arrive at the Sabbath table, and so leave behind the material entrapments of civilization? The distance between these two pairs of threesomes—the father with his two escorts, and the mother with her two children—charts the movement from idol to icon. Authentic presence is less immediate than deliberate, captured within a cultural moment of familial harmony and creation. The father must leave the idolatrous world behind—a motif that the darker figure on his left conveys by his slight lean backwards. The white figure, to the father's right, seems closer to him, and so can more easily guide him home. Here the family reconstitutes itself under the wedding canopy, blessed by (at least one of) the father's escorts and sustained by the daughter's affirmation. And this idealized familial image arrives at the expense of everyday life, as the page following this image boldly asserts: "he who wants to enter the holiness of the day must first lay down the profanity of clattering commerce, of being yoked to toil."[83]

Yet even as the father moves steadily from profane to holy ground, he does not lay it all down. The wedding canopy still elicits notions of abundance, peace, and community. His family welcomes him from *within* culture, not outside it; the black figure is still present, however reluctantly. Schor depicts holiness in time beyond the yoke of civilization, but he must traverse the space between welcoming and arrival, and therein lies the ambiguous relation between profane idols and holy icons. Perhaps Schor presents the question to his visual readers as well: how long will it take to arrive at the Sabbath table, and so leave behind the material entrapments of civilization?

In the darker image of the figure chained to civilization, Adam and Eve represented that freedom beyond material constraints. But the walk up the stairs into the wedding canopy appears far more graceful, and certainly less painful, than being "yoked to toil" in that more disturbing sketch. Still, the creation story plays a central role in Schor's iconic imagination, and we can see this in two images that I juxtapose below, though they appear some thirty pages apart in *The Sabbath.* The first introduces part three of the text (Figure 2.4), and the second sketch is the very last in the book (Figure 2.5). Both images recall the creation story, mirroring the depiction of Adam and Eve in the darker image noted above (Figure 2.2). In all three portrayals, Adam and Eve (with fruit in hand) each stand

Figure 2.4. The Tree of Life. Wood Engravings by Ilya Schor from THE SABBATH: ITS MEANING FOR MODERN MAN by Abraham Joshua Heschel. Copyright © 1951 by Ilya Schor. Reprinted by permission of Farrar, Straus and Giroux, LLC.

Figure 2.5. The Circle of Creation. Wood Engravings by Ilya Schor from THE SAB-BATH: ITS MEANING FOR MODERN MAN by Abraham Joshua Heschel. Copyright © 1951 by Ilya Schor. Reprinted by permission of Farrar, Straus and Giroux, LLC.

beside the fruit tree in Eden, with the snake wrapped around it (quite ominously in Figure 2.4, a detail with some importance). The image in part three (Figure 2.4) depicts the various mammals and fish of creation, but the tree of life, with fruit indicating the Hebrew alphabet, is the symbolic center of creation. Those animals in the lighter portions of this sketch move upward toward that tree and the bright sun beyond, while Adam and Eve, together with smaller vegetation and other threatening creatures, seem trapped in the "toil" of creative existence. This sketch tends to subvert that darker one (Figure 2.2) by placing constraints upon Adam and Eve: they live within civilization rather than beyond it.

The very last image (Figure 2.5), located at the beginning of the Epilogue in *The Sabbath,* mediates these two opposing images. Neither depicting Adam and Eve in their prelapsarian bliss nor in their fallen creation (note the menacing face of the serpent in Figure 2.4), this Epilogue image suggests a progressive narrative from creation out of nothing to the holiness of the Sabbath day. If we "read" the image clockwise, beginning with the slice that appears at one o'clock, we can follow how Schor mirrors the acts of creation: he begins by depicting a formless void, then divides light from darkness, fashions the waters and earth with the creatures who inhabit them, creates Adam and Eve in Eden, and then concludes creation with the Sabbath day (high noon). The days of creation, like the days of the week, conclude with the Sabbath and inevitably move toward it. The bright sun shines directly down upon and into the kiddush cup full of wine, hallowing it with brilliant splendor. The Sabbath arrives at the end of the journey, at the climax of God's creation. Yet like the sacred canopy that enveloped Schor's *shtetl* family (Figure 2.3), there are paths to walk. The journey does end, and ends well, but how much of its "toil" carries over to that final brilliance? When the father at last embraces his daughter, will his dark escort on the left set him free? Will Adam and Eve taste the fruit of the Hebrew letters, or drink the cup of sweet wine? These questions are anything but rhetorical, for they suggest how Schor takes us both into and beyond civilization, into and beyond representation, and finally, if necessarily, into and beyond the text.

This tense mirroring of text and image, in which Schor's representative art remaps Heschel's anxiety of authenticity, bequeaths a book that seeks to become that which it evokes. *The Sabbath* itself makes its own claims to authentic presence and vision. Heschel's prose and Schor's images reenact the iconic desire and together, as one complete "text," become a window to spiritual, authentic presence. *The Sabbath,* as material image and inscription, attempts to reproduce the movement of holiness: it conjures up a world of material goods as conduits to spiritual time and wonder, and seeks to become, echoing Wolfson's account of the Zohar, the "hermeneutical basis for revelatory experience."[84] Rather than a physical object to read and worship (a "primitive" sensibility), *The Sabbath* strategically advances itself as a revelatory text in time. As evocative inscription, Heschel's prose directs physical sight to spiritual amazement in the very ways that Schor's engravings redirect the viewer's gaze upward toward authentic presence. In his *God in Search of Man* (1955), Heschel reiterates this metaphor and trajectory: "words must not become screens; they must be regarded as windows."[85]

Scholars recognize Heschel's evocative language, but lament its lack of philosophical rigor.[86] But spiritual insights, so Heschel warns, are found "not on the level of discursive thinking, but on the level of wonder and radical amazement."[87] *The Sabbath* yields haunting prose rather than concise philosophy, nostalgic images rather than a cold modernism, so that material words and images might become spiritual windows. Its very style and rhetoric are bold attempts to channel sight through the material screen so that one might experience radical amazement in time. *The Sabbath* as text/image presents itself as an iconic representation of holiness in time.

Heschel depicts the Sabbath as a guiding window to the ineffable presence of God. The Sabbath day transforms the beauty and allure of physical sensation into a spectacle of spiritual presence: "Then we arrive at the seventh day, and the Sabbath is endowed with a felicity which enraptures the soul, which glides into our thoughts with a healing sympathy."[88] To see the Sabbath as window to spiritual presence is to be moved, enraptured, and comforted by it:

> All week we may ponder and worry whether we are rich or poor, whether we succeed or fail in our occupations; whether we accomplish or fall short of reaching our goals. But who could feel distressed when gazing at spectral glimpses of eternity, except to feel startled at the vanity of being so distressed.[89]

The Sabbath thus offers a new spectacle, not of dazzling, material possessions, but of the tranquility of divine presence. That glimpse of eternity soothes, even as it challenges the vanity of desire, and deflects the insatiable craving produced by technical civilization. In Heschel's rhetorical mood, who could feel distressed when gazing at the authentic presence of the holy?

Schor's images enhance this visual appeal to authenticity in Heschel's written text. They reproduce the visionary tension between seeing *through* and gazing *at* an object, but they also elicit a visionary mode of unseeing the world as a gaze beyond it. These images mimic, in short, Heschel's textual claims to authentic vision: the movement from idolatrous worship to iconic veneration. Heschel's text weaves its way through these visual modes in order to arrive at an experience of holiness in time. He imagines a world replete with material splendors that evoke a sense of the ineffable, but fears that these same objects yield spectacles of enchantment and seduction. He seeks to awaken in his readers a "spiritual eye" that sees through rather than gazes at objects, yet his appeal to divine presence underscores the power of physical sight to ensnare and captivate the self. So too Schor's woodcut engravings. His images suggest a more nuanced text that evokes equivocal visual practices, and they illustrate the anxiety of graphic productions. Together with Heschel's written text, Schor's images produce a fractured and evocative mode of "visual piety."[90] This is in part what images do.

Heschel wagered that a world of spiritual authenticity would resonate for Jews living in America in the 1950s. Perhaps the abandoning of the city for the shelter of suburbia had resulted in too much being left behind. He felt that a nostalgia for what had been lost might stifle the continual production and acquisition of things, and so return Jews to an Eastern European heritage. He worries about an easy conformism to modern consumerist practices, and counters by evoking an enchanted world of images, gazes, and positions so that Jewish culture remains apart from and beyond American civilization. Schor makes a similar case for Jewish authenticity in the face of modern art. In these and many other ways, Heschel and Schor link vision with chosenness in order to decouple Jewish Americans from their American cultural surroundings. *The Sabbath* constructs a particular type of American Jew—one who sees *through* rather than gazes *at* objects, one who searches for God's presence rather than desires God's power, and one who discovers authenticity in a Jewish holiness beyond civilization. Seeing things in time, or in Heschel's evocative phrase, *"coveting the things in time,"*[91] envisions Jewish Americans as set apart from technical, American culture. This image of Jewish identity makes claims to visual authenticity, but inevitably raises the freakish spectacle of the inauthentic. In *The Sabbath,* text and image conjure up both those Frankensteins of space and authentic Jewish seekers of holiness in time.

3 Seeing Food in *The Jewish Home Beautiful* and *Kosher by Design*

> The beauty of the Jewish home resembles the ever-changing beauties of nature. God did not paint one sunset and hang it permanently in the sky. He paints a new sunset daily. Thus too do the beauties of the Jewish home pass through an endless cycle of repetition but not of exact duplication. Our mothers evolved new and beautiful settings and culinary masterpieces for the various days and seasons of the Jewish year.
>
> —Betty Greenberg and Althea Silverman, *The Jewish Home Beautiful*

In chapters one and two I explored the anxiety of authenticity as it surfaced in Bernard Rosenblatt's *Social Zionism* and Abraham Joshua Heschel's *The Sabbath,* and noted how these texts deployed images to present extra-linguistic claims (*Social Zionism*) and to mirror textual dilemmas (*The Sabbath*). In these two texts, visual accounts of the land (Rosenblatt) and sight (Heschel) raised claims to authentic Jewish presence. The images in both texts capture but also evade this anxiety as they deconstruct visions of harmony between Jewish identity and American culture. For Rosenblatt, the American frontier has moved to Palestine where Jews recover their authentic selves; for Heschel, iconic vision protects Jews from the dazzling displays of technical, American culture. Yet these appeals to visual authenticity raise the fear that an authoritative Jewish presence could be lost or never fully regained. The land could remain fallow, or American Jews might turn iconic things into idols. The visual images in Heschel's text mimic this textual anxiety, for Schor's etchings are just as alluring as they are inspiring, whereas the images accompanying *Social Zionism* work in different registers than textual ones to expose both authentic and inauthentic vistas.

I want to explore another rhetorical use of images in two influential American Jewish cookbooks that seek to lessen the anxiety of (in)authenticity by becoming guides to religious practice. Both texts creatively blend homespun advice, religious instruction, and captivating images in ways that inform the visual threads I have been weaving throughout this book. Images function in these texts to stage Jewish authenticity as a performative act. They take center stage, as it were, in the drama of representing Jewish authenticity. Though *The Jewish Home*

Beautiful (1941) and *Kosher by Design* (2003)[1] were published more than sixty years apart and serve very different audiences, they both are significant texts in American Jewish thought. Cookbooks in general, and Jewish cookbooks in particular, offer fascinating resources for recovering cultural and women's history.[2] But these two cookbooks are really guidebooks to Jewish practice: they offer religious instruction and normative claims about how to live a Jewish life in America. They have something to say about Jewish lifestyle, about the nature and practice of tradition, about Jewish law and the centrality of home, and about the ways that food culture develops proper dispositions and insights into Jewish religious commitment. In Jeremy Stolow's important study of *Kosher by Design* within the influential ArtScroll publishing world, he claims that Jewish cookbooks "are particularly valuable for shedding light on the materialization of religious sensibilities."[3] And Jenna Weissman Joselit explicitly labels *The Jewish Home Beautiful* a "guidebook to Jewish ritual practice."[4] The value of guidebooks, within this study of visual authenticity, lies in how *Kosher by Design* and *The Jewish Home Beautiful* claim religious authority for Jews seeking a more authentic Jewish culture in America. As I argued in the introduction to this book, we should apply a pragmatic criterion to determine what "counts" as the proper object of inquiry for Jewish thought. The question is whether a text moves us to think well about Jewish life. Such pragmatic concerns will not silence discussion about a Jewish canon, but instead will provoke ongoing debate. This is, to my mind, how it should be. My claim here is that both *Kosher by Design* and *The Jewish Home Beautiful* show us *how* to think well about visual authenticity as a performative Jewish practice.

To be clear, neither Susie Fishbein (author of *Kosher by Design*) nor Betty Greenberg and Althea Silverman (of *The Jewish Home Beautiful*) have deliberately produced texts about visual authenticity. This is certainly not their intent. But texts often yield meanings well beyond authorial design, and in the cases of these particular books, texts and images work together to expose Jewish culinary practices. My concern focuses on the visual display of Jewish foods, and the anxiety of (in)authenticity such displays provoke. But in addressing the rhetoric of authenticity, I am not thereby affirming a claim about authentic tradition, Orthodoxy, Judaism, or even Jewish culture. To be sure, both *Kosher by Design* and *The Jewish Home Beautiful* do make claims to authentic Jewish tradition, yet these claims tell us little about what is truly authentic, and instead *show* us how images and texts work together to produce those very claims. That an image presents authentic culture does not make it so; but it does help us understand *how* texts rhetorically construct visual authenticity.

Susie Fishbein's *Kosher by Design* is a popular cookbook that appeals to an Orthodox middle-class aspiring to higher status and upward mobility, even as it evokes a peculiar New York City or East Coast aesthetic. Fishbein is sometimes referred to as the Jewish Martha Stewart, for like Stewart her appeal often lies in making "inexpensive gifts appear more costly," and she tends to privilege "appearance over substance, substituting the attainable 'look' for the unattainable class ascension."[5] But substance does come through in the form of homespun motherly advice, careful instructions and preparation, useful tips, and a pragmatic sensibility that projects the confident tone of traditional piety. With sparkling images that assert equal parts beauty and order, *Kosher by Design* seeks to remove the anxiety of authenticity by *staging* traditional religious community in place settings and food that "yield a maximum amount of aesthetic impact." Fishbein weaves beauty and order together to validate her "clever twist"[6] on traditional recipes, and justifies those innovations by displaying authentic culture. The images in *Kosher by Design* present authenticity as ordered, graceful taste.

In *The Jewish Home Beautiful* we discover how Betty Greenberg and Althea Silverman search for continuity as they recover insights and recipes transferred from mother to daughter in order to temper the fear of inauthenticity. Greenberg and Silverman were active in the Conservative movement in the middle years of the twentieth century, as were their spouses (both married Conservative rabbis). They were, in Shuly Schwartz's language, "veteran congregational rebbetzins."[7] Their cookbook is really a pageant of Jewish performance in which staged settings present holiday rituals around the dining table. Published by the National Women's League of the United Synagogue of America, *The Jewish Home Beautiful* targets a female Jewish audience (and some non-Jewish readers) who feel less secure in the Jewish kitchen, but aspire to a more beautiful, edifying Jewish home. Greenberg and Silverman cultivate a healthy appreciation for creativity, and show how each generation can assert its own character and taste through the celebration of the Jewish liturgical year. Like Fishbein's *Kosher by Design*, Greenberg and Silverman organize their book around Jewish holidays and celebrations that include festivities around the dining table. These are less everyday cookbooks (despite Fishbein's claim, in the subtitle to her work, that her "picture-perfect" food works for "holidays & every day"), and far more a celebration of celebrations. And for *The Jewish Home Beautiful*, those holidays commemorate feminine artistic expressions rooted in Jewish cultural continuity. The way Greenberg and Silverman see it, if the daughter creatively reimagines Jewish ritual in her mother's style, then her innovations are equally traditional and fitting. In this sense, food preparation and display in *The Jewish Home Beautiful* can be a carrier of memory and tradition.[8] But this appeal to continuity also raises the fear of discontinuity, forgetfulness, disorder, and the threat of Jewish inauthenticity—precisely the unease that both texts seek to efface through their culinary and religious expertise.

The striking visual images in both works—the professional color photography in *Kosher by Design* and the performative stage designs of *The Jewish Home*

Beautiful—are the centerpieces for textual claims to authenticity, continuity, tradition, and order. *Kosher by Design* is properly named, for the Jewish cook must actively *design* a kosher home to fit a modern, fashion-conscious community. But Fishbein is there as "personal coach" throughout as "a guarantor of knowledge" and "psychological motivator."[9] The images in her text present this work to her readers, for they reveal the traditional nature and authority of her culinary skills and confirm that her mix of "modern and traditional styles" is really only "a clever twist on the traditional." The pageantry invoked in *The Jewish Home Beautiful* walks you through the Jewish holidays and shows its audience affective modes for continuing Jewish culinary traditions. Both the images in the cookbook and the stagings of synagogue pageantry work with the textual utterances to justify Jewish ritual performance as a traditional aesthetic act. In these two cookbooks, images and texts work together to assert religious authenticity as a performative event.

To convey how these texts and images present authenticity as a performative, aesthetic act, I focus on two Jewish holidays—the Sabbath and Purim—that bear witness to this visual register. For Fishbein, but also for Greenberg and Silverman, the Jewish Sabbath presents order and respectability, and the discussions of Sabbath observance, together with accompanying images, powerfully assert that sense of traditional order. The festival of Purim presents a time in the Jewish ritual calendar when masquerade and revelry undermine this traditional propriety. This holiday tests the limits of that order, but *Kosher by Design* continually reinscribes it by tempering merriment with conscious design (in both text and image), and *The Jewish Home Beautiful* reasserts the ethical codes that inform Purim, fearing an unsupervised revelry without them. Fishbein offers delectable dishes that display order within upheaval, and Greenberg and Silverman establish the Jewish mother as the guarantor of religious continuity among the play of culinary rituals. The presentation of the Sabbath and Purim in *Kosher by Design* and *The Jewish Home Beautiful* are "feasts for the eyes"[10] that locate Jewish authenticity within the performance of traditional order and continuity.

Authority, Culture, Cultural Authority

Barbara Kirshenblatt-Gimblett has persuasively argued that Jewish cookbooks create pictures of domestic life and portray a cultural life rich with sounds, smells, images, and tastes. These are books meant to evoke the entire sensorium, and are to be used for efficient dining.[11] Cookbooks respond to cultural anxieties and needs, and their authors imagine readers who seek out culinary expertise and choice morsels of helpful advice. The authors of *The Jewish Home Beautiful* and *Kosher by Design* present themselves as cultural authorities as they recall familial harmony—"from far and near, the family is reunited around the Seder table to re-enact in song and story the miracle of Israel's departure from Egypt"[12]—and feminine romp—"I love the experience of spending a Thursday night in the kitchen with my three daughters baking challah the old-fashioned way, the way its [*sic*] been done by mothers and daughters for generations. The kneading and mixing become a group effort with lots of giggling to go around."[13] Making Jewish food is a traditional observance: it draws families together to recall foundational narrative beginnings (the exodus from Egypt), even as it grounds generational continuity.[14] Cooking with Fishbein, Greenberg, and Silverman is a rich, sensual experience that draws readers into a lively world of folksy advice, imaginative play, timesaving tips, and beautiful preparation. It is a world steeped in Jewish folklore, law, and cultural belonging. Jews enact and perform their American Jewish identities when they take part in producing Jewish foods with these authors.[15] And these cookbooks reveal how authenticity and its related fears shape Jewish culture in America.

Yet Greenberg, Silverman, and Fishbein present their culinary and Jewish expertise to vastly different Jewish audiences. *The Jewish Home Beautiful* (1941) appeared at a time when Jewish identity in America could no longer be presumed but instead had to be cultivated. Jenna Weissman Joselit points to the change in home décor and function that increasingly narrowed the lively sense of Jewish ethnic belonging. In the tenement apartments of New York before the First World War, the kitchen remained the center of Jewish domestic life, both symbolically as the "hub of the home" and quite physically as the central point out of which other rooms expanded. But this tenement experience of spatial belonging loosened when the home no longer functioned as a site of production. The tenement had turned into a private retreat now engineered for consumption. With the nuclear family at the center (without room boarders or extended family), and a younger generation yearning to appropriate American middle-class culture, Jewish Americans moved out of the kitchen in the 1940s and 1950s and into the dining room where they could eat together, set the table with fine cutlery, and perform their "culture of domesticity." Jewish ornaments and markers of ethnic affiliation were replaced by designs that signaled middle-class respectability: the Van Goghs and Renoirs took over for prints of Herzl and Moses.[16] *The Jewish Home Beautiful*, as its title suggests, returned Jewish homemakers to an elegance that would be recognizably Jewish to all. Greenberg and Silverman decry those Jewish mothers who "have turned to foreign sources for their inspiration," especially to the "large department stores and women's magazines," and so have "failed to explore the possibilities of our own traditions." *The Jewish Home Beautiful* arrives to fill this breach, seeking to "inspire Jewish women to a deeper search of their own treasure house."[17] The dining room can still remain elegant and respectable, but Jewish tradition begins in the kitchen.

This call to return home responded to an increased concern that as Jews left the city for the suburbs, and as American-born children abandoned the traditional practices of their parents, "foreign sources" would inspire far more than

Jewish ones. Greenberg and Silverman appealed to authentic roots because they feared inauthentic travels beyond Jewish borders, and a "deeper search" might prevent lost wanderers. *The Jewish Home Beautiful* revealed a cultural anxiety peculiar to this moment in American Jewish upward mobility, yet it also captured the emotional pull of the authentic that resurfaces again and again in modern Jewish thought.

We discover this same dynamic in Susie Fishbein's *Kosher by Design* (2003). One of ArtScroll's best-selling publications, *Kosher by Design* sustains a marketing reach well beyond the affluent East Coast Orthodox Jewish community (and to new members of that community) to whom it makes its most successful appeal. Initially ArtScroll, founded in the 1970s by two ultra-Orthodox American rabbis, directed their publications to *ba'alei teshuva*—those who have appropriated a stricter form of religious observance, but who usually do so without prior experience within the Orthodox community. But the press has since broadened its appeal to include first-generation Orthodox Jews who have yet to acquire Hebrew fluency "to read the original texts and commentaries without the aid of translations."[18] ArtScroll seeks to transmit and thereby affirm ultra-Orthodox values and content (arising especially out of the *haredi* group Agudat Israel) to become, as Jeremy Stolow argues, "a vehicle for transmitting the voice of *haredi* authority, for bringing it into the presence of both committed adherents and various categories of outsiders . . . through the medium of popular print."[19]

Kosher by Design radiates this authority and appeals to this audience as well—especially for those who seek adherence to Jewish dietary principles without forgoing style. Their food must not only taste good, and taste Jewish, but as the subtitle makes clear, it also must be "picture-perfect." Yet in the busy lives of an increasingly affluent observant community, one now firmly and confidently entrenched among other wealthy Americans, these Jews only want to *appear* like they returned to the kitchen; as the inside jacket cover to the book cheekily admits, "Susie Fishbein helps you prepare meals that look like you've spent hours in the kitchen, without the fuss." Presentation and appearance are front and center; behind the elegant façade lies Fishbein's authority as master chef and conveyer of Jewish tradition. *She* works hard so you don't have to, and she worries about details so that you can enjoy being with your invited guests. Fishbein stages kosher designs so that readers can perform their Judaism without fuss and anxiety. With Fishbein present "guiding every step,"[20] it might appear that homemakers spend hours laboring over Jewish dietary laws and culinary masterpieces, but in truth, *Kosher by Design* bestows an "aura of trustworthiness and authenticity" upon the Jews who read it. This is why Stolow believes cookbooks such as Fishbein's illustrate how "scripturalism" works in religious communities: the text itself grounds identity in authentic practice.[21] Jews need not be well-versed in religious law; they only require Fishbein as culinary religious expert to guide them. In this sense, *ba'alei teshuva* (who still serve "as an important part of the

ArtScroll phenomenon")[22] might find this cookbook especially appealing, for it eases the transition to more traditional cultural habits and laws. It is through this process of consumption, Stolow asserts, that "readers and users succeed in naturalizing ArtScroll texts, among other things, as sources of reliable information and aesthetic pleasure, and as repositories of Jewish tradition."[23] Authenticity can be had without the fuss or the cultural work. Behind the elegant presentation lies the authority of Jewish tradition, one mediated by Fishbein's assured sense of proper conduct and "picture-perfect" images of religious order.

Both *Kosher by Design* and *The Jewish Home Beautiful* engage an audience eager for an authoritative voice, one that justifies traditional Jewish culture within a household returning to its Jewish roots (*The Jewish Home Beautiful*), or one designed for a more elegant, sophisticated home culture in twenty-first century America (*Kosher by Design*). The tasteful use of images, coupled with the language of guidance and firm conviction, rhetorically position this voice as an authentic expression of a more traditional Judaism.

The Sabbath in *The Jewish Home Beautiful*

The Jewish Home Beautiful is a rather elaborate collection of notes, blessings, calendars, songs, recipes, and photographs of staged table designs. Greenberg and Silverman begin their work with a short but pivotal introduction on "living as a Jewess"[24] in America, then turn to the "narrative" and "dramatic" versions of their pageant (Greenberg writes the former, Silverman the latter), and inelegantly publish both of these versions together. In quick succession they offer directions for holiday table settings, musical selections, traditional blessings, an eleven-year ritual calendar, and holiday recipes. As a material book and object, *The Jewish Home Beautiful* is patched together following the method of a seasoned chef who adds a little here, a bit there. Images of table décor appear in some (but not all) of the "narrative" renditions of the holidays, and in some (but not all) of the "dramatic" versions. Most of those photos were taken when Greenberg presented her narrative to the National Convention of the Women's League in Atlantic City in 1940, so readers must visualize for themselves how Silverman's dramatic version had appeared when she first presented it in 1932, and again at the Joint Sisterhood Assembly in the Temple of Religion at the World's Fair in 1940.[25] *The Jewish Home Beautiful* is a collection of lore and custom, and like any archive that claims universal coverage, not everything finds its way in.

Though the Sabbath narrative and drama arise last in their list of holiday celebrations,[26] Greenberg claims that the seventh day of rest "has preserved the dignity and self-respect of the Jew through centuries of oppression and darkness." And she highlights how "the woman plays a large part" in preparing the home for that "great day."[27] Indeed, the Sabbath (and all the other festivals appear in this way) is primarily a home celebration. In one sense, this is both obvious and to be expected for a book designed to beautify domestic space. Yet recall Ilya Schor's sketch of the son, daughter, and mother as they welcome their father/husband back to the Sabbath table (Figure 2.3). In that image, two angelic figures escort the father back from synagogue, and the children (especially the daughter) eagerly await his return home. There, the table has been set, but it is incomplete: the scene requires the father's presence. But in *The Jewish Home Beautiful*, it is the woman's stature and her command of the home that is front and center, not the background to the male work in synagogue. The woman does not await but beautifies; she does not stand complacent but "is privileged to be the first to usher in the Shabbat as she lights her candles." These are *her* candles, and so the wife/mother replaces Schor's father as the carrier of tradition to the home. Greenberg introduces the father's presence only once—in connection to the blessing over the wine—and only in the passive voice ("the Kiddush is recited by the father of the house").[28] When he reappears at the closing of the holy day to say blessings over the wine and spices of the *Havdalah* ceremony, Greenberg quickly dismisses him for the more nostalgic image of the family joining in songs to conclude the Sabbath day. The Sabbath is not really his; it is her day because she radiates authentic Jewish tradition.

That authentic character takes on a distinctly aesthetic form in Greenberg's introduction to *The Jewish Home Beautiful*. Joselit is surely right that Greenberg and Silverman appealed "to the aesthetic sensibilities of the modern Jewish woman," and Kirshenblatt-Gimblett artfully recognizes how the text "joined floral design, coordinated table settings, and notions of elegance and refinement to the promotion of Jewish ritual observance."[29] But note how this aesthetic turn artfully raises the issue of authenticity:

> Living as a Jewess is more than a matter of faith, knowledge or observance. To live as a Jewess, a woman must have something of the artist in her. She must have an appreciation for things beautiful and a desire to create those beautiful things herself.[30]

Perhaps for male heirs, like Schor's figure of the father escorted by the two angels, "faith, knowledge or observance" function as authentic carriers of Jewish tradition. But for Greenberg, these traditional pillars are inadequate for American Jewish women of the 1940s. An aesthetic awareness must enter to fill the void of what Greenberg sees as a far more sterile adherence to Jewish conventions. Beauty evokes appreciation, admiration, and desire. But it also awakens personal commitment: "a desire to create those beautiful things herself." This creativity is really *her* inheritance, for Jews of the past also yearned "to beautify the Jewish home and ennoble every Jewish life," just like, Greenberg believes, American Jewish women do in her day. Her creative genius is an authentic Jewish genius because it is grounded in traditional precedent. Greenberg's Jewess does not create out-of-nothing; she dutifully continues "the finest artistic achievements of our people."[31]

Greenberg displaces common appeals to authority (faith, knowledge, observance) with an aesthetics of feminine creativity. The Jewess's active, expressive powers are not original to her; they have deep, authoritative roots in the Jewish tradition. In this reversal of value, Greenberg feels compelled to ground ingenuity in the past so that innovation appears as progressive continuity. The Jewish home beautiful is really the traditional Jewish home—it merely continues the aesthetic expressions of Jewish observance.

Locating female creativity in a traditional past reveals the anxiety of authenticity that shadows Greenberg's account of Jewish continuity. In some sense, she protests too much. She roots stylistic innovation in traditional Jewish culture, and she likens a woman's touch to God's own creative acts:

> The beauty of the Jewish home resembles the ever-changing beauties of nature. God did not paint one sunset and hang it permanently in the sky. He paints a new sunset daily. Thus too do the beauties of the Jewish home pass through an endless cycle of repetition but not of exact duplication.[32]

In imitating this natural Creator, Jewish women follow divine inspiration. They also follow other cookbooks and food manufactures of this period, as Rachel Gross notes, in their consumer appeal to creativity.[33] And like Greenberg's Jewess, God exercises innovation within the framework of continuity. The natural world, in one sense, is the very same world each and every day, but this world also arises as a form of renewed creation ("He paints a new sunset daily"). Unlike matters of faith, knowledge, or observance, art is the true expression of God's continued but ever changing presence in the world. Greenberg's American Jewess inherits this divine creativity: "guided by the memories and traditions of yesterday, [she] must herself create new glory and new beauty for the Jewish home of today."[34] This "new glory" is really not new at all, for it remains grounded in God's own original creative act. Her aesthetic creations imitate God's own deeds, and this mirroring helps to reduce the fear that aesthetic creations reveal the altogether new and unprecedented. This is what I have been calling the anxiety of authenticity: the felt need to justify innovation by tethering it to an authoritative precedent.

This secure linking to the past does not mean that aesthetic pageantry resembles a museum installation, "as something to admire and then to forget, or merely to recall in conversation." *The Jewish Home Beautiful* is less artistic work than vibrant artistic project: "its purpose is rather to urge every mother in Israel to assume her role as artist . . . to make her home and her family table a thing of beauty."[35] Greenberg seeks to galvanize modern Jewish women to take up their traditional role as artistic homemaker, modeled on God's own creative role in nature. The home is to modern Jewish women as nature is to God: their domicile is the canvas upon which they must express their creativity. Their residency and recognition of place confers a powerful sense of continuity. Throughout the late nineteenth and early twentieth centuries, the American home symbolically and materially functioned as the bearer of continuity within Jewish tradition.[36] The Conservative movement in particular, to which *The Jewish Home Beautiful* holds a special allegiance, "stressed the primacy of the Jewish home as an agent of Jewish identity, cultural continuity, and 'beautification.'"[37] The American Jewish woman conserves but also advances culture in the home, as God does so continually in nature. Even if the Sabbath arrives last in the narrative and dramatic order of *The Jewish Home Beautiful*, it still remains the ever recurring home celebration that makes it the primary, natural site for Jewish continuity. In Greenberg's Jewish home beautiful, the Sabbath is a woman's holiday that conserves but also advances Jewish culture, even as it continues God's own creative acts.

The image that accompanies Greenberg's discussion of the Sabbath emphasizes the feminine roles during the Jewish day of rest. In both the narrative and dramatic versions of *The Jewish Home Beautiful*, Greenberg and Silverman include ornamental sketches that are stylistically similar to Schor's engravings. The sketches accompany the holiday descriptions as elegant adornments, and appear as decorative introductions to each of the Jewish festivals. The sketch of Passover, for example, includes the large letter *P* at the center, with four kiddush cups surrounding the center plate—a clear sign of the four cups of wine consumed throughout the seder, together with the symbolic foods of the holiday. All the narrative and dramatic sections follow this pattern: there is a large letter in the center of the sketch (corresponding to the first letter of the holiday), surrounded by materials that represent that day's special features. The image accompanying Greenberg's discussion of the Sabbath follows the pattern set by all the previous holiday sections, but it omits one noticeable feature: the kiddush cup. We see a soft white dove hovering over a large letter *S* that itself lies above two loaves of challah, all surrounded by two candlesticks. But there is no kiddush cup for the traditional male blessing over the wine. The sketch, like Greenberg's own narrative, emphasizes "how the woman plays a large part in impressing the Sabbath spirit upon her family" by preparing the food and lighting the candles. The image excises the male role from the holiday, and mirrors Greenberg's thin description of the passive male ("Kiddush is recited by the father of the house"). Peace and tranquility (the dove) protect the Sabbath day, but this is a day that women initiate, and do so in the active voice: she is "the first to usher in the Shabbat as she lights her candles, a quarter of an hour before sunset, and says the benediction over them."[38] She lights and speaks, but the kiddush is recited. This is her home beautiful as performative utterance.

Her Jewish home is also a house of song. She transmits the ballads and yearnings of the past to her offspring, and continues Jewish tradition through music:

Figure 3.1. P for Pesaḥ. Reprinted by permission of Women's League for Conservative Judaism.

> Jewish children all through the ages have been nurtured on folk-songs that expressed the hopes and yearnings of their people. . . . Into their small, pink ears, Jewish mothers crooned desires and hopes, dreams and yearnings that have sprung from the traditions of Israel.

> And in the JEWISH HOME BEAUTIFUL the mother still sings the old folk-songs which she has heard her own mother sing,—songs of Torah, of learning, of duty.[39]

Althea Silverman wrote this section on holiday songs, but she harkens back to Greenberg's introductory claim that Jewish mothers inspire faith, knowledge, and observance through artistic beauty. She sings in order to impress "upon her

Figure 3.2. S for Shabbat. Reprinted by permission of Women's League for Conservative Judaism.

child his duties as a Jew," for "all his obligations she teaches him through song!" Silverman still clings to the traditional focus on the male son, for only he appears to have duties and obligations. He learns Torah, goes to Hebrew school, becomes a "pious Jew" and a renowned scholar. She is the proud, enabling mother, but she cannot rely solely on the folk songs she heard as a child. Silverman balances that more traditional voice with new voices coming from the land of Zion:

> Now Jewish mothers have new folk-songs to sing. Out of the land of Israel, out of the land of their fathers, have come new Jewish folk-songs, songs of planting

and reaping, of harvesting and cutting, of building and creating. And in the Jewish home, mothers will sing old folk-songs and new folk-songs, prayers and zemirot,—to *keep* their Jewish homes beautiful![40]

We have already witnessed in Rosenblatt's *Social Zionism* how these tropes promote the harvesting of the land, and how more authentic Jewish bodies are thereby cultivated. But for Silverman, Jewish mothers do their own planting, reaping, and harvesting by investing in their children. As Jews are commanded to remember and keep the Sabbath, Jewish mothers *keep* their homes beautiful with song and grace, mixing just the right amount of tradition and modernity. Rosenblatt believed Jews ought to traverse the ocean and conquer a land in order to become more authentically Jewish; Silverman, in tones both nostalgic and familial, insists they stay right at home and perform their actions there.

Innovation enables mothers to observe and pass on traditions to their children, and Israeli folk tunes serve those American Jewish interests. Although Jewish mothers sing the Yiddish tune "Auf'n Pripitchek"[41] to encourage diligent study, those "small, pink ears" might not listen, or even understand those traditional aspirations. Israel fills that voice by recovering a lost innocence and an honorable tradition. This is certainly how Rosenblatt envisioned his Israel, and Silverman, too, is caught up in the Zionist imaginary. But she appeals to Israel in order to confer an authentic inheritance: Israeli folk songs unite with "old" *zemirot* to kindle Jewish passions and *keep* the Jewish Sabbath. Jewish women stand firmly in the center between an Ashkenazi inheritance and an Israeli future. She manages both old and new, and enables Israel to sing the language of tradition.

Silverman also designed the "dramatic" version of *The Jewish Home Beautiful,* and while much of her discussion of the Sabbath follows Greenberg's, there are some striking differences. Silverman's version performs Greenberg's narrative rendition, with a "Reader" who explains the meaning of the day and its ritual performances. There is a choir off-stage that "softly" sings the blessings associated with the holiday as the mother carries out the Sabbath activities. The "Reader" guides the audience to imagine a serene, beautiful time when the mother invites the Sabbath into her home. Silverman almost entirely silences the father in her stage directions. To be sure, he still welcomes the Sabbath by chanting the kiddush over the wine, and he says the prayers for the *Havdalah* service, but he nowhere appears on stage. When the "Reader" explains how the father kindles the *Havdalah* candle and chants the prayers, the stage directions suggest a very different kind of presence:

When Reader mentions "The Habdalah candle," the woman holds up the braided candle. When Reader says "sniffs the fragrant spices," she displays the spice box. When Reader has finished, soloist off-stage sings "Hamabdil" and choir joins briskly in the chorus "Shevuah Tov."[42]

The mother and choir have displaced the father's active voice: the father might kindle the "Habdalah" candle, but she *shows* it to the audience without his presence. Silverman is almost reluctant to mention him at all: "As a Jew lifts his Kiddush cup, his glistening table is a festive board. With wife and children gathered about him, he welcomes the Sabbath day." To be sure, this is a pageant dedicated to and for American Jewish women. We should expect that women dominate the role playing in this spectacle. But to actually *see* the male absence is striking. We know he is there, as father and husband, but his presence is incidental: "Joy, warmth, hospitality, peace,—these make his Jewish home beautiful."[43] Those values of middle-class respectability—values bestowed by the mother but not the father—imitate God's own activities in nature.

Silverman's dramatic version performs a more secure Judaism that knows how and when to act, and what to say, and does so with style and grace. There is a quiet confidence in how the woman carries out her prescribed duties:

> Off-stage choir sings "Sholom Aleiḥem" softly as woman dressed in taffeta dress, wearing a soft white apron and a white lace scarf over her shoulders, walks slowly to Shabbat table. She covers the two Sabbath loaves with a Ḥallah cover, lights the candles, covers her head with white scarf, and as singing off-stage is concluded, raises her hands and recites the blessing for the kindling of the Sabbath lights in Hebrew and then in English. . . . When she has concluded her blessing, she lowers her hands slowly and becomes still as Reader continues.[44]

Dressed entirely in pristine white, this Jewess is neither hurried nor troubled by Sabbath preparations—she "walks slowly to Shabbat table." Her white apron witnesses to her kitchen work, but the material bears no signs of mess or disorder. Indeed, the kitchen lies far away from the Sabbath table: like the choir, the kitchen remains off-stage. This dramatizes nicely Joselit's suggestion that much has changed for American Jews in the move from kitchen to dining table. This is a public Judaism, displayed before guests, rather than a more intimate affair of returning home to one's kin.[45] But more than this: missing in this dramatic version are the father and children. Silverman once instructs a boy to impress his mother with the four traditional Passover questions. Yet in every other case, when Silverman and Greenberg describe a warm, joyful household of song and mirth, we can only imagine what father and children really do at the Sabbath table. *The Jewish Home Beautiful* stages Judaism before an audience, but that audience must still conjure scenes unseen. This is what it means to see an absence: we know father and children are there, but we can only represent them as present in our visual imaginations.

This absence reveals the mother's quiet confidence, for she does not require her husband's presence to stamp "her personality upon her household." She con-

Figure 3.3. *The Jewish Home Beautiful* Shabbat Table. Reprinted by permission of Women's League for Conservative Judaism.

trols and manages the joy, warmth, hospitality, and peace in the Jewish home beautiful as she "takes her pattern from the mothers of yesterday and creates new beauty, new spirituality for the Jewish home of tomorrow."[46] She projects this sense of command and composure not only through her white clothing, but also through her setting of the Sabbath table. In Silverman's "Production Notes" for the dramatic presentation, she ensures that tables "are meticulously set with choicest linen, china and silver table service."[47] And we can see this in the accompanying photograph of the Sabbath table (Figure 3.3). This is an image of order, elegance, and tranquility. The table decorations are sparse but bright. Each place setting has its own kiddush cup—a smaller version of the larger one lying on the far right at the head of the table. Next to that kiddush cup we find the challah loaves with a white, decorative covering. The Sabbath candles are here too, with a flower arrangement in the middle. Some foods grace the table, perhaps a kugel and gefilte fish. Silverman arranges the table in exquisite detail:

> The table is set for dinner for six people; damask tablecloth and napkins, fine china, silver and glassware. Two handsome, tall old silver candlesticks with white candles and a low bowl of flowers on either side, keeping the candlesticks together in the center, make the centerpiece for the Shabbat table. . . . A large platter of gefilte fish, a container of horse radish, a platter of eierkichel and a round noodle or potato kugel, partly cut, are also on the table.[48]

Even if set for six, this table has no chairs to surround it (this is true for every table photographed, with the one exception of the Passover setting). Despite Greenberg's claim in her introduction that "the *Jewish Home Beautiful* is not presented as a museum piece,"[49] it certainly appears as such in this photograph, down to the partly cut kugel. The effect is one of order, composure, and calm certitude. A table for six has room for guests, but probably not guests with children. This is a Sabbath table of adult elegance and composed order. There is no anxiety of (in) authenticity here.

The recipes that Greenberg and Silverman include at the end of their compilation also help to keep this anxiety at bay. It is not just their inclusion of chicken soup, cholent, lukshen kugel and the rest. Nor is it their nostalgic use of Americanized Yiddish, or their schmaltzy recollections of "the sweet syrupy smell of teiglach boiling in honey." It is instead how these foods *function* to preserve the authenticity of Jewish holiday observance. These foods, Greenberg tells her readers, "acquired a dignity, bordering upon sanctity, which elevated them to the status of religious traditions in the home." This is not food for "every day," as Fishbein's *Kosher by Design* would have it. Authentic cuisine requires scarcity and particularity:

> All we need to remember is that by the beautiful expedient of surrounding certain foods with the halo of religious associations and with the magic charm of "once in a while," our mothers were able to preserve these traditions for us down through the ages. It is an old Jewish cooking secret, that one should never abuse a delicacy by serving it too frequently.[50]

Delicacies become religious traditions when served only at holidays, when "the mere mention of these names arouses nostalgic and mouth-watering memories." Nostalgia and sanctity make a potent mix to ward off the insecurity of "new beauty, new spirituality for the Jewish home of tomorrow." These succulent foods and distinctive odors carry Jews back home, literally, to the "performance of sacred rites."[51] According to Elliot Weiss, this is what package labels on Jewish products did for their buyers. By appealing to traditional home cooking, and including images of "the yiddische mama," labels on kosher foods endowed their products with authenticity:

> The recipe therefore is generations old. The timelessness of the text endows the recipe with a quasi-sacerdotal aura. The reenactment of the recipe, the preparation of the latke mix, thus becomes akin to religious ritual, its performance validates the consumer as a member of the chosen people.[52]

Greenberg and Silverman attempt to do much the same for their texts and for their readers. The performance of *The Jewish Home Beautiful* is the enactment of a sacred rite, as Weiss suggests. But as a cultural exhibition, their cookbook invokes and seeks to constrain the anxiety of authenticity in both visual and textual modes. Greenberg's Jewess creates new recipes and sings new songs, but these innovations make for anxious appeals to continuity and tradition: "Here is a raised dough recipe minus the bogey of countless hours of rising and endless kneading. The method is not traditional; in fact, it is quite modern, but as long as the finished product is just like mother's, does it matter?"[53] It does not matter, and we can see this in the images and stage directions of *The Jewish Home Beautiful*. It is important that Jewish foods, as a "finished product," look, smell, and taste authentic: they must be carriers of the sacred, perhaps even more than the women who serve them, to help keep the Sabbath beautiful.

The Sabbath in *Kosher by Design*

The performative struggle with authenticity that I find so pronounced in *The Jewish Home Beautiful* is not entirely absent in *Kosher by Design*. Nonetheless, Susie Fishbein maintains a confident voice throughout, and offers homespun advice with the assurance that all is kosher, by design. The magnificent images scattered throughout her text stage this sense of order, confidence, and authenticity. Images in *The Jewish Home Beautiful* also functioned to secure authenticity and a sense of order. But an apologetic tone often surfaced in Greenberg's and Silverman's defense of innovation. They both anchored creative home entertainment in traditional practices: "From the days of Abraham when Sarah's Home Beautiful . . . was deemed worthy of a visit by three angels of the Lord, the Jewish woman has stamped her personality upon her household."[54] This mode of address, which reveals a felt need to ground innovation in the past, is utterly missing in Fishbein's more assertive prose:

> The recipes in this book offer abundant directions to help walk you through them. The selected dishes mix modern and traditional styles. I always try to include a clever twist on the traditional wherever possible. You will find tips, hints, menus, and wine recommendations to round out your meals.[55]

The vision of walking together with ample and clear directions speaks directly to an audience accustomed to the religious practice of Jewish law (*halakhah*)—a term that also implies a straightforward path within which to walk. The recipes guide, much like Jewish law and tradition. But in mixing the modern and traditional, Fishbein restrains her innovation to a "clever twist," and this only whenever possible. Tradition still commands and asserts authority; Fishbein never deviates from that style, but only adjusts when she can, and only when it is proper to do so. *Kosher by Design* is still confined by traditional directives, but now with Fishbein's more sophisticated twists, you can walk with confidence, knowing that this modern journey is still kosher.

Fishbein draws on the figure of a journey to elevate kosher food preparation. The title of her book carries a double meaning, but only for the audience she addresses: "This book is for you—the cook who *chooses* to cook kosher and who wants to present beautifully designed dishes with style and grace." The Jewish dietary laws neither burden nor demand excessive restrictions. Jews can adopt that defining American value—individual choice—to actually moderate their culinary options. But those limits are really opportunities, and in this context Fishbein employs the language of journey: "Above all, have fun. Let each meal be a wonderful journey—the sharing of something special with people you care about."[56] As Steven Cohen and Arnold Eisen argue in their influential study of contemporary American Jewry, Jews (as well as other Americans) often speak about their religious practice as a journey.[57] This rhetorical move enables creativity, but it also condones a more casual approach to religious obligations. Yet Fishbein contends that one can enjoy that journey fully within the strictures of Jewish law. The kosher dietary rules are treasures to be shared with loved ones. Jewish law is a gift that one actively chooses, "week after week" and "night after night" at the holiday table. This traditional pleasure can be designed to look beautiful ("with style and grace"), and so modern Orthodox Jews need not give up aesthetic taste for religious obligation. Everything works together with ease: "A well-arranged kosher kitchen just hums along."[58] Jewish dietary laws are *designed* to be enjoyed, shared, and beautifully presented. The images in Fishbein's text do this kind of work: they present design as elegant, creative, and traditional.

In Fishbein's kitchen, the laws of *kashrut* neither dampen pleasure nor impede journey. Family and guests, who now eat "in accordance with Jewish law," enhance "their spiritual, as well as physical, well-being" by eating kosher food. But it need not appear that way: "We look for fresh ingredients that can be prepared with a minimal amount of fuss, but yield a maximum amount of aesthetic impact."[59] The food can indeed look like those "beloved dishes" that so enchanted Greenberg's nostalgic yearnings.[60] But those "formal meals loaded with rich choices," Fishbein now tells us, should give way to the American demand for "simpler, well-planned meals." Jews in the kitchen want "easy-to-read recipes"[61] because time matters, and as Stolow helpfully points out, "the *reduction of effort* emerges as a new organizing principle [in *Kosher by Design*] for the successful replication of authentic Jewish practice."[62] Ease, simplicity, guidance: these are values that appeal to contemporary Jews who *choose* to keep kosher but may not want their foods to *appear* so. After all, these Jews really want *out* of the kosher kitchen to enjoy and share their food with family and friends. But once there, Jews should delight in the journey as a complete, sensual process:

> Listen for the sizzle as meat hits the pan, feel the food to determine its doneness, smell the nutty aroma of grains as they toast, behold with your eyes the plate's appeal, taste with your palate the delight of your creations.[63]

Kirshenblatt-Gimblett notes how taste operates "as a sensory experience" among multiple registers, "not only by way of the mouth and nose, but also the eye, ear and skin."[64] And Stolow perceptively claims that images in *Kosher by Design* also act as "objects of pleasure" that seduce the whole body.[65] Fishbein aspires to an accessible, friendly, and sensual experience in the kitchen: "I wanted to do something like what Martha Stewart or the Barefoot Contessa does—meals that are easy to prepare, and elegant and healthful, and that appeal to all the senses."[66] Kosher cooks enjoy these physical pleasures, and delight in a creativity that still conforms to the pathways of Jewish law. In these ways, preparing kosher food *enables* a full aesthetic experience, body and soul. In taking hold of this culinary journey, American Jews might discover their own authentic selves, so Fishbein asserts, in the kosher food they serve.

As Jews savor their own culinary creations, they can also gather around the holiday table, "savoring the life-enhancing magic of Shabbat." Throughout *Kosher by Design*, Fishbein draws together culinary and spiritual delights. Food design highlights religious values, and those values can be seen, touched, smelled, and tasted in kosher foods. Jews should delight in both their special foods and in their presentation:

> This is true about entertaining, too. It is not only what you serve, but how you serve it. A simple garnish, a beautiful table, an unusual floral arrangement, a colorful plate filled with assorted delicacies—all of these things elevate the mundane to the magnificent.[67]

Attention to aesthetic detail mirrors the movement from the profane (mundane) to the holy (magnificent) that occurs each week during sabbatical time.[68] When Fishbein appeals to aesthetic impact, she is not privileging appearance over substance, as Ann Mason and Marian Meyers claimed for Martha Stewart. To the contrary: Fishbein elevates the aesthetic to a religious duty that mirrors "the life-enhancing magic of Shabbat." Just as the seventh day enhances the everyday, so too the Jewish kosher cook transforms the ordinary into something magnificent.[69] Fishbein dramatizes this religious aesthetic by elevating the choice and presentation of kosher food to an expression of Jewish style.

We see this presentation of authenticity in the images that accompany Fishbein's arrangement of the Sabbath. Professional, striking color photographs abound in *Kosher by Design*. Fishbein assembled a professional team to stage these photographic shoots, including John Uher as "the world-class food photographer, " Renee Erreich as "one of Manhattan's top event planners," Larry Sexton as designer, and Jill Raff as food stylist. Although the images are brilliant and enticing, Fishbein hopes her readers will not be "fooled by the stylishness of the photos": "our team worked very hard so that you won't have to. We want you to spend more time being a gracious host than a chef that sweats it; but while you're wearing your chef's hat, we'll help you cook with confidence and inspiration."[70] This sense of confidence without the sweat describes how Fishbein deploys Uher's photographs in *Kosher by Design*. Stolow has argued that these professionally produced images are feasts for the eyes, and so appeal to our aesthetic tastes. He argues persuasively, following W. J. T. Mitchell, David Morgan, and others, that we ask, "what kinds of work do ArtScroll pictures perform in relation to their viewers?" Though attune to "the much wider range of perceptual, affective, cultural, and technological registers in and through which images are manifested," Stolow nonetheless focuses his attention upon the *"visually desirable:* food that is designed to be seen and good enough to be photographed." This no doubt captures what images do in *Kosher by Design,* but I look at another, no less significant, performance: the ways these images work to create an aura of authenticity—not because the food is beautiful (even if it is) and appeals to all the senses (even if it does), but because these photographs radiate order, tradition, and sublimity. When viewed in this way, Stolow has it right: "the photographs found in *Kosher by Design* not only convey information but also possess a cathectic power to transport their viewers into a virtual world of vibrant authenticity and harmonious fellowship."[71] In this sense, texts like *Kosher by Design* work "by orchestrating the desire for authenticity and shaping the means of its attainment."[72] I want to explore how the images in *Kosher by Design* do this.

The image of the Sabbath table presents tradition in all its grandeur, stability, and rootedness. The viewer gazes from the head of the table toward a magnificent window leading out to what looks like the Hudson River. Where all the table settings are light, elegant, and brilliant, the drapes surrounding the window, together with the deep leather chairs, are heavy, darkened, and lush. This formality and sophistication appears in all the photographs in *Kosher by Design.* The images suggest a wealthy, urban Orthodox elite comfortable with American high culture. Here we gaze upon a sophisticated, elegant, and traditional dining table. Each place setting includes a *birchon* (a book of selected blessings) for Sabbath evening prayers, together with individual challah rings for napkins ("Could there be a cuter accent on a Shabbos table than challah napkin rings?").[73] At the head of the table lies a large, polished kiddush cup, while guests or other family members enjoy their own smaller variants (though still brilliantly polished). The exquisite floral arrangement at the center perfectly complements the individual place settings. Two bottles of red wine match the two wine glasses for each guest (Fishbein includes a wine list for her Sabbath menu), and the coffee/tea cups are fashionably set on their sides. The knife to cut the challah bread is impeccably prepared to make the initial cut (although the loaves remain uncovered at this time—it has to be seen!). With Sabbath candles alight, and the growing darkness outside, all appears in order before the onset of the seventh day. What happens here on the Sabbath happens at the dining table, displayed and designed for royal guests.

This image of the table perfectly mirrors Fishbein's confident prose that projects an easy comfort with the brilliance of traditional Jewish practice. Nothing is out of place; order, simple elegance, repose, but also a touch of the modern "twist"

Figure 3.4. *Kosher by Design* Shabbat Table. Reproduced courtesy of ArtScroll/Mesorah Publications, Ltd.

rejuvenate an ancient tradition. This sense of stately influence and authority comes through in the side-view of the Sabbath table. In this photograph we see a large, antique mirror reflecting the candles and the overhanging chandelier. The mirror literally reflects the continuity that such lighting suggests. And we have

Figure 3.5. *Kosher by Design* Shabbat Table (side view). Reproduced courtesy of ArtScroll/Mesorah Publications, Ltd.

a fuller picture of the plush, leather chairs, now visually surrounded by deep, wooden columns that surround the heavy-set dining table. The floral centerpiece appears much larger in this side view than it did in the more prodigious, frontal image. All this magnifies the dignity, authority, and weightiness of the Sabbath: we view the heavy chairs and table, the magnificent columns, the elegant sparkle of china and glassware, the large centerpiece design, and even the conservative wallpaper matching the luxurious rug underneath the table. This is a staging of visual authenticity conveyed through order, tradition, and sublimity.

Compare these images to a very different visual spectacle of a Sabbath table in Cary, Mississippi, on display at the Museum of the Southern Jewish Experience (in 2005). This photograph, too, is staged before a window, but instead of the Hudson River we recognize a large cotton field appearing just on the border to the house property. Though muted, this black-and-white photograph still radiates a simple elegance. The caption to this image suggests how the curators wish to focus the viewer's sight: "This Cary, Mississippi, Shabbat table is a sacred place where traditions and family come together with cotton, family silver, challah, and pecan pie."[74] Southern culture and cuisine mix with Jewish ritual to produce a distinctive flavor of the sacred. Marcie Cohen Ferris argues that to understand what it means to be both southern and Jewish, one must find the answers "in stories and in recipes passed like a patchwork quilt from one generation to the next."[75] This is the language of *The Jewish Home Beautiful,* in which the focus on continuity, together with its attendant anxieties (the image of a patchwork quilt), carries the weight of Jewish authenticity. The Cary, Mississippi, Shabbat table also exhibits a patchwork, however staged, of symbolic Jewish and southern culture. But the metaphor of a quilt, in which various strands weave together to form a "sacred place," has no place within John Uher's photographs in *Kosher by Design.* Fishbein's clever twists on traditional designs are not braids knitted together to fabricate a patchwork identity. Instead, her Shabbat table radiates a grounded authority that commands in a simple but demanding voice: *This* is Jewish. It is an authenticity founded on a confident appeal to tradition.

Fishbein accentuates this voice of tradition in three smaller images gracing the last page of her introduction to the Sabbath. Each focus attention on the particular rituals associated with the seventh day: (1) the ritual washing of the hands before (2) removing the challah cover, and (3) the *Havdalah* ceremony that concludes the Sabbath. The floral designs and coordinated color schemes all suit the careful design of the Sabbath table. These particular ritual acts are no less powerful, and so no less elegant, than the ordered serenity of the evening meal. The hand washing station appears as solely devoted to that purpose, with the drying towel included to help remind guests of the traditional blessing. Even the *Havdalah* station stands nicely to the side, forever clean, polished and new—an elegant distance from the messiness that multiwick candles often produce. Fishbein has modernized these traditional ritual acts with elegant design, but they still articulate a sense of permanence. These photographs are staged installation pieces, presenting the washing and *Havdalah* stations as enduring cultural practices that *always* look like this. Nothing is out of order because the images assert the stability and authenticity of place. These images present Jewish authenticity as a durable, beautiful, and ordered tradition that easily blends with modern aesthetic values. Here tradition mixes and twists with elegance to radiate authenticity.

The images in *Kosher by Design* display observant Jewish practice as authentic Judaism. And though many readers of texts often view images as simply pictorial representations of the written word, this cookbook works in precisely the opposite direction: Fishbein's prose reinforces the arguments delivered in and through the photographs.[76] Stolow marshals fascinating anecdotal evidence from reviewers on the Web site amazon.com to suggest how readers see this book as a visual production. Food tastes good in large part because it looks that way: "My sister-in-law told me that my Sunken Apple and Honey cake looks so good it should be pictured on the cover of a magazine!" even if her cake does not turn out "exactly as pictured in the book."[77] As the comment from the sister-in-law suggests, her sunken apple and honey cake looks as good, if not better, than Fishbein's own, and so deserves its own magazine cover. Fishbein's recipes enable her

Figure 3.6. Cary, Mississippi, Shabbat Table. Photo by Bill Aron. Courtesy of Goldring/Woldenberg Institute of Southern Jewish Life.

to produce something beautiful—the written word serves the visual aesthetics of food production.

Fishbein's account of the Sabbath appeals to Jewish tradition in ways that support the pictorial images of the table. She describes that table as "elegant, yet

Figure 3.7. Ritual Washing Station. Reproduced courtesy of ArtScroll/Mesorah Publications, Ltd.

Figure 3.8. Challah Cover. Reproduced courtesy of ArtScroll/Mesorah Publications, Ltd.

Figure 3.9. Havdalah. Reproduced courtesy of ArtScroll/Mesorah Publications, Ltd.

relaxed—for the queen is not only a special guest, but an old friend as well." We hear the message of continuity and elegance, but also a sense of worship: "It is our privilege to honor her every week." "She" is not an occasional guest but a continued presence every seventh day. And the Sabbath queen deserves labored preparation, for when royalty come and visit, Jews must make the house sparkle, dress in their finest clothes, and "serve the most lavish cuisine." But Jewish law ensures that these displays of style and taste never become vain temptations to impress. Underneath beauty lies order:

> Lighting the Shabbat candles is a *mitzvah* performed by the wife/mother of the household eighteen minutes before sundown. As we light the Shabbat candles, we absorb the tranquil mood that helps turn our thoughts from the mundane to the spiritual.[78]

Note Fishbein's subtle claim to authentic style: the heightened beauty conveyed through photography brings the viewer, as Stolow argues, "into contact with an authentic presence"[79] by moving her from the profane to the sacred realm. Aesthetic beauty serves the higher calling of religious devotion and reorientates moods and thoughts to more lofty goals. Observant Jews should neither feel ashamed nor defensive when their Sabbath table radiates the beauty in *Kosher by Design*; their sophisticated style, however modern and American, inspires their own religious practice.[80]

We see this in the ritual objects that surpass their elegant beauty as they point to God's activity in creation. Fishbein inclines towards Heschel's visual optics by moving beyond the beautiful objects to a fuller reality. But where Heschel believes such things are windows to a holy presence, Fishbein argues that ritual objects teach us about God:

> Our candles are also symbolic of God's creation of the physical and spiritual universes, as the Torah records that the universe began with the Divine declaration "Let there be light." The creation of the world is prominently featured in the words of Kiddush, the prayer over wine that begins our meal.
>
> The challah on the table is a reminder of the manna that fell in the desert to feed our ancestors after their Exodus from Egypt. It fell six days a week, but not on Shabbat. On Fridays, each household received a double portion. And that is why we place two challot on our Shabbat table—recalling the double portion of food lovingly sent by Heaven for every Jew every *erev Shabbat* for nearly 40 years.[81]

Each ritual object on Fishbein's Shabbat table signifies to a larger meaning about God's activities. The Torah "records" how God acts, and the Sabbath blessings remind us of God's original intentions. Fishbein's explanations are traditional and well-known within observant communities. But note the difference between her commentary and the far more passive exegesis that Greenberg and Silverman offer in *The Jewish Home Beautiful*. Here is Greenberg:

> Six days he may have toiled at the most menial tasks, but on the seventh day he was *commanded* to rest and to devote his mind to things spiritual. . . . The two loaves of Shabbat bread, or Hallot, are symbolic of the double portion of manna supplied to the Israelites for the Shabbat in the wilderness.[82]

Silverman is even more evasive:

> His home, though lacking in worldly splendor, is sanctified by the mellow glow of the Sabbath candles. . . . The two golden loaves remind us also of the double portion of manna that our ancestors received for the Sabbath when they wandered in the wilderness.[83]

Who supplies that bread, and who commands Jews to rest? Greenberg and Silverman remain silent on both accounts, but Fishbein manifests a confident faith in God's creative works. To Fishbein, the beauty of the Sabbath table reflects God's own beauty; Jews labor for God because God deserves their praise.

Yet if God requires physical labor to honor the Sabbath queen as a royal guest, then Fishbein demands anything but "a minimal amount of fuss" when preparing the table. To begin, one must find a "cascade of hydrangeas as a centerpiece," polish all the silver, arrange the place settings, scrape the wax that inevitably drips onto the saucer from the *Havdalah* candle, bake separate "Challah Napkin Rings" for each guest, and on and on. All this, including the Sabbath candles, surely adds "to the grandeur of your table."[84] But it also means a good amount of time and work for those who Fishbein knows would rather be doing something else: "We want you to spend more time being a gracious host than a chef that sweats it."[85] Yet if the Sabbath table must host a royal guest every seventh day, then Jews *do* sweat it, and so the anxious fear arises that they can never do enough, that the beautiful dishes may not be as visually appealing or as appetizing as Fishbein's own elegant creations. What if the sunken apple and honey cake droops rather than shines, or seems to lack sophisticated taste? And perhaps even more damning, what if the beautiful images (and by extension, the Sabbath table) lack substance and character, presenting only "the attainable 'look' for the unattainable class ascension"?[86] Hence, one can read this disparaging review on amazon.com: "Am I the only critical owner of this book? The pictures and layout are indeed stunning, but I found when I tried to produce the recipes many were overly sweet (chocolate pecan pie) or rich, and contained many very fattening additive rich ingredients" (posted February 14, 2004 with title "Some criticism allowed?").[87] The concern about authentic cuisine also comes to the fore in this sassy review: "I purchased this book because everyone in the community was gaga over it. What I found when I actually looked at it was that all it is is a bunch of pretty pictures and that's the big wow" (posted January 4, 2007 with title "Pretty Pictures, No Substance").[88] Despite Fishbein's promise that her recipes demand little effort, she *does* require significant preparation to entertain guests and to display beautiful arrangements. This is an anxious effort, I am suggesting here, because Fishbein commands attention to the *staging* of aesthetic beauty; food must look good to be good. But this anxiety folds into an underlying concern that *Kosher by Design* is just "a bunch of pretty pictures." Perhaps, as Mason and Meyers argue about Martha Stewart, Fishbein really does privilege appearance over substance. Could it be that Fishbein's cuisine really is too sweet, both in substance and presentation?

Fishbein's "twists" on traditional Ashkenazi foods only heighten this tension between modest substance and boastful appearance. Since Sabbath foods must be prepared in advance of the holiday, Fishbein provides easily arranged dishes for her Sabbath menu. Yet she tends to focus on the special allure of these updated recipes:

> The delicious Porcini Mushroom and Caramelized Onion Soup offers a nice change from traditional chicken soup. A colorful Asian Steak Salad is hearty enough to be considered an appetizer. Honey Mustard Cornish Hens—just a bit more unusual than chicken—make for a beautiful presentation. Our two colorful side dishes round out the hues of the plate.[89]

Fishbein also includes a wine list to complement her menu, a nod both to the gourmet tastes of her audience and the quick rise of the kosher wine industry.[90] The specialized language that often accompanies wine appraisals finds its way

Figure 3.10. Tri-color Gefilte Fish. Reproduced courtesy of ArtScroll/Mesorah Publications, Ltd.

into her recommendations ("floral aromas" and "ripe fruit" that pair well with particular dishes),[91] but this only heightens the concern about presentation. Even Fishbein's "tri-color" dish decidedly evades Greenberg's "peppery pungency of gefilte fish every Friday".[92] "This easy spin on traditional gefilte fish has three different colored layers for a sophisticated look."[93] Fishbein's innovative recipes raise the suspicion that they are sophisticated in appearance only. Even if "people eat with their eyes,"[94] as Fishbein says they do, they also digest with their stomachs. And so her texts and Uher's photographs must claim an authentic presence in order to dislodge the fear of artificial presentation (the community is just gaga over a bunch of pretty pictures). The images need to be more than pretty; they need to evoke that sense of tradition as authentic anchor. Even for a text that strives mightily to overcome the anxiety of authenticity, when images take center stage, the unease of the façade disturbs both text and image.

Purim in *The Jewish Home Beautiful* and *Kosher by Design*

The heavy weight of tradition is precisely what the festival of Purim undermines. Here is a holiday ripe with tricksters, irreverence, and childlike play. Still, for Betty Greenberg, Purim remains, much like the weekly Sabbath, a woman's holiday. Men are simply nonexistent, and Queen Esther becomes the "central figure of the Purim story" because this holiday "is the closest to the feminine heart."

This takes visual form in the decorative image accompanying Greenberg's narrative description. Like the Sabbath sketch, with the large S in the center, this one contains a tall P for the Purim holiday. But the letter surrounds a portrait of Queen Esther looking regal, beautiful, and demure. Her face tilts downward with a sense of propriety, yet is still strong and determined for one who will influence kings and bring down tyrants. Greenberg describes Esther as "Cinderella-like" and "courageous," for the manner in which she saves her people satisfies "the dramatic urge in every woman's soul." Even the gift-giving tradition during Purim is "essentially womanly," as are "a woman's delight in exhibiting her culinary abilities at the large family dinner."[95] The appeal in *The Jewish Home Beautiful* is quite clear: Jewish women recognize their true selves, and become who they really are, in the celebration of Queen Esther's triumph over the wicked Haman and her salvation of the Jewish people from certain destruction.

Although the Book of Esther is one of reversals, where the Jews marked for extinction turn the tables on those who would destroy them, the "dramatic" play in *The Jewish Home Beautiful* celebrates "the masquerading and merrymaking characteristic of this joyous day." Such frivolity comes to the fore in Silverman's stage directions, for the mother of the household approaches the dining table singing "Gut Purim, happy day of gladness; Gut Purim, Gut Purim, drives away all sadness." She has just arrived from the kitchen, wearing a full-length apron, and "her face is flushed and smudged with flour." These details signify the movement from private kitchen to public dining, and reveal how Silverman admires the work and effort performed in the kitchen. This is not Fishbein's kosher chef who seeks a minimum of cooking fuss; instead, "the woman prepares a Seudah [festive holiday meal]" with good cheer and a touch of childish pleasure. Silverman trivializes the presentation of food—"she carries a pan heaping full of Homontaschen [traditional Purim cookies] which she transfers to a dish on the table"—and foregrounds the merrymaking:

> She is full of spirit and sings merrily as she twirls a Homon-dreyer that she picks up from the table, stuffs another Homontasch into the Sheloaḥ Manot dish that stands covered on the table, sticks her finger into a dish of food and licks finger in comic manner.[96]

This Jewish cook is carefree and enjoys the inelegance of her manners. She entertains only herself, and cares not for custom or formality. She can wipe her cheeks with her apron, slip on a mask over her face, "or do anything else that is characteristic of a vivacious, happy hostess."[97] This is her holiday, and whatever she does authentically expresses domestic pleasures.

The image of the table designed for the Purim Seudah suggests, however, a more complicated relationship between these domestic frivolities and Jewish tradition. Silverman's text imagines a carefree, playful mother. We recognize signs

Figure 3.11. P for Purim. Reprinted by permission of Women's League for Conservative Judaism.

of kitchen labor—the smudge of flour on her face, the full-length apron—even if the labor itself remains behind the scenes. Silverman focuses on the fruits of her work and the enjoyment she receives from admiring her efforts on behalf of family. This is all quite lighthearted and silly. Yet the photograph of the table blends this playful exuberance with more serious holiday messages. It is well-ordered, elegant yet busy, symbolic but playful. The elaborate centerpiece illustrates this twinning of modern romp and traditional piety:

> A small doll richly dressed as Queen Esther may be perched on a tiny throne in the center of the flowers. If a glass horse is available, a figure dressed in

Figure 3.12. *The Jewish Home Beautiful* Purim Table. Reprinted by permission of Women's League for Conservative Judaism.

purple as Mordecai should be sitting on the horse which is led by another figure dressed as the villainous Haman. This group is placed to one side of the centerpiece. On the other side is propped an illustrated Megillah [Book of Esther] partly unrolled.[98]

Queen Esther, perched above the rest, looks down upon the traditional scroll lying elegantly to the side. Like the contemporary practice of Purim, in which Jews turn tragedy into comical farce, the Purim table in *The Jewish Home Beautiful* captures the lightness of amusement together with the seriousness of respectability.

Even as *The Jewish Home Beautiful* revels in the joy and silliness that make up the Purim celebration, it still contains merriment within a more sobering vision. After Silverman describes the centerpiece and various dishes on the Purim table, she directs readers to the small table next to the window (toward the very top of the photograph of the Purim table, to the right of the right-most candle). Lying on that table, she explains, "is a small open chest of coins for the poor." She couples the children's gay singing and costume makeup with a clear message: "gifts are distributed among the poor, for no joy and no spirit of gratitude is complete while others are in need."[99] Even at the most festive of times Jews should recall the need of others, and those in need temper the delightful abundance of the Purim table. Recall the image of Queen Esther: a far more staid, composed, and respectable figure than the mother who sticks her finger into the table food and licks off the excess. These couplings—between the quiet Esther and the boisterous mother, or the excess of food and the privation of those in need—restrict the joyous celebration of Jewish triumph over their cruel oppressors. Too much frivolity might be disingenuous, and would show a lack of proper respect for others less fortunate. Joy tempered by concern: this is, according to Silverman, the authentic Jewish celebration of what "is essentially womanly" and what "is the closest to the feminine heart."[100] The images and stage directions in *The Jewish Home Beautiful* radiate this sense of the feminine.

Just as *The Jewish Home Beautiful* moderates the image of the flighty housewife with the composed and devoted Esther, so too *Kosher by Design* seeks to curb the frivolous excesses of Purim without undermining its playful character. Like Greenberg and Silverman, Fishbein enjoys the colorful bounty and mischievous joy of the holiday. But for her this is all show. Underneath the frivolity lies the seriousness and ethical concern of her traditional Judaism:

> Purim is the one festival that encourages behavior that is normally restrained in Jewish life: synagogues become boisterous; adults freely imbibe wine and spirits; zany costumes, masks and giddy celebration are the order of the day. Why does traditional, stately Judaism tolerate these hi-jinks? It's all a front. In rabbinic lore, Purim has the gravity and holiness of Yom Kippur, but these are masked by revelry.[101]

The sense of order, tradition, and continuity that Fishbein infused into her Sabbath table also appears here in her moderation of Purim excess. The holiday masks are just that: a front for more serious, holy concerns. Certainly "traditional, stately Judaism" would require nothing less. Fishbein even reads the story of Esther as a series of schemes dramatizing a more complicated and profound meaning. The surface tale of "a paranoid king, a scheming villain, a pious Jewish queen and her wise uncle" resembles a poker-face narrative of schemes and counter-schemes. Much like her reading of Sabbath ritual, Fishbein sees the work of God underneath the whimsical and the mundane:

> In writing the *Megillah,* Queen Esther and her uncle Mordechai wove in allusions to the spiritual forces at work under what appear to be mundane politics and pure luck. . . . Throughout the *Megillah,* they hint that the Hand of God moved the entire process through a series of covert miracles.[102]

The Purim holiday follows the twofold register of the apparent silliness of games and the serious gravity of traditional Judaism. Beneath the perceptible chaos lies order, authenticity, and tradition. Fishbein invents recipes, and Uher develops photographs to present Purim as ordered spectacle.

The menu items for Purim replicate this pageantry by hiding the hearty fillings within a lighter casing. Substance triumphs and lies within appearance: "We masquerade to hide reality. We conceal luscious fillings beneath the dough in hamantaschen." All of her foods display this double register:

> We selected a menu that picks up on the themes and nuances of the holiday. The meal starts with Won ton Wrapped Chicken. The hidden chicken filling represents the hidden layers of the Purim miracles. Another take on this dish stems from the fact that Haman superstitiously drew "lots" to determine the "auspicious" date for the Jews to be annihilated. Our small, envelope-shaped appetizers represent those lots.[103]

Even the challah and roast turkey point to deeper meanings of these miraculous events. Fishbein douses her challah with poppy, sesame, and sunflower seeds to commemorate the Talmudic story that Esther only ate seeds while in the King's palace to avoid non-kosher foods. The turkey represents King Achashverosh's empire stretching from India to Ethiopia (a pun on the Hebrew word for turkey, which sounds like the word for India). And because "it is a *mitzvah* to drink on Purim, the sweet potatoes are glazed with Jack Daniels." Nothing is left to chance, misunderstanding, or pure revelry. Even the desserts reflect more serious themes (the cookies should remind us of the rope used to hang Haman and his ten sons). Fishbein claims that "the food, the décor and the mirthful ambience create an unmistakable aura of merriment."[104] But she demands more from her guests: if all they remember is the levity, then they fail to recognize the Hand of God as faithful guide. Purim foods must signify a more traditional order of God's protective shelter. Just as unmistakable is the aura of the holy that undergirds the mirthful appearance. To those who think Fishbein's *Kosher by Design* is "overly sweet" or simply "a bunch of pretty pictures," she responds by grounding sweetness in the Hand of God.

The vibrant photographs stage this more "traditional, stately Judaism," recognizing God's acts beneath apparent chaos. The images are radiant, playful, and celebratory, but order and tradition moderate the excess. They project Fishbein's directions of a Purim table in which "whimsical accents balance the importance of the occasion with a bit of humor." The rich and lively table that "screams with color" displays "accents" of a more disciplined Judaism.[105] Like the story of Esther itself, nothing is left to chance or positioned out of place. Her table radiates an ordered chaos in which the holiday's symbolic meanings emerge as significant and perceptible themes. The colors are attractively bright, festive, and airy—a mood that sharply contrasts with the more stately Sabbath table, with its heavy drapes and columns. Here we see a lightness of touch—with masks to hide the eyes and "groggers" for the reading of the *Megillah*. But there is also a constructed elegance and sense of place. Each table setting maintains its own color scheme, but they all cleverly match the décor. Fishbein also decorates each corner of the room with "crepe paper flowers" (a yellow one appears in the photograph, at the very top of the image). That sense of "stately" order comes through in the placement of the three forks for each setting, with two set down on their top prongs

Figure 3.13. *Kosher by Design* Purim Table. Reproduced courtesy of ArtScroll/Mesorah Publications, Ltd.

while one is turned upward. Precision and conscious orientation dominate this table—an order sanctioning the holiday merriment.

This balance between playful appearance and weighty substance is most pronounced in the image of the side table. This table extends the bright tones of the central one, and continues the bi-fold register of serious play: "In one corner, we placed a spectacular Shalach Manot basket surrounded by charity boxes, groggers, and a stunning silver *Megillah* case."[106] The polished silver casing stands alongside an ArtScroll sacred text (it may indeed be the book of Esther). This juxtaposition of the "stunning silver *Megillah* case" with the sacred text performs the visual spectacle that Fishbein seeks throughout the Purim holiday: hidden beneath the brilliant case lies the miraculous story revealing God's protective agency. God's concealed presence becomes visually manifest in the ArtScroll text lying to the side. Fishbein will not allow the Purim tables to disguise or mask God's presence, for holiness remains ever present in the mundane craziness of things. Stunning silver should not divert our eyes from the authentic presence of an ordered, stately Judaism. The images in *Kosher by Design* present, as staged performance, the directive hand of God in and through Fishbein's own light touch.

When Susie Fishbein introduces the recipe for her challah napkin rings, she conveys the dual registers of "cute" appearance and more profound substance. But she also reveals that peculiar anxiety of authenticity that I have been tracking in this and the previous two chapters:

> My sister-in-law's aunts are famous in both Brooklyn and Queens for this fabulous creation. Could there be a cuter accent on a Shabbos table than challah napkin rings? They serve a dual purpose by holding the napkins and providing each dinner guests [sic] with their own challah roll.[107]

Cookbooks are often sources of family traditions, and *Kosher by Design* is no exception. Recipes travel, but this one has a particular dwelling: Brooklyn and Queens. These two boroughs signify Jewish home, perhaps *the* Jewish home for American Ashkenazi Jews. This is Jewish New York, as Toni Eisendorf recognized when she saw the poster commercials for Levy's Rye Bread (discussed in the introduction to this book), and it holds a nostalgic and memorable place in the Jewish imaginary. It is place as social position and hierarchy, and one that Jonathan Z. Smith helpfully describes as that "sense of social location, of genealogy, kinship, authority, superordination, and subordination."[108] Fishbein understands the symbolic power of a Brooklyn and Queens, together with the nostalgia they evoke, and so grounds visual cuteness in cultural lore. The aunt is "famous" for these challah rings in the very places that register as authentic for American Ashkenazi Jewry. Even if cute, these napkin rings must still be acceptable: if they work for Jews in Brooklyn and Queens, they should work equally well for Fishbein's readers who seek that cultural heritage. In this sense, Fishbein's recipes in *Kosher by Design* serve a dual purpose: they offer clever "twists" to traditional fare, but they also authorize innovative designs by appealing to authentic traditions. As she argues throughout her book, aesthetic style elevates the mundane to the holy—it serves God by channeling the cute appearance to more serious

Figure 3.14. *Kosher by Design* Purim Side Table. Reproduced courtesy of ArtScroll/Mesorah Publications, Ltd.

concerns. But in that sense of heightening, we witness the anxiety of authenticity: beauty, practicality, and cute accents cannot stand alone as authentic innovations, but all must be grounded in claims to origin, family continuity, and tradition.

This form of religious anxiety appeared in *The Jewish Home Beautiful,* but in a more acute form. Greenberg and Silverman did not turn to God's hand to underwrite their creative endeavors; the notion of continuity alone would have to suffice. Greenberg's question stands as a critical commentary for her entire work: "Will we be wise enough to recognize the importance of these traditions and to hand them down intact to future generations?" That question Fishbein did not ask, for there is no disputing the value of Jewish tradition for her and for many in her Orthodox community. But when Greenberg attempts to answer her query, she relies only on a vague utilitarian principle: "It is not as difficult as some may imagine."[109] This appeal to an effortless performance runs through *The Jewish Home Beautiful* and *Kosher by Design.* Both texts promise culinary labor, in Fishbein's phrase, "without the fuss." But they both fail to deliver: Greenberg and Silverman still draw out the mother from the kitchen to the dining area, with specks of flour on cheek and full-length apron in tow, and Fishbein requires "whimsical accents" that take careful planning, precision, and preparation. You really can't have your cake and eat it too.

At least not in written text. The images in *The Jewish Home Beautiful* and *Kosher by Design* take center stage because they present elegance and precision with ease. The promise that you can have it all is a *visual* production, not a textual one. The prose in both cookbooks elicits the anxiety of (in)authenticity, but the images arrive to project a stately Judaism of continuity, tradition, and tranquility. Even if modern cooks need not work quite so hard in the kitchen, for these texts guide every step of the way, the photographs stage an authentic aura to everyday Jewish cooking. Perhaps no image in Fishbein's *Kosher by Design* dramatizes this authenticity more than the one depicting the Passover seder. The term itself is almost made-to-order for Fishbein's religious sensibilities:

> The Hebrew word *seder* means "order." Even through all of the frenzy of preparation, once the holiday begins there's a calmness at the seder itself. The sense of order derives from a specific set of information slated for discussion, as clearly spelled out in the Haggadah.[110]

Like the Hand of God that underwrites the merriment of Purim, the Haggadah text, "clearly spelled out," calms the frenzy of preparation. And this sense of order and authority is precisely what John Uher's photograph reveals in this text. He grounds the frenzy of preparation in the detailed font of Hebrew characters, in the fine leather of *The Family Haggadah,* in the polished kiddush cup filled with wine, and in the intricate and perfectly placed containers of the Passover

Figure 3.15. *Kosher by Design* Passover Table. Reproduced courtesy of ArtScroll/Mesorah Publications, Ltd.

symbolic foods. Elegance and style promote this staged authenticity rather than diminish it. As Greenberg and Silverman would have it, the Jewish home can be beautiful, and authentically so. I have argued throughout this book that images do things, and we see them perform authentic culture in *The Jewish Home*

Beautiful and *Kosher by Design*. That performance is laced with anxiety over the reality that beauty and cuteness require more stable affirmations of continuity and tradition. We see that anxiety muted in the photographs that dominate both cookbooks. The images seek to command authority, and to project it onto Jewish culinary practices. This is visual authenticity as the staging of taste, refinement, and traditional order; and this is what images do in *The Jewish Home Beautiful* and *Kosher by Design*.

Section II.
The Embodied Language
of Visual Authenticity

4   The Language of Jewish Bodies in Michael Wyschogrod's *The Body of Faith*

> Were God to have entered this world in the fullness of his being, he would have destroyed it because the thinning out or the darkening we have spoken of would disappear and with it the possibility of human existence. He therefore entered that world through a people whom he chose as his habitation. There thus came about a visible presence of God in the universe, first in the person of Abraham and later his descendants, as the people of Israel.
>
> —Michael Wyschogrod, *The Body of Faith*

IN THE PREFACE to the second edition of his *The Body of Faith,* Michael Wyschogrod notes the change in subtitles from the first to this more recent edition. Where he had once appended *Judaism as Corporeal Election* to the title (first edition, 1983), the reissued second edition now defined *The Body of Faith* as *God in the People Israel* (1996).[1] Much of what interests me in Wyschogrod's embodied language of authenticity can be gleaned from this acute change in subtitles. Where the first edition focused on Judaism and chosenness (*Judaism as Corporeal Election*), the second edition emphasized God's presence in a particular nation (*God in the People Israel*). This modification delicately alters how one understands Wyschogrod's book. With Judaism as corporeal election, the word *body* in *The Body of Faith* defers to a theological statement about belief. *Body* reads more as metaphor, such that corporeal election becomes the "body" of faith. The point here seems to be that chosenness is Judaism's central theological principle. But with the phrasing in the second edition—*God in the People Israel*—the word *body* refers less to a theological claim and is far more a descriptive statement about the physical indwelling of God's presence. And that presence resides in the people Israel—really, truly, in *that* body. Judaism is neither some kind of chosen religion, nor a theological construct. Indeed, God displaces Judaism altogether, reflected in the subtitle, and chooses to dwell "in" a particular national group. The body of faith is a real, material, and visual body in which human beings recognize God's presence. This is a claim about visual authenticity and chosenness in a corporeal body. Wyschogrod tethers ocular metaphors to physical bodies, and thereby directs visual discourse into carnal Israel. Faith has a body, so Wyschogrod argues, and we can see it in the Jewish people. In *The Body of Faith: God in the People Israel,* Michael Wyschogrod envisions God's presence in an embodied people as an authentic and corporeal display of divine chosenness. This is the embodied language of visual authenticity.

As a strong voice within modern Orthodoxy in America and a student of the great modern Orthodox teacher, Rabbi Joseph Soloveitchik, Wyschogrod (b. 1928) certainly recognizes the theological implications of visual embodiment, especially as they imply a controversial stance toward Christian theology. He admits to "the incarnational direction of my thinking,"[2] and as an energetic participant in Jewish–Christian dialogue,[3] he acknowledges his debt to such Christian thinkers as Karl Barth (and has even been read as "a Jewish Barthian").[4] Yet even as Wyschogrod distinguishes his corporate incarnational theology from a presumed Christian focus on the singular body of Jesus, he too struggles with the meaning of God's presence in a physical body. Is God present continually or only in isolated, rare moments? Does such a God emerge in full view or mysteriously? Where do we see that chosen display of embodied divinity in death? Or, as I will discuss in the conclusion to this chapter, how do we see God in converted bodies? Wyschogrod confronts these and other theological dilemmas, and much of the power of his work derives from his fearlessness. He unashamedly discusses God's love for the Jewish people, even calling it a "falling in love," asserting that God loves some children more than others.[5] Wyschogrod tells his readers what God desires, how God feels, and why Jews cannot escape their chosen heritage. Foundational claims abound in *The Body of Faith,* in part because the biblical text is a divine one for Wyschogrod: it "is first and foremost the word of God," rendering in human language God's desires, demands, and punishments, together with human responses to God's word.[6] Wyschogrod's boldness yields a refreshing confidence, one that defines the shape and scope of Jewish theology. He sharply criticizes the insular security of his own Orthodox community, even as he resolutely believes that it offers the most authentic Jewish practice and serves as the "core" of Jewish identity.[7] In short, Wyschogrod boldly defends the claim that God falls in love with and chooses to dwell within the people Israel. This is an unapologetic modern reclamation of a chosen people in a visual and material body and is very much a response to the more spiritualized, esoteric, and disembodied rhetoric that came before it.

Such a visible presence of God in the people Israel, as the epigraph to this chapter asserts, draws together notions of authenticity, vision, chosenness, and embodiment in ways unique to Wyschogrod's theological text. I explore in this chapter how Wyschogrod employs visual discourse to see an embodied Israel as God's chosen people. Israel remains the proper, authentic body within which God dwells, and this indwelling is a visual event. Wyschogrod's theology attempts to capture this visual certainty by exposing a distinctively Jewish visuality of God's indwelling in the people Israel. To be sure, these claims to authentic certainty have received little support among Jewish theologians of the late twentieth century. Even David Novak, perhaps the contemporary Jewish thinker who shares most with Wyschogrod, still resists his emphasis on God's indwelling in the Jewish people.[8] But Wyschogrod's peculiar argument for Jewish election deserves our attention because he so forcefully interweaves claims to authenticity with a visual discourse both embodied and carnal. Jews can see their election in the embodied people of Israel as a form of visual knowledge that binds sight to authenticity. *The Body of Faith* exposes how the visual language of embodiment works to authenticate divine election.

I do not share Wyschogrod's claims, nor do I wish to assert my own views on chosenness. But Wyschogrod's visual discourse is a critical, modern voice in imagining Jewish authenticity in America. Rather than dismiss or defend, I seek to expose *how* language works in *The Body of Faith* to present carnal Israel as the authentic embodiment of God's presence. In other words, I am interested here in the embodied rhetoric of authenticity.

We can find three distinct but interrelated features in Wyschogrod's rhetorical use of vision to reaffirm God's falling in love with the people Israel. To establish this divine link to a national group, Wyschogrod discusses the nature of human finitude by employing ocular metaphors that, so he claims, function less as symbolic speech and more as an embodied dialectic between light and darkness. Humans are the kind of beings who oscillate between clear enlightened visions and darker, more obscure musings. Judaism adequately renders this condition as worthy of divine love, for God creates a person both carnal and spiritual. Wyschogrod goes on to describe Judaism as the most authentic visual expression of the embodied and enlightened human condition. This sense of Judaism's authenticity—that it adequately portrays the human existential situation—confirms Jewish chosenness. Wyschogrod's fleshly Judaism reveals God's choice as appropriate and good: Israel turns out to be precisely the kind of people with whom God *should* fall in love. But this love story—and here I turn to the last feature of God's indwelling in a people—must end with the death of particular bodies, for this love persists as both a human and divine narrative. If God establishes a visual presence in the people Israel, what happens to this God when one of Israel dies, and the corpse lies inert before a gazing spectator? This is the limit case for Wyschogrod's sensual and visual account of Jewish election, and one that ties him to Christian incarnational theology. If persons can still recognize God's presence in a dead, chosen body, then God too feels the pain and terror of a dark mortality. But even more, God's presence as visual and material indwelling in the people Israel overcomes death and the darkness that lurks therein. The embodied triumphalism of God's visual presence in the chosen people is permanent heritage and authentic indwelling in which death loses its mortal sting. But as I discuss in the conclusion to this chapter, this triumphalism raises vexed questions for Wyschogrod's account of conversion to the Jewish people. How do we see God's indwelling in non-Jewish bodies, and how do those bodies suddenly appear as Jewish ones? Visual knowledge of God's presence testifies to the hope for meaning beyond violence and death, but it also delimits conversion as a visual problem.

Situating Vision in the Self

Structurally, Wyschogrod's *The Body of Faith* mimics Abraham Joshua Heschel's well-known rhetorical strategy: reveal the nature of human finitude and existence, and then show how Judaism adequately responds to the human situation. Like Heschel, Wyschogrod talks about God's pathos and suffering, divine sympathy and jealousy, for he seeks a God who yearns for human companionship. Wyschogrod's God is not a distant observer, but an empathetic personality—sometimes mature, but other times vicious—who falls in love with the people Israel. This Jewish God is known as Hashem, as the God of Abraham, Isaac, and Jacob, who abandons the more abstract concept God to take on distinctly human characteristics. Hashem is "the one who is related to the people of Israel"; to Hashem, Israel speaks freely and openly, for their God remains familiar, close at hand, and trustworthy.[9] This intimacy between a people and their God sustains both a spiritual and material presence. Hashem offers neither metaphysical grounds nor ethical foundations, but reveals a physical, visual presence among Israel. This is but one meaning of Wyschogrod's title: God as Hashem *is* the body of Israel's faith. This God acts, feels, and reflects in ways that human beings recognize as their own. Hashem's jealousy abides as a human emotion; his loneliness—and Wyschogrod always genders Hashem as male—provokes human empathy. God hurts like we do; he scolds his children like human parents do theirs. Wyschogrod still upholds God's invincibility and supremacy: though vulnerable, this God commands, creates, reveals, and controls darker forces. Even so, Hashem reveals himself in material bodies, and like those bodies he travels within the spiritual moods and physical boundaries, both hopeful and tragic, of the people Israel.

Wyschogrod's account of Hashem as the body of Israel's faith underscores how God's personality authenticates human existence. Here is a god who condones rather than judges human desires and fears. If God loves some more than others, this only confirms how a human father "will find himself more compatible with some of his children than others and, to speak very plainly, that he love some more than others."[10] Certainly fathers love all their children, as does God. But Hashem's love neither confronts nor challenges human love as partial. Israel's God accepts fragmentary and particular love as fundamentally human and good.

After all, this God created beings in this way, in his image, and so their sensibilities in part reflect his as well. Clearly Wyschogrod's Hashem does not force submission to categorical ethical demands. If ethics channel an is to an ought, such that persons aspire to what they ought to be and do, then Wyschogrod's Hashem vindicates a more limited, flawed, and scarred human existence. Authenticity here means not becoming who you ought to be but rather accepting who you are. This God acknowledges human beings with their faults, and comforts them in the hope for a brighter future. Though Hashem may expect more, he still receives less. Wyschogrod's God acts as a compassionate father who accepts his children as they are, even if he wishes they could be much more.

So Wyschogrod begins his text with an account of human finitude in order to situate Judaism as a fitting response to it. And from the beginning Wyschogrod establishes the visual as a critical feature of human activity and identity:

> Man is a being who prefers light over darkness. The day is the normal time for human activity, the night for sleeping, for the suspension of consciousness. . . . But human being is being in the light because vision, the primary human sense, functions only in the presence of light.[11]

This dichotomy between light and darkness extends throughout Wyschogrod's text and becomes its central motif. Though persons gravitate toward the light, they cannot escape darker corners. Perception and philosophical scrutiny work in the light, but human beings must sleep too. This ever present fluctuation between illumination and concealment defines the human condition. Yet persons yearn for brighter enlightenment, argues Wyschogrod, and this because vision is the preeminent human sense. Light enables persons to engage a world actively rather than to receive it passively. Vision opens up a horizon of possibility in ways that other senses conceal out of sight:

> To some degree, the world reveals itself in smell and touch, hearing and tasting. But a dark world in which odors are smelled, surfaces touched, sounds heard, and flavors tasted but nothing is seen, remains a world that crowds man, that does not open itself but impinges upon him and turns man into a recipient of what the world wishes to deliver to him. Only the seen world, the illuminated world stretches off into the horizon.[12]

A person who is visually impaired cannot lead a flourishing human life, so Wyschogrod implies here. Such a visual deficit impedes human productivity, for an unseen world "crowds" and "impinges" human expression. Note how Wyschogrod appropriates the long-standing reverence for sight as the master sense,[13] and does so by turning against the efficacy of other modes of engagement. Touch, smell, and taste are mere passive responses to a world seeking more active feedback. Through these less vigorous senses, persons become ordinary recipients of experience and not purveyors of and actors in a world. To be human is to stretch beyond a "dark world" and to engage the illuminated space of a distant horizon.

This visual perspective drives human beings toward an enlightened future. A prospective gaze, as a fundamental human directionality, positions Judaism as a religion of the future. For Jewish thought to respond adequately to the human condition, it must seek out an intended future without always looking back. This yields important consequences for Wyschogrod's critique of Christianity and some forms of Orthodox Judaism. Religions that look backward to a glorious past or to a fulfilled prophecy reverse the natural human gaze toward the future. These perspectives fail to account for the inevitable darkness, insecurity, and ignorance of a future not yet born into the light. As Wyschogrod's anthropology would have it, human beings oscillate between reflective light and obscure darkness, and so live in the present with the inheritance of a past and a yearning for a brighter future. Vision remains so crucial to Wyschogrod's account of human being-in-the-world because the light of day "releases man from its [the world's] tight embrace and reveals to him vistas in all directions, toward which he can move and which he perceives long before he sets out toward them." Sight propels human beings forward, opening up a world of possibility and freedom. In the biblical account, Israel promises to obey the commandments before actually hearing them (Exodus 24:7), but for Wyschogrod human beings see before doing. Physical sight liberates persons to expand toward objects of desire. Indeed, Wyschogrod tightly binds vision with desire in ways that activate directional and purposeful activity. Light then becomes "the great liberator that bestows power because it transfers the inititative [*sic*] to man."[14] Human beings lean toward a future brightness illumined by the master sense of sight. With this visual perspective, the world no longer "crowds" but instead draws closer to human control. Vision allows persons to master the world.

Animals too have eyes for seeing, and compared to inanimate things, they also illumine a world before them. But within these other creatures resides a "darkness of consciousness"[15] that forever remains obscure to human perception. Persons ascend toward the light, and this determined movement to the beyond contrasts with the instinctual pursuits marking other animals. Wyschogrod associates critical thinking, consciousness, philosophy, and knowledge with the light; embodiment, emotions, and partial knowledge belong to darkness. Persons instinctively gravitate toward philosophical knowledge and the brilliant illumination it promises, but they are still embodied beings who come up against dark limits. A reason true to the human condition would be a dark one that acknowledges obscurity, ambivalence, and finitude as inescapable features of human existence. Beings exist somewhere between the light as high and beyond, and a darkness as low and behind. This positionality between light and darkness defines finite, physical reality.

When Wyschogrod claims that persons meet God in "the realm of light," he recognizes this as metaphorical speech about the sacred. But he also believes such visual appeals are more, or perhaps less, than metaphorical leaps:

> Viewed mundanely, the language of light when applied to the sacred is metaphorical language, applying an aspect of the material world to the divine domain. But after a while, we find ourselves less certain about our ability to distinguish the literal from the metaphorical. Does "seeing" literally refer to what we perceive with our eyes and only metaphorically to understanding or is it the other way around?[16]

How would "the other way around" appear in Wyschogrod's visual anthropology? He asks us to consider a mode of understanding as literal and physical seeing. Appealing to "the other way around," Wyschogrod suggests neither an analogical nor a metaphorical account of knowledge, but rather a physical mode of understanding. Can we see knowledge in this way? Is epistemology a visual practice? Wyschogrod raises but does not fully come to terms with these questions (in this too he shares much with Heschel). But it does seem clear that Wyschogrod wants his readers to think and see materially, and to consider light and darkness as physical attributes that make human knowledge possible. It is as if Wyschogrod fears his readers will too easily escape darkness through metaphorical flights to the light. Reason may observe and enlighten a future, but it is still an embodied reason that bumps up against darker forces.

The human experiential wavering between light and darkness shapes Wyschogrod's account of knowledge. To see an object requires both a radiance to illumine and an opaqueness to delimit it among other things. Something must reflect back the light of vision for the object to come into view. Recall Jean-Luc Marion's distinction between an idol and icon, discussed in the second chapter on Heschel, and the way in which the idol arises by a gaze that captures the object and focuses a view upon it. This gaze does not pierce through the object as icon, but rather delimits it as idol.[17] Something like this phenomenological account of vision is at work in Wyschogrod's text:

> Seeing requires the opaque because without it there is nothing to reflect back the light, thus making something visible since light travels until it reaches that which it cannot penetrate and only then does it return to the observer, carrying the image of that which refused it passage.[18]

I very much doubt the scientific accuracy of Wyschogrod's claims, but I want to focus on the rhetorical work such claims do to structure his account of reason. One thing this account certainly does is undermine Wyschogrod's sharp dichotomy between vision and all the other senses. Here we see how vision and touch work together, a visual, haptic field that Rachel Neis has illustrated with regard to rabbinic thought.[19] Wyschogrod believes that a ray of light projects toward an object in the visual act of seeing. That object reflects the light back to the observer, and the light now carries with it an image of the material thing. In Marion's language, only an icon is transparent; here we see an idol in all its opacity. But Wyschogrod seeks to understand "the basic structure of rationality," and that structure reveals how talk of rational light and embodied darkness is not merely metaphorical language. Knowledge of things is a physical seeing requiring both obscure things and brilliant rays of light. Understanding in this empirical, "other way around" sense reveals a seeing that requires both light and darkness. As Wyschogrod would have it, "without meeting such opacity, reason would lose its contact with being and its light would become invisible."[20] Marion sought out that invisibility by piercing through the object; Wyschogrod stands firmly in the darker soil of being and the visible, illumined objects stretched out before the human gaze.

Wyschogrod accepts Marion's idols as authentic objects of perception because God created Adam and Eve as physical, embodied beings. Turning to the biblical terms in Genesis for image and likeness (*tselem* and *demut*), Wyschogrod offers this provocative reading:

> These are basically visual terms, and were it not for the long-standing resistance to anthropomorphism, we would interpret them in physical terms to refer to the kind of resemblance children have to their parents. It may therefore be the case that the Bible would find it difficult to focus on reason as the defining essence of man because reason is a mental capacity that does not take into account the physical uniqueness of man.[21]

There are more than a few significant claims lurking in this reading of the Genesis creation story, and not least among them is Wyschogrod's personification of the Bible—a rhetorical gesture that positions his own voice as a more authentic revelation of biblical intentions. For if the "Bible would find it difficult to focus on reason," should not we as intelligent readers do so as well? This is less a motivated reading than a discovery of revealed voice. Biblical interpretation recovers the voice of God's intentions: "The meaning of the Torah is the intention of the divine lawgiver, who is its author. It therefore follows that the only fully satisfactory way of determining what the law is in any specific case is to ask God."[22] Of course this we can no longer do, so instead persons "must ask Hashem to guide them to the discovery of his will." In this "prayerful dialogue," the interpreter "transmits the will of Hashem to those who inquire."[23] In his own attempt at biblical transmission, Wyschogrod shows how the text could not have envisioned a meaning for "image" beyond a biological analogy. To be created in the image of God means to be physically akin to an embodied God, as a child appears similar to his/her biological parents. With visual knowledge, persons come to know and recognize God in physical bodies. But Wyschogrod distinguishes between God's image and God's dwelling in a people. All persons reflect the image of God, but only Israel reveals God's presence. This too is part of what Wyschogrod means by the subtitle to his work: God in the People Israel. Though all persons reflect the divine image, God chooses to dwell only among the body Israel after God's initial creation. Persons physically see God in those bodies—and because of this, as we shall see, conversion looms as a theological problem for Wyschogrod. Dwelling is no metaphor: it is a visual recognition of God's chosen people, where physical presence confers knowledge. To know God is to see him in the people Israel.

Yet even for Wyschogrod, to be in the image of God conveys more than physical resemblance. He emphasizes Adam's "creatureliness" and the psychological dimensions of the parent–child relationship.[24] Much of his book seeks to dissolve a "resistance to anthropomorphism," and often Wyschogrod leans heavily on the body in order to realign a perceived imbalance toward abstract reason. Here again he reasserts another long-standing dichotomy: the distinction between Greek philosophy and Jewish biblical religion. The Greeks could easily define "man without reference to his body," but not so the Bible. Wyschogrod's appeal to "the physical uniqueness of man" mitigates against this perceived Greek bias. Yet a dark "creatureliness," one without reflective capacities, would fail as an authentic human life, for it could not stretch forward toward an enlightened future. Embodiment without intelligence would be a tragic darkness resembling nonhuman animals. But Greek notions of reason, so argues Wyschogrod, are too abstract for embodied persons, for they seek only "philosophical theory" and "the rationality of the universe." Wyschogrod desires a more balanced account of enlightened reason and embodied image, and he discovers it in a biblical reason as radiating intelligence: a form of "working endowment rather than a theory" that remains "a quality of brightness."[25] This biblical intelligence, in contrast to Greek reason, adequately responds "to the inherent ambiguity of the human situation," and "is so deeply rooted in human existence and its limitations."[26] In this more expansive picture of the human image, Wyschogrod portrays authentic selves as those carnal beings who perceive human frontiers through a radiant vision.

The radiant light of biblical intelligence remains infinite enough to perceive and move toward future possibilities, but is finite still as an embodied reasoning that struggles with indecision and partial knowledge. The limits to this directive capacity of human intellect lie not only within the self, but also outside it "before the power of God." All human reasoning confronts an opaqueness that reflects its projected light. In this way, according to Wyschogrod, human beings perceive physical objects. But this is also the mode by which human intelligence becomes aware of God's presence. Like those inanimate objects that project back the light directed to it, so too God functions as the opaque limit to an enlightened human intelligence: "In its direct encounter with the holy, intelligence is calmed, brought up against its limits, and at least temporarily silenced. It is not destroyed, as man is not destroyed. But it is endangered, as man is endangered."[27] The picture conjured here is one of intelligence striving to move beyond its legitimate borders, only to confront the holy who polices and delimits them. But only temporarily: weakened but not destroyed, endangered but not subdued, intelligence will soon rise again to challenge those imposed limits. This phenomenological account captures the dialectic movement of light (intelligence racing forward) and darkness (intelligence calmed and in retreat), one that mirrors Joseph Soloveitchik's existential portrayal of the lonely man of faith who likewise advances and retreats before God.[28] Wyschogrod, like his teacher Soloveitchik, directs religious experience away from both self-annihilation and complete unification with God. When finite intelligence confronts God's holiness, in this *mysterium tremendum* of fear and wonder, humans address that unintelligible but very real limit to their own pursuits. As intelligible light bumps up against objects that reflect back its rays, so too the human gaze directly confronts the divine body as visual limit. This is what Wyschogrod labels a dark reason: "a reason that remains entangled in the dark soil in which the roots of reason must remain implanted if it is not to drift off into the atmosphere." The basic dyad of light and darkness, one that demarcates the nature of perceptual knowledge and the human condition, also works in Wyschogrod's text to locate God's relationship to humanity. An authentic encounter with God's holiness adequately restricts human aspirations to be less in spirit than what they are in body.

Wyschogrod maintains that some religious traditions encourage a spiritual drifting to higher pursuits in ways that remain distinctly ill suited to the human condition, and Christianity is his primary target for such ethereal flights. Even a cursory reading of *The Body of Faith* reveals how the Christian tradition functions as Wyschogrod's conversational other. At times he deflects typical criticisms against Judaism onto Jesus or Christianity, but more often he opposes Christian spirituality to Jewish material humanism. Christianity appears closely aligned to Greek philosophy in its fondness for clarity, philosophical truth, and total exposure. Judaism accords with the human condition, but Christianity, with its unencumbered brilliance, rejects that finite, embodied condition:

> Jesus' relative lack of interest in the political order, his absolutist and uncompromising ethical demands, the absence of law (which embeds the moral vision into the soil of the created order) in the New Testament are among the symptoms of Christianity's liberation from the darker side of reality. Christianity therefore shuns the darkness, from which it attempts to escape into the light of redemption and sinlessness.[29]

Note, to begin, how Wyschogrod typically personifies Christian practice ("Christianity therefore shuns"), effectively silencing the multiple and complex voices within that tradition. Readers do not know who shuns, but only that Christianity does so. And one can sense too how Wyschogrod closely aligns "Christianity" with more liberal forms of Judaism that stress ethics over law. This essentialist rhetoric positions Christianity (or a more liberal Judaism) as the distorted foil to Wyschogrod's Judaism: where Judaism is rooted in physical beings, Christianity seeks to escape them; if Judaism is an embodied politics, Christianity has little interest in mundane proceedings; when Judaism creates law to inhibit darker forces, Christianity liberates persons from darkness to a grander light. "Judaism will not be unfaithful to the darkness of human existence,"[30] but Christianity misrepresents the human condition before God. Judaism delivers an authentic humanism.

Light and darkness are more than visual metaphors; they are for Wyschogrod constitutive features of human embodiment. Judaism can justifiably claim allegiance from finite beings because it recognizes both intelligent striving and embodied vulnerability: "Human existence is possible only in the shade of the divine light as that light comes up against its limit and the solidity of matter. . . . We see it in terms of a darkness that is required by human existence which Judaism preserves in its very fabric."[31] While Christianity arises out of Greek reason, Judaism grounds itself in a finite existence in which knowledge persists as embodied vision—a physical seeing that distinguishes human beings from other animals. Wyschogrod ties vision to personal identity in order to situate intelligence within embodied beings. Though persons still prefer light over darkness, as Wyschogrod claims they do in the opening sentence of his book, that preference resides within the limits of a darkened order. The nighttime remains and even makes possible the presence of daylight. Knowledge as a form of physical seeing and as "the other way around" to metaphor suggests a more concentrated gaze at the embodied life of a people. Seeing "requires the opaque," as Wyschogrod claims, and both the human and God's body function to limit a radiant intelligence. Only a Judaism faithful to this human condition can be a body of faith.

Judaism, Authenticity, and Chosenness

Wyschogrod maps Judaism onto his visual anthropology of light and darkness. He articulates a vision of the human condition, and then suggests how Judaism (and not its foil, Christianity) fittingly addresses human experience. God too, as Hashem, confronts human beings as they are: embodied, enlightened, and so hovering between light and darkness. Judaism and the Jews who practice it expose a visionary and carnal humanism that stretches beyond toward a vague future, but they do so forever tethered to the soil of a created and constraining world. Human beings are not gods, Wyschogrod warns throughout his text, but neither are they physical beasts. Authentic Judaism captures these expressive features of the human condition, and reveals them to be features of God's intended creation. Wyschogrod employs ocular models to expose Judaism as authentic vision, and I want to look at three moments in which he does so. In his discussion of the sacrificial ritual, Karl Marx as alienated Jew, and Jewish art, Wyschogrod articulates a mode of being Jewish-in-the-world that appears as right, fitting, and just. A Judaism that resonates with a darkened but illuminated experience teaches Jews how to see well.

The cultic life of the Temple sacrifices is above all "concrete and incarnated." In these physical, bloodied acts, "the holy appears with predictability."[32] This is both a physical and visual security: God presides before Israel ("the holy appears") and dwells with Israel in the Temple. Wyschogrod certainly understands that Jewish prayer and practice eventually supplant this sacrificial system. Still, the destruction of the Temple that brought an end to the daily ritual slaughters is a human tragedy. That sense of predictability, security, and holy presence in the ritual act would no longer be available. Unlike the commandments, in which Jews can only obey in part, "the obligatory sacrifices of the day either have or have not been brought." There exists no middle ground here: either the sacrifice has been performed or it has not. The "mixture" that Wyschogrod finds in the commandments yields to a stark either/or of ritual obedience or disobedience. Prayer works as a "contemplative" gesture,[33] Wyschogrod tells his readers, but persons see, feel, touch, and smell sacrificial acts; Hashem resides in the physical acts of sacrificial worship. Without the Temple as physical site for God's dwelling, Jews are deprived of that physical closeness offered by the sacrificial system. God's residence among Israel partially compensates for this loss of the Temple as physical abode.

That loss should neither be forgotten nor ignored, for it exposes a darkness at the heart of human experience. In sacrifice, human beings see themselves as they really are. Wyschogrod highlights this visual experience, and attends to the corporeal movements of the deathly ritual. Indeed, he vibrantly portrays the bloody scene:

> The priestly slaughterer approaches the animal with the lethally sharp knife in his hand, yet the animal does not emit a sound of terror because it does not understand the significance of the instrument. It is then swiftly cut, the blood gushes forth, the bruiting begins as the struggle with death begins, as the animal's eyes lose their living sheen. The blood is sprinkled on the altar, the animal dismembered, portions of it burned, and portions eaten by the priests who minister before God in the holiness of the Temple. This horror is brought into the house of God.[34]

Holiness resides here—in the dismembering of animal limbs, in the dullness of the physical eyes, in the flow of blood. The priest functions as God's minister, but he is a slaughterer before a dumb animal. The killing yields neither conceptual ideal nor symbolic import, but simply witnesses to a struggle with impending death. The terror lies not in the loss of meaning, but in a failure to recognize the function of a physical instrument. Wyschogrod portrays the scene as the base act that it is: "a dumb animal is to be slaughtered." When the knife approaches, the animal remains calm: it simply "does not understand the significance of the instrument." Yet that significance lies solely in its use value; it is there to slaughter by means of the priestly slaughterer. The horror, then, is ours alone. Wyschogrod's use of the passive voice ("this horror is brought") underscores the sense of observed terror. It is not the brute that emits a sound of terror; we do.

The focal point of the sacrificial service resides in the visual observance of it. God sees the killing because "the bruiting, bleeding, dying animal is brought and shown to God." But so too every person who witnesses this event stands before "the truth of human existence":

> This is what our fate is. It is not so much, as it is usually said, that we deserved the fate of the dying animal and that we have been permitted to escape this fate by transferring it to the animal. It is rather that our fate and the animal's are the same because its end awaits us since our eyes, too, will soon gaze as blindly as his and be fixated in deathly attention on what only the dead seem to see and never the living.[35]

We see the darkness that is ours alone in the Temple sacrifice; we do not escape death, nor mitigate its horror, but actually see it executed. Yet Wyschogrod channels a passive observance into an active performance as "our eyes" take the place of the animal's stare. But this gaze cannot enlighten: it "blindly" attends to an anticipated death. Wyschogrod stresses the sensual and visual features of this fate, and denies conceptual or symbolic meaning. A sacrificial act yields only a visionless death. There is no light in this kind of darkness.

Wyschogrod imagines the sacrificial scene as a kind of bodily transference effected by a visual apparition: we come to see ourselves as that dying animal, and position our gaze from within the physical eyes of the brute. In this way, the animal sacrifice becomes a vision of human experience:

> In the Temple, therefore, it is man who stands before God, not man as he would like to be or as he hopes he will be, but as he truly is now, in the realization that he is the object that is his body and that his blood will soon enough flow from his body as well. The subject thus sees himself as dying object.[36]

The animal "brought and shown to God" is really the human individual as embodied victim. Wyschogrod uses the term *man* to designate the positioned gaze, but he appeals to an "I" who confronts a personal death. The sacrificial system in Judaism shows that "I" precisely for what it is: embodied existence as a dying object. The subject cannot escape to some incorporeal essence, but must see personhood as "the object that is his body." Sacrificial Judaism, as Wyschogrod calls this event, enables persons to see as God sees. It reveals a divine vision in which human beings are "brought and shown to God" as dying objects. It is to see the "I" as truly embodied object before God. This is the authentic vision at the core of the Jewish sacrificial system.

Wyschogrod's rhetoric turns decidedly apologetic in his account of the prayer service, for he understands that much has been lost within it. Although the rabbis structure sacrificial worship within prayer, they too "share some of the prophets' ambivalence to sacrifice." This wistful tone suggests how some features within Judaism have become less authentic than others. Prayer has come to supplant the sacrificial system, but it has not done away with it altogether, and even seems inferior to it. The visual horror of sacrificial worship has dimmed, both in prayer and in other sacrificial acts. Wyschogrod notes how circumcision is "the vestigial remains of human sacrifice in Judaism. The knife that cuts into the flesh of the animal in sacrifice cuts into the flesh of man in circumcision." Despite the prophetic ambivalence toward Temple sacrifice, circumcision remains "holy to the Jewish people." This people remains decidedly gendered, such that holiness travels from the bloody knife to male bodies to expose "the sacrifice of man before God." The knife that sacrifices animals, and that turns male bodies into holy ones, also appears in Abraham's hand to slaughter his son Isaac. In the Jewish *Akedah* (the binding of Isaac narrative of Genesis 22), Jews learn "that to be loved by God requires the willingness to accept death at the hand of God." Wyschogrod reads the binding of Isaac story as a parent–child narrative in which "continuation of the Jewish people" is the most precious good. The test before Abraham, then, appears as a conflict of values: his trust in God struggles against his yearning for descendants through Isaac. Sacrificing Isaac becomes a self-sacrifice, and Abraham's test mirrors Israel's own: "Israel's acceptance of the law is such a sacrifice of the uncurbed biological appetites that are at the service of the species' life-force."[37] The law arrives, sometimes through a cut of the knife, to restrict passions such as the biological desire for children.

But note the difference of that bloody knife from the one set to slaughter the dumb brute. Sacrifice has transformed from a stark physicality to a vague "life-force" that delivers a weakened security and predictability. Within the sacrificial system, Jews recognized their condition in the objectified eyes of the dying animal, but the Genesis account shows how they must curb their love for a son, the one they love, for an Isaac, and replace him with a hope for "the continuation of the Jewish people." Though he does not intend to lessen the drama of the *Akedah*, Wyschogrod exposes a form of sacrifice far less powerful than the kind of visual physicality in Temple sacrifice. A Judaism forgetful of its sacrificial heritage will too quickly abandon terror for hope. Certainly hope remains a critical feature of Jewish yearning toward the future, but Wyschogrod seeks to recover a past darkness before too much light seeps in. For Wyschogrod, authentic Judaism shows us that "there is darkness in which there are occasional clearings but much of which the sun never penetrates."[38] In *The Body of Faith,* a Judaism mediating this kind of light in a darkened world speaks to the human experience revealed in the sacrificial system.

A fully illumined human condition, one in which the sunlight really does penetrate every finite experience, is an alienated life in Wyschogrod's Jewish theology. It may comprise the messianic future, but here and now human beings undergo partially bright and dark lives. That yearning for total exposure and enlightenment, however, overwhelmed many European Jews who dreamed of "a neutral society" that would look beyond religious affiliation to affirm individual citizenry. With a promised social emancipation in which Jews could enter once closed professional trades and occupations, European society in the nineteenth century appeared to value productive citizens and rational beings. That liberation, of course, proved all too elusive, but Wyschogrod understands the motivations that might compel what he calls "Marrano philosophers" to hide their Jewish convictions and translate them into universal claims of science. Marrano experience comprised "Jews who were not steadfast enough to resist conversion ... but who nevertheless were loyal Jews,"[39] and included those Jewish types who criticized society in the name of science or nature, but still appealed to Jewish visual knowledge of light and darkness to level that critique. Philosophers hid their Judaism and Jewish sensibilities, only to expose them as universal, "neutral" claims. Wyschogrod considers this kind of mutation a form of Jewish alienation, for it marginalizes the authentic source (Jewish knowledge) from the public perception (scientific critique).

Both Sigmund Freud and Baruch Spinoza count as Marrano philosophers in Wyschogrod's sense, but I want to focus on his depiction of Karl Marx as that alienated Jew who nonetheless draws upon Jewish sensibilities to attack modern capitalism. To Wyschogrod, Marx is not a Jewish "philosopher who struggles with basic Jewish ideas," but is instead "one who was born Jewish and then proceeds to philosophize without any apparent reference to his origins."[40] Yet Marx cannot escape his Jewish heritage, for he still levels a Jewish critique upon economic value. That one discovers no "apparent reference" to his Jewish analysis only confirms (for Wyschogrod) Marx's Marrano status as one who conceals what is essentially his all along.

According to Wyschogrod, Marx represses his Jewish identity by attacking Jews as the modern symbol of capitalist excess. Associated with finance and portable wealth, the Jew embodies the modern values of translatability, fluidity, and uprootedness that capitalism requires for ever expanding markets. Marx assails this unholy business in which "everything has a price" unrelated to productive labor. With a monetary value assigned to each object, exchange among incommensurable goods now becomes possible. Wyschogrod argues that speed and fluidity of exchange come to dominate trade with this new sense of translatability:

The money system brings into play a permanent system of translation that monitors relations continuously and, what is more important, makes it unnecessary to confront individual essences but enables the monetary system to perform the translation without an encounter between individual objects being necessary.

Financial capital undermines individual differences and essences, and produces universal translations among what use to be distinct objects. Now that "the value of everything else can be translated,"[41] notions of Jewish difference, chosenness, or authentic rootedness lose their distinctive qualities and become part of a monetary algorithm of quantitative value. From a "total absence of comparability," in which claims to authentic culture and a chosen people made sense, European Jews now symbolize for Marx the tyranny of money as the universal arbiter of value.

Wyschogrod embarks on his own translation of value, associating Marx's critique of capitalism with the method of modern science. Both Marx's critique and science tend "to minimize the ultimacy of qualities in favor of quantitative relations." Science, so Wyschogrod argues, "seeks the quantifiable regularities behind the confusing qualitative world." It searches for pure enlightenment, and conceals all that cannot fall under its purview. Marx associates the capitalist order with these scientific values: quantifiable regularity, translatability, and clear and repeatable use. Yet Marx revolts against this process, in Wyschogrod's reading of him, because he recognizes the fundamental dehumanization of assigning market value to everything. In his disgust, Marx reveals his Jewish sensibility and preference for qualitative uniqueness over and against quantitative uniformity:

> He [Marx] is appalled by a system that is able to assign a monetary value to anything, no matter how unique, noble, or precious. His experience resembles that of the homeowner who attends an auction at which the objects with which he has been living all his life are on the block. He is pained as each object is auctioned off and a number is called out for which it is sold. He learns that the objects that are an extension of him have a market value . . . which tears away his precious belongings and hurls them into a public world in which he, along with his belongings, becomes an object alienated from himself because perceived through the eyes of others.[42]

Like the homeowner, Marx stands aghast at the loss of personal value, a forfeiture of individual love for neutral exchange. But Marx does not attend the auction; he criticizes it with his weighty tools of economic theory that draw upon scientific method. He fights back, as it were, in the name of the "unique, noble, or precious." In other words, Marx plays the scientific game in order to undermine it. He utilizes techniques of science to expose the empty value of quantifiable things. Persons are not objects but subjects with unique qualities. Yet all this gets lost in market translatability where personal value converts into the worth "perceived through the eyes of others." Marx is a humanist disguised as a European enlightened scientist.[43]

But he is also a Marrano philosopher, according to Wyschogrod, whose humanism belies a Jewish consciousness. As an alienated Jew, Marx fails to recognize his humanist critique as a Jewish one. But Wyschogrod does see this, and his supple reading suggests how Marx could both yearn for the neutral values of the market economy and be repulsed by them. Marx too dreams of the "neutral society" in which he casts off his Jewish heritage for an "equal identity as [and among] rational beings."[44] He could value and be valued like all other intelligent persons. This is a false mythology, one that captures his passions but ultimately destroys Marx's unique personhood. Wyschogrod sympathizes with Marx's devotion to a neutral society, however illusory, for this had been a coveted goal of "modern Jewish consciousness." In some sense this remains an estranged Jewish consciousness, but Wyschogrod suggests how Marx's Jewish alienation runs deeper:

> We have shown that the seeds of a critique of modern science can be discovered in Marx and that his theory of money implies a critique of the consciousness of quantification. But all this is presented under the rubric of science. The moral passion, the messianic imagination so active in Marx, is repressed, thereby turning him into a paradigmatic example of Jewish alienation. He must objectify his concerned advocacy, which is moral in nature, and pass it off as a force of nature, a law that operates in society as the laws of nature do in the realm of the natural. . . . We interpret this as an expression of Jewish alienation. The prophetic role is externalized by converting it into science, perceived by the assimilated Jew as the vehicle of Jewish liberation.[45]

Marx's alienation is twofold: on the one hand, he passes off a Jewish prophetic critique as modern science, but then as an alienated Jew, he perceives this science as his liberation from Judaism. But even more, a Jewish critique rooted in the "unique, noble, or precious" becomes, in its alienated form, a science of quantifiable objects. Marx's humanism *is* a Jewish prophetic call to qualitative uniqueness, but he represses that heritage, and in doing so translates it into a quantifiable science of exchange. It is not the Jew who symbolizes the abstract form of money, as Marx would have it; instead, it is Marx himself who appears as the alienated object now at auction, displaced from its Jewish home.

Appeals to authenticity as prophetic Jewish heritage run throughout Wyschogrod's reading of Marx. He defends Marx's prophetic critique against a misguided scientific method that sheds a universal light on the darkest corners of human experience, and so alienates persons from it. For Wyschogrod, there are features of a human life that defy quantification, and so must remain opaque to rational analysis. He fears a universal translatability of essentially distinct and unique objects. But with such ubiquitous exchange arises the idea of a universal subject, one neither embodied nor chosen. Wyschogrod's embodied Judaism is a bad fit to this modern sensibility of quantity, exchange, and use value. It is more at home where the "unique, noble, or precious" reign as valued ideals. Yet as the discussion of sacrificial worship suggests, there remain more and less authentic forms of Jewish practice. A modern Judaism content with enlightened order and rational exchange is less humane because it misses essential features of the human condition. It is therefore less authentic as well, for only the Jewish prophetic voice perceives the noble as a unique encounter with embodied radiance.

Wyschogrod carries over this language of authenticity, rooted in the dichotomy between the unique and the commodity, to his analysis of Jewish art. He echoes both the distorted consensus that "Judaism has not made a great contribution to art and music," and appeals to the distinction made famous by Clement Greenberg between kitsch and the avant-garde.[46] Yet Wyschogrod's concern for "the level of taste" among contemporary Jewish communities has less to do with aesthetic preferences, and more to do with his claims to authentic Jewish culture. For Clement's kitsch (the bad taste of a debased, conservative art) and the avant-garde (the progressive art of modernist works), Wyschogrod inserts "bourgeois mentality" and the "bohemian." Judaism has succumbed to a bourgeois sensibility, and this because "the rabbinic mind is, to a large extent, a bourgeois mind." Rabbinic Judaism, so Wyschogrod contends, is structured, orderly, static, "in short, bourgeois and not bohemian." To counter this stultifying logic, he promotes a modern Judaism that resonates with Greenberg's and Silverman's *The Jewish Home Beautiful*. Like the Jewess who creatively fashioned in the likeness of God's natural acts, Wyschogrod's modern Jews should cultivate "the free play of the imagination" and "its antibourgeois clientele." To integrate this bohemian sense of creative play, Judaism must return to authentic sources:

> The great souls of Judaism, as of any religion, are not cautious members of the middle class. They do not calculate their actions from the point of view of prudence. They do not hesitate to stick out, to be different, to risk everything on their mission. A bourgeois Judaism is dead because it is out of contact with the explosive ferment of the religious spirit.[47]

Authentic Judaism in Wyschogrod's taxonomy is more prophetic than rabbinic, less rational than imaginative. Jewish art can help cultivate this volatility only if contemporary Judaism opens itself to this instability. This is sharp critique from Wyschogrod, especially for his own Orthodox community that produces more scientists than artists. He suspects that Orthodoxy appears compatible with scientific careers because it easily distinguishes light from darkness, and sees only quantifiable objects rather than qualitative disruption. While Orthodox Jews can live "parallel lives" in which their Jewish and scientific selves rarely conflict, Wyschogrod believes "this is far less possible for a poet." He desires more Jewish poets because with "bad taste goes an inauthenticity of its spiritual life." Good art reveals authentic religious culture, as Ilya Schor had argued some decades earlier about Judaism in Eastern Europe. The bohemian artist, like the prophets of old, forces us to see "the unpredictable and the noninstitutional"[48] as constitutive features of a religious life. This "explosive ferment" can neither be measured nor translated into exchange value. It resonates instead with the qualitative distinctions that generate objects of the "unique, noble, or precious."

In his account of sacrificial worship, Marx, and Jewish art, Wyschogrod traces subtle relations among vision, authenticity, and chosenness to reveal how visual discourse makes claims to authenticity, and so vindicates God's choice of the Jewish people as his embodied dwelling. For Judaism to appear as authentic—in the spectacle of sacrificial performance, in the work of bohemian art, or even in the moral passion of the alienated Marx—it must return to the prophetic imagination as that unpredictable voice of human experience. That experience, Wyschogrod argues throughout *The Body of Faith,* is one of hopeful brilliance and embodied darkness. In a universe of pure light (the world of Christianity, in Wyschogrod's theology), the qualitative dimensions of human existence would be concealed under the majestic allure of transparent enlightenment. But finite beings do not live in that world of illumination, and neither should Judaism. Authentic Judaism is faithful to beings as they are: not as the bourgeois middle class, but as avant-garde bohemians who recognize more than order, logic, and quantity. That visual awareness is a muddied one, obscured by a darkness that Wyschogrod associates with the body. And God does not abolish the night, nor denigrate the body, but determines their fitting place within a created world. In that world God takes hold of the Jewish people as the chosen body of divine dwelling:

> Were God to have entered this world in the fullness of his being, he would have destroyed it because the thinning out or the darkening we have spoken of would disappear and with it the possibility of human existence. He therefore entered that world through a people whom he chose as his habitation. There thus came about a visible presence of God in the universe, first in the person of Abraham and later his descendants, as the people of Israel.[49]

God encounters human beings as they are in a world of light and darkness. But to discover God as he is in the world we must see Hashem in the people Israel. Chosenness confers visual authenticity of God's presence in these biological descendants of Abraham. This is the visual language of embodiment.

Though he cannot fully justify God's election of Israel, Wyschogrod still suggests, more than once, that the proper response is one of gratitude and wonder.[50] Appealing to the kabbalist notion of *tsimtsum* as a mode of divine shrinking or withdrawal, Wyschogrod claims that human beings would be utterly destroyed were God to unreservedly enter the world "in the fullness of his being." God's light would vanquish the darkness, "speaking to the highest in man but having nothing to say to the lowest in him." To Wyschogrod, this kind of divine incarnational potency belongs to a Christian vision that destroys the darkened body. Yet God did choose the Jewish people "as his habitation," and Wyschogrod confidently asserts God's creative intentions: "But God did not want to destroy man and his world. His desire was to make human existence in the created order of finitude possible."[51] Human beings learn about God's desires, intentions, and decisions through Israel. This is what Wyschogrod means in claiming that Jewish theology "arises out of the *existence* of the Jewish people." God constricts his own divine intensity so that finite beings can relate to Hashem through Abraham's descendants:

> The God of Israel has chosen to hyphenate his name with the people of Israel. . . . The only viable name is the "God of Abraham, Isaac, and Jacob," tying God's identity to the people of Israel. It is as the God of this people that he becomes known by all the people of the earth.[52]

Access to God runs through the Jewish people. This is not to justify God's choice, but to gratefully acknowledge the choice God did indeed make. God sanctifies the darkness of human existence by dwelling within it.

Yet even if Wyschogrod refuses to justify God's act, he certainly does confirm the appropriateness of that choice. This, as it turns out, is the peculiar responsibility of Jewish theology as Wyschogrod understands that discipline. Jewish theology arises out of the existence of the Jewish people, and so must be true or fitting to that existence,[53] and must account for the light and the darkness of visual knowledge. In Wyschogrod's view, God selected well in choosing the Jewish people, and Jewish theology can help explain the suitability of God's preference. But Wyschogrod also claims that Christian theology cannot justify its own claims to chosenness without accepting a reduced vision, a more obscure light to shine within a darkened world. As Wyschogrod argues throughout *The Body of Faith*, "Judaism will not be unfaithful to the darkness of human existence."[54] And neither will God. Wyschogrod knows God—his intentions, desires, and concerns—in and through the Jewish people, such that all recognize God as Hashem. God's choice to dwell among the Jewish people is appropriate, Wyschogrod believes, and the descendants of Abraham, Isaac, and Jacob have articulated a theological humanism that accepts darkness in the midst of light. When Jews abandon that sensibility—when they become more rabbinic than prophetic, more bourgeois than bohemian—they surrender a Jewish theological humanism and its authentic vision. In this regard, David Novak worries that Wyschogrod has subordinated the Torah to the Jewish people, such that God's choice is both biological and unconditional.[55] Novak's concerns are real and disquieting, but we should not lose sight of how Wyschogrod defends the authenticity of God's choice: the people Israel, as revealed through Wyschogrod's theology, faithfully discloses the presence of God as one that confirms the reality of finite existence. God dwells among this people because Israel is, truly and eternally, the body of faith most authentic to the visual knowledge of light and darkness. This is Wyschogrod's core theological claim, and it embodies the language of visual authenticity.

Vision and Chosenness

Wyschogrod binds vision to chosenness such that one can see God in and through the body of Israel. Seeing God is a form of bodily recognition; God chooses to dwell among Israel, and so Israel's body reveals God's presence. Wyschogrod makes this a visual knowledge for both God and human beings. God continues to love the people Israel, as Wyschogrod tells it, "because he sees the face of his beloved Abraham in each and every one of his children."[56] This is a physical, biological awareness. God creates physical beings in his likeness, such that the body "cannot be excluded from this resemblance": "Man is created by God as a physical being and if there is a human resemblance to God then his body also resembles God."[57] The biblical term *tselem* (image) is a visual one, according to Wyschogrod, "related to the concept of shadow, a naturally occurring drawing of physical likeness."[58] This physical correspondence with Adam only intensifies in the people Israel. God recognizes Abraham in his Jewish descendants, and human beings see God in and through Israel's body. Wyschogrod continually asserts this natural or biological relationship between Israel and God. Now with the diversity of Jewish faces, one might remain understandably puzzled by what Abraham's countenance actually looks like to God. But Wyschogrod contends that this obscurity of vision remains a finite one: in some mysterious way God recognizes his beloved Abraham in Israel's bodily appearance. And by dwelling among that people, God reveals himself in and through these material bodies.

But will God's presence disappear with the inevitable disintegration of the body, or will it remain even in death? This question haunts Wyschogrod, as it would any theologian who so profoundly ties God's visual presence to embodiment. That God's presence may surrender or succumb to human mortality also raises constructive links between Wyschogrod's work and Christian incarnational theology, as I briefly explore below. Even so, bodily death raises distinctive problems for Wyschogrod, in part because he continually reasserts the physical and biological features of visual knowledge. We have already confronted this carnal recognition in his discussion of Jewish sacrificial worship. There it was a vision of the self as dying object in place of the sacrificial animal. Here it is the possibility of divine death, in which God can neither be seen nor discovered in the people Israel. Wyschogrod understands well the horror of bodily decay, and how death impairs a more hopeful vision of eternity. Yet in the midst of this despair he reasserts God's presence in death *because* God's dwelling has always been a physical embodiment. In death, the divine image "is no longer mediated by the invisibility of thought and speech," but is revealed instead within the stark visibility of the motionless body:

> The dignity that is bestowed on man by the divine image does not cease with death, which would be the case if only the spirit of man had the divine stamp. Instead, a corpse remains holy or perhaps becomes more holy than ever. . . . In death, the illusion of spiritual eternity is shattered, and yet the image of Hashem does not flee but remains sharply impressed in the human body.

With death, a morbid darkness overwhelms the lightness of being. If Hashem were to flee the body at that moment, "human encounter would be driven to despair and murder."[59] Here Wyschogrod reclaims God as the great protector against meaningless existence; God is the one who will preserve hope amid death. Yet the dead body terrifies the self in much the same way as the sacrificial animal: *that* death could be *my* death. To restrain this terror, Judaism inhibits a public gaze on a dead corpse, and in particular a look at the "eyes of the dead," for they "are the organs by means of which man thrusts himself ahead." Recall how Wyschogrod recovered vision as "the great liberator" that "transfers the inititative [sic] to man" by extending the human gaze "into the far distance."[60] But a dead man's gaze is "fearfully empty, an impotent thrust into the beyond that returns into itself and only emphasizes the deadness of the corpse."[61] This vacuity moves us to close the eyes of the dead in order to limit their darkness from absorbing our own light. Fearful that we might succumb to complete darkness and despair before death, Jewish tradition councils a withdrawal of the human gaze from dead bodies; by closing their eyes, we prevent a mutual look of incoherence. Yet death mysteriously intensifies God's presence such that the body "becomes more holy than ever." This reveals, as Wyschogrod powerfully asserts, the human attraction and repulsion to death: God more assertively dwells in the dead body, yet the inert eyes and blank stare reveal only an "impotent thrust into the beyond." Even in death, the delicate balance between light and darkness remains a deeply human visual experience where enlightened hope mingles uneasily with a darkened morbidity. We see this in death, Wyschogrod asserts, even if we cannot really see it at all.

The darkening insecurity of death raises the specter that nonbeing will overwhelm the more luminous quality of being. Wyschogrod devotes a lengthy and somewhat tortuous chapter to an exploration of nonbeing in the Western philosophical tradition.[62] While much of his analysis extends his earlier work on Kierkegaard and Heidegger,[63] I find that R. Kendall Soulen summarizes quite well Wyschogrod's critical interest in nonbeing:

> So long as non-being is embraced only in thought, the final result falls short of the actual embrace of nonbeing. Real nonbeing can be embraced only outside

of discourse, by the act. But the act that affirms being and is at the same time the pure embrace of non-being is the act of destruction, the act of reducing another living being to death.[64]

For Wyschogrod, nonbeing cannot be thought but only enacted. Yet nonbeing as physical act is embodied violence, as Wyschogrod believed it was for Heidegger and his support for the Nazi regime.[65] Wyschogrod's God is "the Lord of being," and as such exists "beyond being and nonbeing."[66] God guarantees that nonbeing will not win out, that violence will not prevail, and that death can be outflanked:

> As the Lord of being, he [God] circumscribes being, not in the mode of nonbeing that must translate itself into violence but in the mode of the trustworthy promise, which is the power of nonbeing transformed into the principle of hope. . . .
>   In spite of these similarities between nonbeing and Hashem, the difference between the two is the difference between death and hope.[67]

The delicate balance between light and darkness plays out here too between nonbeing and being. Nonbeing (darkness) limits being (light), but Hashem is the God who contains both without destroying either, and so radiates hope in a meaningful life of embodied existence. The being of light still radiates in death, for God dwells among even the dead bodies of his chosen people. Hope really does spring eternal.

This sense of hope in the midst of death conveys Wyschogrod's incarnational reasoning and the influence of Christian theology. Wyschogrod has readily acknowledged Karl Barth's impact on his own Jewish theology, but he has also confessed to a form of incarnational thought akin to Christian doctrine. Jewish thinkers of the past have often evaded discussions of God's corporality, Wyschogrod surmises, because they feared such topics would draw them too close to Christian theology. Not so for Wyschogrod: "The incarnational direction of my thinking became possible for me only after I succeeded in freeing myself from the need to be as different from Christianity as possible."[68] Yet Wyschogrod wishes to avoid the term *incarnation* to describe God's embodiment in the people Israel. Instead, he develops the notion of indwelling to account for God's presence. This evades, so Wyschogrod hopes, any misunderstanding that God actually becomes one with a particular group. The Christian incarnation, in Wyschogrod's view, yields pure presence and light that destroy the darkness of human existence. A god who dwells among his people, however, chooses to intensify their uncleanness and darker moods, and so accepts them as they are. As "the dwelling place of Hashem," Israel appears not as sinless but as more authentic, for this people exposes the true nature of human experience steeped in light and darkness. Christianity, with its appeal to a "sinless Christ," denies that experience and so becomes, in Wyschogrod's critique, a dehumanizing religious tradition.[69] Walter Lowe has written eloquently about an abiding darkness that permeates Christian thought as well, suggesting how Wyschogrod misreads the Christian tradition or has accounted for only one strain within it.[70] Wyschogrod certainly limits a more diverse Christianity to one monolithic culture, but he does so to play the foil to an equally homogeneous reading of Jewish theology. In Wyschogrod's taxonomy, Judaism and Christianity offer two competing accounts of God's relation with finite existence. Where Hashem associates with a people, the Christian God becomes human in one man; if Hashem accepts human beings as they are, Jesus too often condemns sinful acts; and where Judaism imparts an embodied visual knowledge of light and darkness, Christianity only sees the light, and so must deny the body and its darkened physicality. Wyschogrod's incarnational theology, however tied to reductive versions of competing religions, seeks to reassert God's presence in a people without thereby undermining its corporeality.

So Judaism is incarnational, but in a form distinctive from and critical of Christian traditions that assert God's unity with a singular person. At times, Wyschogrod stresses this distinction, noting how Judaism is "a less concentrated incarnation, an incarnation into a people spread out in time and place." In this sense, "the presence of the Jewish people in the world is a kind of continuing incarnation." In these texts, Judaism differs from Christianity only in God's adoption of an entire people. One may witness God's presence in Christ, but "he who touches this [Jewish] people, touches God and perhaps not altogether symbolically."[71] Here, Israel functions much like a Christ figure who embodies God's presence.

Yet in other texts Wyschogrod asserts the deeply humanizing force of Jewish incarnational theology, in which Israel reveals God's acceptance of human weakness and corporeality. To be sure, both Wyschogrod and his imagined Christian theologians confront the horror of a divine death, either in Jesus Christ or in the people Israel. Christian thinkers have developed robust theologies to mitigate against and even rejoice in this fear and trembling. But if Wyschogrod appropriates features of Christian incarnational thought, he does not appeal to a resurrection, to the trinity, to Marian theology, or to the many other ways of situating a divine death in a larger narrative of salvation. Instead, he appeals to the people Israel, "a less concentrated incarnation," one "spread out in time and place," such that any one death among Israel will not engender a divine death. Indeed, the very opposite is true: God appears more fully present in corporeal death, and strengthens that bond between Hashem and his chosen people. By spreading out God's presence among the people Israel, Wyschogrod expands God's body through time and place, and this not altogether symbolically. The chosen people of Israel are a permanent, visual presence of God's love. Their visual and material body is their faith.

In the preface to the second edition of *The Body of Faith*, Wyschogrod admits that he barely touched on notions of conversion in the original publication, and poses this query: "if the primary identity of the Jewish people is based on its descent from the patriarchs, then how is conversion to Judaism possible?" In fact, it should not be possible, for this chosen people constitutes "a priestly class into which one either is or is not born." This is the kind of honest confrontation that Wyschogrod takes on throughout his book, for he forthrightly acknowledges the theological dilemma: his focus on the visual and carnal body precludes conversion, and yet clearly persons convert to Judaism. Such a rebirth can only occur "by means of a miracle," and this because the convert "miraculously becomes part of the body of Israel." The convert "must become seed," and she does so "quasi-physically, miraculously" (this is my gendered language, not Wyschogrod's). This is a genuine rebirth, according to Wyschogrod, for a male son who converts does not violate the biblical law against incest were he to marry his mother (although the rabbis banned such marriages). Through some miraculous occurrence the gentile body transforms into a Jewish one. But we cannot see it:

> Conversion is thus not just a spiritual event. It has biological or quasi-biological consequences. This does not, of course, imply that the biological miracle that accompanies a conversion can be observed under the microscope as changes in the DNA of the convert. It is a theological–biological miracle. It severs the mother–son and brother–sister relationship in some way that we cannot physically observe but that must be very real.[72]

The miracle consists in a real event taking place beyond visual assurance. This is why Wyschogrod must qualify his embodied language with phrases such as "quasi-biological" and "theological–biological" miracle. Since marvels such as these should not occur, and yet they do, Wyschogrod insists that "converts are therefore accepted but not encouraged."[73] The problem here lies in a physical change beyond discernment. We can see God in the chosen people Israel, and yet we cannot perceive this same God in the body of the convert. God can miraculously envision the face of his beloved Abraham in the gentile become Jew, but Israel cannot do so.

Wyschogrod is clearly uncomfortable with conversion to Judaism, and is even more uneasy with Jewish proselytizing activities. He avoids saying too much about DNA, and yet he appeals to some kind of biological change for the convert. This anxiety is a visual one, for Wyschogrod defends a "theological–biological miracle" that "we cannot physically observe." God's visual presence in the dead body delivers hope over a final death. But what of this visual absence in the quasi-physical conversion of the gentile? The convert elicits anxiety because she neither displays visual authenticity of this hope, nor reveals God's chosen indwelling with the people Israel. We can only infer a miraculous presence of light, but the convert remains uncannily obscure to human vision. Hers is not a body of faith but a quasi-biological miracle. And this mystery shadows Wyschogrod's embodied triumphalism. Conversion narratives threaten the visual authenticity of Israel's status as God's chosen people. Chosenness is not a miracle but a result of God's loving choice. Wyschogrod avoids discussions of conversion in his text because gentile bodies, even converted ones, do not fully expose God's presence to human vision.

I read Wyschogrod's account of conversion as anxious apologetic, and this because the rhetoric of visual embodiment plays such a decisive role in his account of chosenness and authenticity. Conversions ought not be possible because only Israel portrays the human condition in its existential light and darkness; only Israel displays God's presence as embodied in its people; and only Israel sees as God sees the I as a sacrificial, dying object. This is authentic vision, and it is Israel's alone. By means of miraculous conversion, the non-Jew takes on these responsibilities and powers, but is forever regulated by a "quasi" status of embodiment and, because conversion should not be encouraged, is marked by inauthenticity.

When Wyschogrod claims that "the majority of Jews must remain the descendants of the patriarchs and the matriarchs,"[74] then the minority of converts—who, it seems, really do not become full descendants—are a bit less chosen, somewhat less insightful, and far more obscure and opaque. This is so, I have argued throughout this chapter, because Wyschogrod ties chosenness to visual authenticity, and he employs a visual rhetoric to expose God's love for the people Israel. But vision has its limits, and not only in the agitated body of the convert. It is, as Wyschogrod repeatedly reminds us, an obscure and partial perspective. Total exposure lies beyond the human realm, and certainly beyond the Jewish gaze. So perhaps conversion is no miracle at all, but rather a partial revelation that chosenness is far more mysterious, and darker, than any one people could hope to perceive. The visual language of embodiment reveals the anxiety of authenticity, and perhaps a welcome unease at that.

5 The Language of Gendered Bodies in Rachel Adler's *Engendering Judaism*

> What happens, however, when I reach out to stories whose worlds do not
> permit me to enter, that exclude me or distort me? This is the first problem
> that confronts anyone who attempts to construct a theology of Judaism that
> includes *all* the people Israel, men and women. How do we face a story that de/
> faces some of us and thereby diminishes all of us?
>
> —Rachel Adler, *Engendering Judaism*

RACHEL ADLER (B. 1943) BEGINS all her chapters of *Engendering Judaism* (1998) by telling a story that, she hopes, will yield a "purifying laughter" to restore the feminine other.[1] Though she reframes the tales as comedies, these are serious narratives indeed. And like many good jokes, Adler's textual play is subversive, offering a transformative account of "a way of thinking about and practicing Judaism that men and women recreate and renew together as equals."[2] One of those jokes is the "shit" method that relies on a bilingual pun in Yiddish for throwing stuff together. Eastern European Jewish women often used this method as they cooked their foods without precise measurements or recipes. Though a far cry from Fishbein's more deliberate and precise cooking recipes in *Kosher by Design*, the heuristic value of utilizing the resources at hand works for feminist theologians because the "shit" method teaches how to be "attentive to potential resources in its immediate environment, imaginative about combinations, and flexible about the structure of the recipe."[3] This playful openness—one that is pliable yet resilient, inventive yet also attentive to context and tradition—shapes Adler's approach to engender Judaism. She mines the Jewish textual tradition in order to reclaim female presence and performance; she offers imaginative retellings of stories to embody an ethics of mutual responsibility and just relations; and she stretches the boundaries of vision to include the face of the forgotten Other.

This exposure of the embodied Other, one that engenders both men and women, reveals the visual, gendered language of authenticity. Adler criticizes a masculine vision that focuses on genitalia and the sexualized body, and seeks to restore a more polysemous vision that imaginatively opens to a more wholesome body of desire. This more authentic vision recognizes other sensual registers—touch, smell, taste, and sound—even as it strengthens unsettling mixtures, odd subtleties, and unresolved meanings of Adler's liberal, pluralistic Judaism. This is certainly not Wyschogrod's body of faith, but Adler does respond to his call for a more imaginative, bohemian creativity. Still, Wyschogrod tends to gender the chosen body as the circumcised male, and associates the feminine with sexuality and the flesh. Adler's authentic body is altogether different. Though she rarely appeals to the language of authenticity, and at one point actively distances herself from it, Adler nonetheless defends a polysemic vision that authenticates: this vision engenders bodies as complex, material, and holy. Through this gaze we see the other as a sensual, responsive body of wholesome desire. To be "fully attentive to the impact of gender and sexuality,"[4] she requires a new visual register of recognition and splendor. Adler appeals to an engendering vision to justify and cultivate her progressive Judaism. This is the visual language of gendered authenticity.

Adler's work has been immensely influential for Jewish feminist theology in particular, and Jewish practice more generally. Rochelle Millen argues that Adler, Tamar Ross, and Judith Plaskow are the three most engaged, influential, and articulate thinkers in contemporary Jewish feminist theology today.[5] Adler's theological convictions tend to fall between the more orthodox Ross (though she did not discover Ross's work until after writing *Engendering Judaism*)[6] and the more liberal Plaskow. Ross writes from within the Orthodox Jewish community, and so defends the revelatory and divine character of the biblical text. But she also appeals to "a dynamic unfolding of the original Torah transmitted at Sinai that reveals in time its ultimate significance." This "cumulative process" favors "a more fluid view of Torah" that aligns closely with Adler's approach to traditional texts. Yet compared to Adler, Ross retains a more restrictive meaning of the sacred, claiming the pragmatic view that "Orthodox women living out an egalitarian reality are precisely the ones most capable of building upon Adler's model."[7]

Adler's relation to Plaskow is a bit more complex. To better appreciate this, note how Adler mediates between two influential essays—one from Cynthia Ozick and the other from Plaskow—appearing together in the edited volume *On Being a Jewish Feminist* (1983).[8] In "Notes toward Finding the Right Question," Ozick argues that "*for Judaism, the status of women is a social, not a sacred, question.*" The Torah has appropriated a social inequality, and thus "confirms the world, denying the meaning of its own Covenant."[9] This cultural view suggests how patriarchy and inequality are, in contrast to Plaskow's view, inessential features of the biblical text. Tikva Frymer-Kensky offers a helpful summary, and a somewhat more robust version of Ozick's insight:

> The Bible that subtly warns its readers not to focus solely on the men in its text does not sound like the same Bible that has been quoted throughout history as a way of keeping women in their place. Much of the patriarchy that we associate with the Bible and all of its misogyny has been introduced into the Bible by later generations of readers.[10]

This liberation of the "biblical text from its patriarchal overlay"[11] was a critical feature of Phyllis Trible's important study, *God and the Rhetoric of Sexuality* (1978), a text that clearly has inspired Adler's reading of biblical stories. Following Trible, Ozick, and Frymer-Kensky, Adler offers fresh readings of supposedly patriarchal stories to recover the engendered presence of the female body. Like Ozick and Frymer-Kensky, Adler rereads texts for their transformative power, for their playful narratives of desire, and for their capacity to teach us how to be more fully human. These texts still hold blessings to recover and cherish.

But what if Ozick is wrong? What if, as Ozick herself questions, the "Torah itself" is fundamentally patriarchal in nature and scope? Judith Plaskow responds to this challenge in the very title of her essay, "The Right Question Is Theological."[12] For Plaskow, patriarchy goes all the way down into the core of the biblical text, for the Torah assumes "the normative character of maleness."[13] In Plaskow's view, the Torah is profoundly unjust, for "the assumption of the lesser humanity of women has poisoned the content and structure of the law, undergirding women's legal disabilities and our subordination in the broader tradition." Such radical, or in Ozick's terms, "sacred," ruptures cannot be altered piecemeal. Instead, this injustice must be "rooted out at its core."[14] Plaskow responds to this fundamental inequality by expanding the concept of Torah to include records of women's experience. For her, the biblical text exposes only a "partial record" of Jewish "Godwrestling."[15] Adler, whose influential essay "The Jew Who Wasn't There" also appeared with Ozick's and Plaskow's works, accepts a good deal of Plaskow's critique, but she will, like Ilana Pardes, recover "countertraditions" in the Bible that offer more robust and engendering practices of liberal Judaism.[16] She recognizes the patriarchal narratives that Plaskow finds throughout, but she also highlights those countervailing tendencies of an engendering Judaism. So Adler privileges the more egalitarian theology of Genesis 1 to offset the objectifying visions of Genesis 2; and she recovers an ethics of sexuality in the Song of Songs unknown to the Holiness Code of Leviticus 18. Here too Adler tends to follow Trible rather than Plaskow or Pardes, but she does so in order to preserve as well as mourn: "For Judaism's future to be rescued, something will have to die. We must consent to be bereaved in order to be renewed." To be sure, some biblical texts are patriarchal through and through (as Plaskow argues), while others have only been interpreted to be so (according to Ozick and Trible). Attention, imagination, flexibility: this is what the "shit" method involves, and so this guides Adler's recovery of an engendered Judaism. She knows only one way to begin: "let us pick up our tools and start out."[17]

In taking up those tools, Adler offers an important corrective to the story of authenticity and vision pursued throughout this book. She criticizes a monocular vision of sexualized bodies, and replaces it with one more attuned to the multiple senses and embodied practices of engendered beings. Adler tethers polysemous vision[18] with authenticity to envision, and thus to re-member the embodied face of the Other. This act of recovery makes women present and accounted. For Adler, this sense of female authentic presence must be a more coherent rather than a fragmented identity, and it must be one ennobled by Jewish law. She turns to Robert Cover's work on law as *nomos* in order to imagine more complete, inclusive, and meaningful narratives of Jewish practice. This coherent, narrative self is part of what Adler means by authentic presence.

Upon weaving these threads of vision and authenticity together, I turn to Adler's critique of sexualized vision and the modes by which it undermines the wholesome embodiment of the other's presence. This deformed and damaging perception contrasts with Adler's appeal to an engendering vision as one sensual mode among many embodied relations. Here we discover a fully embodied splendor that Adler associates with the sexual play in the Song of Songs. These two contrasting visual discourses—sexualized and engendered vision—mirror two theological reading practices in Adler's text. Appropriating a long-standing bias favoring metaphor over allegory, Adler portrays these rhetorical practices as either polysemous (as with metaphor in the Song of Songs and Genesis 1) or sexualized and reductive (as with allegory in Genesis 2). Polysemous vision, in turn, becomes a strong metaphor for "an inclusive theology and ethics"—the subtitle to Adler's book. This metaphorical reading, one that limits even as it recovers a more holistic vision, significantly revises Wyschogrod's focus on the people Israel as the embodiment of God's presence. If Wyschogrod believes God sees Abraham's visage in the Jewish people, then Adler refocuses that lens to account for God's presence in a "fructifying vision" of "a world that Jewish women build together with Jewish men, a *nomos* we inhabit where we co/habit justly and generously."[19] This is the visual language of gendered embodiment—a wholesome practice envisioned by all.

Remembering the Face

Adler is understandably suspicious of claims to authenticity, for they tend to reduce a more pluralistic Jewish practice to a singular authorized one. As the term *polysemous* suggests, Adler desires a multifaceted and imaginative Judaism that opens to new varieties, even as it is rooted in traditional texts and practices. The image of multiple seeds both rooted and blossoming encourages varied growth. She fears appeals to authenticity would hinder such variation. Indeed, her attack on "authentic Judaism" mirrors her critique of "women's experience": both privilege certain forms of experience that tend to erase important cultural and historical differences. With so many "versions of Judaism," Adler asks rhetorically, "how can one argue that one is more authentic than another without enunciating criteria for authenticity?"[20] Yet despite this warning, Adler does offer criteria for authenticity, and relates those standards to visual discourse, even if she does not authorize one form of authentic Judaism. At times this is explicit, at other times less so, but in each case she binds an authentic Jewish practice or ideal to a mode of seeing others. To be clear, Adler's appeal to authenticity cultivates differences, for she opens Jewish identity to myriad constellations of performance and belief—although, as Tamar Ross argues, her pluralism is not quite as radical as Adler believes it to be.[21] The term *authentic Judaism* is problematic only when it diminishes the range of Jewish expression and belief. For Adler, a polysemic vision is more authentic than a sexualized one because it presents the Other as a coherent, embodied, and infinitely diverse self.

The task of theology, as Adler describes it, directly engages these issues concerning authentic presence. Adler portrays a theology in tune with the continuing revelatory capacity of God's presence as always pluralistic and personal:

> As I understand it, theology's task is to allow the texts of the tradition and the lived experiences of religious communities to keep revealing themselves to one another so the sacred meanings both of text and of experience can be renewed. In the course of this process, God becomes present in our midst.[22]

Theology enables two modes of religious expression—the lived experiences of religious communities, and the texts of a particular tradition—to emerge before each other. They do so separately; there are traditional texts on the one hand, and lived experiences on the other. The theologian draws these two paths together, but does not confuse or merge them. Each maintains its own "sacred meanings," and the challenge is to engage both in an open conversation in order to renew their revelatory power. Only when this happens does God become present "in our midst." There are, to be sure, troubling questions that Adler leaves unanswered here: who determines "the texts of the tradition"; which "lived experiences" count; what criteria distinguish a "sacred" meaning from a profane one; and why submit God to a "process"?[23] Yet however loose, Adler's definition of theology still appeals to authenticity and presence in important ways. Texts and communities reveal themselves to one another, and God's presence arrives as a mode of justification and assurance. God is not one who reveals but one who authenticates: when texts and communities do their sacred work, God becomes present. "Non-Orthodox Judaisms" differ from Orthodoxy, Adler tells us, "by their belief that Jews beget Judaism; they reshape and renew Judaism in the various times and places they inhabit."[24] The dividing line seems clear to Adler: on the one side lies a singular "Orthodoxy" with a God who determines Judaism's shape and character; on the other side lies all the others who appropriate that divine power for themselves. Jews "reshape and renew Judaism," and God enters when they do so in conversation with traditional texts. God's presence authenticates a human process of building and cultivating "sacred meanings." This God grounds the renewal of Jewish practice and helps to diminish the anxiety of inauthenticity.

Adler correlates this sense of authentic presence with the face of the Other. God appears only when "sacred meanings" arrive through inclusive stories, such that the revelatory process between text and experience remains open to all. When traditional texts limit their revelatory power to men only, we must pry them open to face all inquisitive gazes:

> What happens, however, when I reach out to stories whose worlds do not permit me to enter, that exclude me or distort me? This is the first problem that confronts anyone who attempts to construct a theology of Judaism that includes *all* the people Israel, men and women. How do we face a story that de/faces some of us and thereby diminishes all of us?[25]

Adler uses the term *face* as a form of recognition and as an embodied presence. To "face" a story is to ask whether it truly "faces" me: does it recognize my presence as an engendered man or woman? And this is a personal confrontation in which I seek pure presence, one that does not "exclude me or distort me." Note the process here: I "reach out" to textual narratives that may refute my advance. If the text excludes *me,* then it is an inauthentic and distorted meeting: without my visual presence as "face," these texts distort the entire people Israel.

So despite Adler's appeal to both texts and experience, the arbiter of meaning here is personal experience, and not the texts of the tradition. What a woman should not do, says Adler in another context, is resign "her claim to visibility in deference to the superior claim of holy text."[26] Adler reverses this superiority for the "I" to pursue texts from a position of heightened power, and the "I" determines whether texts include or distort personal experience. If both texts and experience maintain sacred meanings, as Adler argues they do, then stories restricting access cannot be holy stories at all. They might certainly be traditional texts, but they cannot be authoritative ones. A text that de/faces also distorts an engendered Judaism.

Now one way to "face" these texts, as Adler acknowledges, is not to face them at all; we could look elsewhere for such blessings. On one reading this reflects, in part, Plaskow's own view, for she seeks to transform Jewish history by adding to it—although she describes this process as a rediscovery of a "primordial" Torah that supplements the "manifest" Torah of male experience.[27] But Adler will not let go so easily. She will not allow these texts to remain inauthentic. She holds them accountable to her experience as a practicing and believing Jew:

> It is precisely because I believe that these texts have blessings yet to bestow that, like another member of Esau's blessing-starved family, I will not let them go until they bless me. I will not abandon traditional texts, and I will not absolve them of moral responsibility.[28]

Adler's "I" is even more powerful here, and she forces these texts to bestow blessings even when, at first glance, they appear to distort or refute her advance. She will make these texts face her and respond to her challenge. Adler will use all the tools her "shit" method affords in order to wrestle with stories that challenge her own authority and authentic presence as "face." Revelation does not come from above, despite what "Orthodoxy" might contend; instead, non-Orthodox theologians like Adler compel texts to reveal their blessings to all.

Adler's theology ties authenticity and vision together by empowering personal experience to demand textual blessings. Traditional texts become so by responding, and thereby facing, the engendered face of the other. God authenticates this sacred occurrence by being present to lived experience and the text. This God functions much like tradition did for Fishbein, continuity for Greenberg and Silverman, and God's embodiment for Wyschogrod: they all keep the anxiety of (in)authenticity at bay. For Adler, God's presence ensures that lived experience is just, sacred, and open to all. The textual blessings, now fully exposed and authorized, make women visible both to the tradition they embrace and to the stories they read. A text distorts, however, when it de/faces women and excludes their visibility. This is what Adler calls "dis/membering" as a form of "dis/remembering": it is "a particular kind of mutilation through language—a de/facing, a tearing away of the face of the other." As "a distortion and deception," dis/remembering evokes a kind of "representation which is morally untrue." The physical violence associated with this erasure—mutilation, tearing away, dis/membering—highlights an absence that was a presence. This is not a passive effacing of the feminine, nor a hiding of appearance. Dis/remembering is an active maiming and a form of excision that fears visual presence. It reveals the anxiety of authenticity from the other side, as it were: the anxiety that the engendered Other might count as fully present and human. The theologian, then, must practice a form of re/membering to enable "the restoration of wholeness" as the full exposure of the once distorted face.[29] This return to wholeness recovers both the other's face and my own: authentic facial exposure and authentic meeting in which God becomes present. Adler captures this sense of authentic presence by quoting Adrienne Rich as witness: "to make yourself visible, [is] to claim that your experience is just as real and normative as any other."[30] When a text steals "the memory of the true face of the other,"[31] it violates the moral knowledge that authenticity requires visibility. Re/membering the other's face is a linguistic act of engendering authenticity.

This visual exposure reveals how Adler's theology initiates an act of recovery. She seeks to restore what has been lost or stolen. In this, Adler's project resembles what Judith Plaskow calls a gain in "more of the primordial Torah,"[32] or what Tamar Ross signifies as "expanding the palace of Torah" through a "cumulative process."[33] Ilana Pardes, too, seeks to recover texts to counterbalance and challenge the dominant patriarchal biblical tradition.[34] All discover alternative stories to dispute prevailing norms, and all situate women's experiences at the very center. Adler knows that women were always there as an original presence, but they were quickly "booted out of the world of the text." Yet their curious absence witnesses to an engendering presence, and therefore "a feminist herme-neutic must identify these thefts and attempt to restore what has been stolen."[35] In this sense, authenticity is not to be won but to be regained: "The problem is not that women never engaged in spiritual expression in Judaism, but that their ex-pressions generally went unrecognized and unpreserved."[36] As we will see in the next chapter, this nicely captures the sentiment of Rabbi Capers Funnye in Kaye/Kantrowitz's *The Colors of Jews*, when he describes his embrace of Judaism as one of "reversion" rather than conversion.[37] Like Adler, Funnye recovers an authentic heritage undeservedly lost. In that process of recovery, Funnye and Adler appeal to visual paradigms to support their claims to authenticity. For Adler, this return is a form of re/membering of a lost wholeness.

Authenticity, Coherency, and Law

Mutilations and scars must be surgically removed; they rarely dissolve or disap-pear on their own. To be whole again—to regain authentic presence—requires sturdy tools to rebuild the palace of Torah. Adler does so by reimagining the legal structure that Plaskow believes has so completely de/faced women's ex-perience. For Adler, Jewish law still has blessings to confer, but it must bestow them to all Jews. Adler depicts Jewish law as a narrative of what matters most to practicing religious communities. Law reflects "a universe of meanings, val-ues, and rules, embedded in stories."[38] In articulating this broad vision of Jewish *halakhah*, Adler draws on Robert Cover's insightful and progressive analysis of legal traditions. Much has been written on Adler's adoption of Cover's work, and its centrality for her theological project.[39] Here, I want to explore how Cover's discussion of *nomos* enables Adler to reclaim experiential coherency as authentic presence.

Jewish law concerns Liberal as well as Orthodox Jews, Adler insists, "because the stories of Judaism belong to us all." These stories reflect a "communal praxis" that yields far more than a collection of practices. Adler demarcates her defini-tion of praxis in italics, and so visually highlights its significance: "*a praxis is a holistic embodiment in action at a particular time of the values and commitments inherent to a particular story.*"[40] In the footnote to this text, Adler notes the "obvi-ous kinships" of her discussion of praxis with the Marxian, Christian liberation, and Aristotelian traditions.[41] Appealing to all three likely covers the range of po-tential sources, but this vast heritage should not blind us to the particular claims within *this* theological project. Adler insists that praxis is a unified body of ac-tion. It might change over time as it reflects historical values and commitments, but at each "particular time" those actions are "holistic." Practices also reflect the "values and commitments inherent" in the stories Jews tell about themselves. If *halakhah* is "a communal praxis grounded in Jewish stories,"[42] then Jewish law must be holistic, and it must embody the values and commitments within those stories. Anything less would constitute an inauthentic rendering of Jewish praxis.

Yet this is precisely what has occurred in the modern world, so Adler tells us. Rather than becoming a complete, coherent embodiment of communal values, Jewish "praxis became both impoverished and fragmented." With such piece-meal articulations of Jewish commitment, those stories lost their inherent richness and plausibility: "It became impossible to imagine a unified way to live as a human being, a citizen, and a Jew." Adler imagines a more wholesome universe in which Jews remain complete and unencumbered beings. This is a nostalgic story of loss, in which riches were impoverished, and complete beings became fragmented. But we can recover that wholeness in a sweeping, almost Hegelian effort of heightened return to coherence:

> A contemporary Jewish praxis would reduce our sense of fragmentation. If we had a praxis rather than a grab bag of practices, we would experience making love, making *kiddush,* recycling paper used at our workplace, cooking a pot of soup for a person with AIDS, dancing at a wedding, and making medical treatment decisions for a dying loved one as integrated parts of the same project: the holy transformation of our everyday reality. Furthermore, we would experience ourselves less as fragmented enactors of divergent roles in disparate spheres—public/private, ritual/ethical, religious/secular, duty/pleasure—and more as coherent Jewish personalities.[43]

A Jewish praxis promotes a "holistic embodiment" to unify what had become fragmented personal experiences and activities. This appeal to more coherent personalities is a transparent claim to authenticity as a more complete and coherent self. It imagines a Jewish narrative without the tragic "trade-offs, negotiations, and unexpected instances of compliance and compromise" that Tamar Ross takes to be the hallmark of "true halakhic stability."[44] In Adler's view, Jewish theology done well can recover a more coherent Jewish modality, although it "cannot simply resurrect the old premodern praxis." Such a blind adherence would be inauthentic, and progressive Jews, above all, long for authenticity: "But the obligation to be truthful and the yearning to be whole are what made us progressive Jews in the first place."[45] Recovering and extending a more coherent praxis, progressive Jews become the true inheritors and faithful observers of the Jewish covenant.

In the context of a progressive "yearning to be whole," Adler turns to Cover's legal theory to help explain "how the feminist project qualifies as a lawmaking enterprise": his work "offers a basis upon which feminist hermeneutics, praxis, and commitments can make defensible claims to authenticity."[46] Adler appreciates Cover's appeal to narrative and imagination as important correctives to formal and positivist legal theories. For legal formalists, "a legal outcome is valid if the system's rules and categories are correctly applied." The legal positivists or realists contend, to the contrary, that law is determined "by the discretionary power of judges."[47] But Cover thinks of legal rulings as embodied practices within a nomic world. A *nomos* articulates a world of values and meanings in narrative form in which persons "envision the possibilities implicit in its [the nomic world's] stories and norms and [are] willing to live some of them out in praxis."[48] Cover opens his inspirational essay, "Nomos and Narrative" (1983), by appealing to this nomic reality: "We inhabit a *nomos*—a normative universe. We constantly create and maintain a world of right and wrong, of lawful and unlawful, of valid and void." In this world, "law and narrative are inseparably related."[49] Law is, in Cover's account, the active maintenance of a coherent universe. It is a story about what communities cherish and aspire to be. Even more, legal narratives unify those aspirations and make our world "sane": "To live in a legal world requires that one know not only the precepts, but also their connections to possible and plausible states of affairs. It requires that one integrate not only the 'is' and the 'ought,' but the 'is,' the 'ought,' and the 'what might be.' Narrative so integrates these domains."[50] Cover discovers law not in formal categories or judicial power, but in the communal visions of a just and coherent world. He provides Adler with a legal framework that reinforces her claims to a more integrated, authentic personhood.

Cover deploys the image of a bridge to account for the way that law links "a concept of a reality to an imagined alternative." A "bridge between the vision and the reality"[51] situates communities between "the meaning-making component" and "the other normative worlds we may choose to imagine." Adler finds obvious appeal in this account, for it binds current praxis with imaginative future possibilities. Feminist legal theory can build on Cover's claims to coherency:

> We can bridge that gap ["between the impoverished imperial world we inhabit and the richer and more vital worlds that could be"] and regenerate a *nomos,* a world of legal meaning in which the stories, dreams, and revelations of Jewish women and men are fully and complexly integrated.[52]

Cover's *nomos* holds out the possibility for authentic legal integrity, and so imagines a world that progressive Jews can inhabit in their "yearning to be whole." The Orthodoxy of a Tamar Ross, one that accepts trade-offs and negotiations, is all but lost here. Both Cover and Adler imagine a *nomos* as "an integrated world of obligation and reality"[53] to encourage pluralism within a universe of well-artic-ulated and unified meaning.

Cover justifies the feminist lawmaking enterprise as fully authentic because "the bridge is what connects maintenance-law to jurisgenerative potentiality."[54] In other words, when Adler reimagines Jewish law, she does so from within a nomic world of shared meaning. The bridge metaphor ties her to an inherited tradition, but it also enables her to move forward: "We must *extend* Torah as we extend ourselves by reaching ahead. The aptest metaphor for that constructive task is that of the bridge we build from the present to possible futures." Engender-ing Judaism does not break with the past; it reflects instead an authentic praxis "to repair and renew the Torah within time."[55]

Although I have emphasized Cover's appeal to coherent personhood, and Adler's appropriation of it, I do not want to lose sight of the dynamic practices and meanings that make up a nomic world. Adler and Cover both insist that a legal tradition is always negotiating the narrative meanings that constitute it. As Alasdair McIntyre has emphasized, this is part of what it means to say that a tradition remains in good working order.[56] This sense of vibrancy from within upends more conservative accounts of religious traditions, and supports a more constructivist agenda:

> Cover's bridge image makes it possible to think freshly about halakhah, because it counters precisely those features that progressive Jews, and progressive feminists in particular, find repressive in halakhah's traditional formulations. It is dynamic rather than static, visionary rather than conservative, open to the outside rather than closed, arising communally, cooperatively, covenantally, rather than being externally imposed and passively obeyed.

These progressive values—dynamic, visionary, open, cooperative, and communal—encourage a spirited pluralism. They are certainly modern goods, as Adler readily admits, but the bridge image ties these goods to authentic sources. A "legal guerilla" (Adler's term of endearment for the feminist Jewish halakhist) always grounds her alternative story "in narratives the tradition believes it owns and understands," and so her rereading counts as authentic. But those narratives harbor a "multipotentiality" to contest and destabilize accepted legal meanings.[57] The bridge image works because it is both visionary and subversive, yet still covenantal. This too, I suggest, is what the language of authenticity empowers in Adler's engendered Judaism.

Sexualized Vision

A dynamic yet holistic *nomos* imagines the legal tradition as a communal dialogue about values and norms. As ongoing and vital, this legal negotiation is pluralistic, open, and potentially destabilizing. But it happens face-to-face, before and in commitment to others who participate in good faith. A particular form of engendering vision mirrors this account of *nomos*. In Adler's reading of the Song of Songs, she discovers a more holistic, pluralistic, and enabling vision that recognizes the "multipotentiality" of other bodies. This is the "legal guerilla" at work, for even as the bridge attaches to a past, it also leads away from it. Yet before we arrive at this more engendering Judaism, I want to analyze why this bridge building is necessary for Adler's theological task. To reach her inclusive theology on the other side of the bridge, Adler must undermine a more restricted, focused perception on this side. I call this restricted gaze a sexualized vision. This perspective concentrates entirely on the genitalia of the feminine Other, and obsessively strives to conceal its visibility. Rachel Neis discovers this gaze in Talmudic sources, arguing that in many passages "the Bavli [Babylonian Talmud] effectively genitalizes a woman's entire body, when it is under the male gaze."[58] For Adler, this is an inauthentic vision because it undermines the nomic ideal that she demands from her progressive Judaism—an open, dynamic, whole, and communal re/membering of the Other as integrated person. A sexualized vision sexualizes the other, enclosing her within borders that conceal rather than extending the self with bridges that expand.

Adler exposes this sexualized vision through a reading of a story in *Midrash Aseret Dibroth*, a midrashic collection composed between the seventh and eleventh centuries. This story involves Rabbi Matiyah ben Ḥeresh and his struggle to overcome his sexual impulses. As he immerses himself in Torah study, his face radiates with beauty, for "he had never lifted his eyes to look at another man's wife or at any woman"—a model of the rabbinic, visual ascetic in which, as Neis explains, rabbis would lower their eyes so as not to look at feminine beauty.[59] Astonished at his self-control, and desirous to undermine it, Satan seeks to test his strength. Disguised as a beautiful female, Satan stands before Rabbi Matiyah, tempting him to withdraw his sight from Torah and gaze instead upon her beautiful flesh. Adler calls this "a ballet of confrontation and evasion," where Satan continually confronts and Matiyah frantically evades. Overwhelmed by the female flesh, Matiyah calls his students to bring him nails; he then sets them afire, thrusts the nails into his eyes so he can no longer see, and thus can no longer be tempted by the feminine body. Although God commands the angel Rafael to restore his eyesight, Matiyah himself refuses to be healed until God promises that Matiyah's evil impulse will never again overwhelm him. Here is how Adler sums things up: "At the story's happy ending, Matiyah is healed both of the mutilation and of all desire to merge with the feminine."[60]

Adler reads this story as a psychological account of masculine autonomy in the language of feminist object-relations theory. In her summary of this psychological model, she emphasizes how all of us seek to "differentiate from the mother to become independent selves." But males "definitively" sever that relation and deny "all commonality with her and, hence, with the feminine." Men experience this rupture as a wound, "a kind of mutilation that the boy sustains in order to attain the coveted autonomous self."[61] Adler appropriates this model to retell the story of Matiyah:

> Sexual sin is here defined as the wish for merger that threatens to undo autonomous selfhood by restoring the original identity with woman. The painful first differentiation from mother is recalled and invoked to counter subsequent desires. Mutilation, paradoxically, preserves integrity.[62]

The sexualized feminine body tempts Matiyah to relinquish his autonomous male self and return to his mother's embrace. But Matiyah's devotion to male autonomy enables him to overcome his yearning for wholeness, and so he repeats the original mutilation by the physical act of dis/membering. Adler reads this story in a mode that she will later critically attribute to allegory: she stages a series of oppositions and estrangements in order to contrast the original state of nature from "the patriarchal perspective."[63] Here, the female body rivals the text, and she must become invisible so that only the text reigns supreme.

Although Adler appropriates object-relations theory to criticize Matiyah's desire for the autonomous male self, she still highlights the role of vision in this ballet of dis/membering. The subtitle of this section—"Matiyah ben Ḥeresh: The Eyes Have It"—immediately focuses the reader's attention on the narrative's visual features. Matiyah's beauty shines because it has never been dimmed by the feminine Other. He essentially appropriates *her* beauty as his own. Always facing Torah, Matiyah never faces that other object of sensual beauty. And the face remains central to this story of temptation: only Matiyah's face "was as beautiful as an angel's," and when Satan stands before him, Matiyah "turned away his face."[64] The physical face is the locale of beauty and temptation, and the eyes, if turned away from Torah, become the organ of sin. Better to tear out the eyes in order to prevent sexual temptation than to allow transgression, even if one could then return to Torah. But there are really two different modes of vision here: the one is "immersed" in Torah and completely absorbed in all its detail, while the other has a singular focus on the sexualized body of the female Other. In Adler's language, Matiyah has replaced the mother with Torah, and so returned to a primordial coherence. The sexualized Other tempts him to adopt a sexualized vision focused on the face as the scene of transgression.

But unlike the dis/membering that tears away the face of the Other, Matiyah's violence is self-inflicted. Yet this self-mutilation fails to erase the feminine Other; she remains in place as passive bystander to a very different visual dynamic. Matiyah's struggle is his alone, and he proves deficient: he fails to overcome his evil impulse, and so he must physically destroy the carrier of vision. Without eyes to see, his evil impulse is powerless. But what of the feminine caress, the scent of the Other, the taste of flesh against flesh? Why do these sensual advances never tempt Matiyah into sin? As Adler recounts the story, only the eyes have it: to the exclusion of every other sensual faculty, vision dominates and controls. Matiyah need not harm any other faculty to diminish the sexual impulse. Sex and vision go together.

Adler traces this coupling in two other stories. One concerns a story about grace after meals, and how the guest Ulla insults Rabbi Nachman's wife Yalta. Ulla defends the principle that, "just as women cannot be fertile through any act of their own, so too they cannot be blessed through any act of their own but only through the agency of men acting for and upon them." How Ulla acts on this principle during grace after meals is rather complex, and Adler skillfully works through the passage to help readers understand the interpretive nuances. But the crucial issue for Adler, and for us, is how Ulla reduces "his hostess to a womb."[65] He sees the feminine Other as a sexualized body, and only as such. The second story concerns the nature of sexual exposure. Adler discusses a Talmudic passage (*Berakhot* 24a–b) that explores whether men can still recite the *Shema* prayer if naked with others in bed.[66] It is within this context that the text raises the issue of female sexual exposure. In this rather bizarre story about what constitutes genitalia, Adler (and Neis) convincingly argue how in these passages, "the entire woman is a genital exposure." The face, the little finger, the leg, the hair, even the female voice all reveal "erva" (nakedness). "Gazing at her" always means gazing at her genitalia; her "face" is her sexualized vulva.[67] In this rabbinic vision, the eyes see only the Other with a singular focus on one sexualized body part.

This is what Adler calls a "pornographic gaze,"[68] and what I label as sexualized vision. There are two crucial components to this gaze: it is singular and focused on female genitalia, and it reigns supreme over all other sensual experiences. Even the female voice, in the second passage discussed above, tempts not the ears but the eyes as a form of sexual nakedness. This is a reductive, objectifying vision, and it violently undermines a unifying *nomos* for both men and women. Recall Adler's appropriation of Cover's bridge metaphor, and the values they both associate with it: "dynamic rather than static, visionary rather than conservative, open to the outside rather than closed, arising communally, cooperatively, covenantally, rather than being externally imposed and passively obeyed."[69] Sexualized vision reflects all the negative attributes of this dichotomy: it is static, conservative, closed, and externally imposed. Simply, sexualized vision is inauthentic exposure; it remakes the Other into an inauthentic, passive object. This reductive vision is neither world-building nor transformative; it is instead a violent dis/membering. Matiyah did well to remove this mode of perception. But in tearing out his eyes, he did not remove the female body. Indeed, he made it all the more present. Perhaps another, more engendering visual register lies waiting on the other side of the bridge.

Engendering Vision

Adler differentiates a sexualized, focused vision from a polysemous gaze that takes pleasure in the multidimensional presence of the engendered Other. This broader perspective nurtures a very different model of engagement than sexualized vision: rather than focused and dominant, an engendering vision is diffuse and generous. This form of vision mirrors Adler's "shit" method, for it remains attentive, imaginative, and flexible. Just as the *shtetl* cook and the feminist theologian undermine conventional systems, so too a more open, engaged vision can break the hegemony of a monocular focus, and, like the "shit" method, "allow difference and dissonance to trouble the interpretive process."[70] For Adler, vision is only one, and perhaps not even the primary sense through which persons engage others in the world. As engendered and material bodies, we grasp at the world with all our senses, and Adler seeks to heighten our varied sensorial practices. At times, touch and smell absorb crucial features of human experience, but more often the unanticipated mix of senses vitalizes lived experiences. This sense of sensual exposure captures what Fishbein argues her kosher cooks likewise experience in the kitchen. Adler affirms this sensual discovery as a critical knowledge of the world, and situates an engendering vision as part of this human awareness.

We discover an instructive example of this worldly, sensual engagement in ritual performance. Adler appeals to Lawrence Hoffman's notion of a "liturgical field" to expand ritual experience beyond a perfunctory recitation of texts. What happens in this field mimics everyday life in its varied sensorial dimension:

> Much of what we experience in worship is not in the prayerbook at all: the body language of prayer, the sights, smells, and sounds. We stand, bow, sway, kiss *tzitzit* or the Torah scroll, walk in procession, dance. We register visual symbols . . . and smells. . . . We respond to music.[71]

Sight is but one of the sensual modes by which we experience ritual activity. As Adam Seligman and his collaborators argue in *Ritual and Its Consequences,* ritual "is about *doing* more than about saying something."[72] This doing of ritual cultivates a multidimensional sensual experience in which vision responds to the entire "body language" of worship. Such a visual register, one more perceptive of the varied dimensions of human performance, is also a chastened sight, for it cedes authority to other sensual modes of engagement. This integrative, sensual model is one quite different from Wyschogrod's own promotion of vision as *the* primary sense of human achievement. Adler's polysemous vision, in contrast, allows other sensations to unfold and mature. Like the "shit" method, an engendering vision finds its way among the sensual field of splendor. For Adler, we extend Torah when we extend our field of vision.

Adler's discussion of a more robust vision uncovers an anthropology of bodily knowledge. Emotions and senses tell us something about the world, and we should trust their responsive capacities. She contrasts this experiential mode with the more rational, intellectual approach of her own Reform upbringing. Instead of that intellectual focus, Adler explores an engendered anthropology to define human beings "by bodily experience, by emotions, and by sociality, and not merely by their rationality."[73] But an engendered body is also a sexual one, and Adler seeks a language to embrace sexuality without an excessive and obsessive focus upon it. We need a language, Adler tells her readers, that approaches the experiential dimension of our lives. If we experience the world through senses both complex and multidimensional, then we need a language to express this broader field of human practices. To do so, she distinguishes a "*language-*

of" from a "*language-about.*" As we will see below, this difference maps onto Adler's discussion of metaphor and allegory, and carries over to her reading of the Song of Songs and the Genesis creation stories. This contrast also flows from her discussion of vision: a *language-about* functions like a sexualized look as it objectifies the other, while a *language-of* works like an engendering perspective by attending to a broader sensorial canvas.

Adler thinks we all intuitively understand this difference between a *language-of* sexuality and a *language-about* it, even if we might employ somewhat different terms. We accept the more official, public, and "formal language spoken rationally and solemnly in school, in synagogue, in the courtroom, in the doctor's office, or the scientist's laboratory." That discourse is abstract, universal, and (in my favorite expression of Adler's) "juiceless." But we all know this "about" language rarely touches what really "impels us as sexual beings." Underneath such intellectual parlance lies a far more arousing language of the body, "a subterranean language whispered in bedrooms and daydreams, burlesqued and boasted among laughing friends, growled from alleyways over a loaded gun." This is a discourse closer to experience, Adler argues, a *language-of* that speaks "of wants, pleasures, repulsions, and obsessions." In the doctor's office, we hear only speakers "utterly detached from bodies, including their own bodies, their maleness or femaleness, their vulnerabilities, hungers, and delights."[74]

Now, to be sure, there are times we solicit that form of detached language, and would not want our doctors to dwell on personal delights. Adler admits we cannot do without *language-about,* and would not want to dwell only in *language-of.* We certainly gain a reflective distance in our *language-about* that "is part of what makes us fully human." But our current language about sex, like sexualized vision itself, is woefully inadequate:

> A *language-about* must distance us from the immediacy of sexual experience, but if it purges itself of all sensuousness and carnality, it disables our efforts to reflect upon the meaning and ethics of what we feel and do as embodied creatures. What we need is a way of talking about sexuality that *distances* us from sexual experience without *estranging* us from it.

Adler seeks to close the gap between thoughtful reflection and personal experience. She presumes that a *language-of* is more expressive, and so more in tune with embodied experience. She wants a *language-about* that continually turns us back to this embodied experience, but now in a more ethically sensitive manner. Once again Cover's bridge model offers a fruitful vision for a more holistic praxis:

> The task of a theological ethics of sexuality is to bridge the chasm between what is and what ought to be. To take up this task, we will have to remake our language about sexuality so that it is distanced enough for reflection but flexible enough to evoke for us the bodily experiences and feelings that so greatly affect our inner and outer worlds.[75]

Language about embodied experiences ought to make us better practitioners of our sensual moments of encounter. More authentic language yields more wholesome bodily practices.

This is what the biblical Song of Songs attempts to do, for in Adler's reading, we never observe the lovers dance from "some alien moral vantage point. We share their perspective. We experience through their consciousness." In the Song of Songs, we discover a *language-about* that draws us closer to the experiential *language-of,* and so the Song models a language about sexuality that affirms our embodied practices. But this is not how the rabbinic tradition has generally interpreted this text. Instead of an evocative language relating our talk of sexuality to our sensual bodies, the Song of Songs becomes an allegory for the love between Israel and God. For Adler, this *language-about* "distances itself from the erotic relations of real women and men, implicitly undermining their holiness." Adler endeavors to retrieve "the Bible's most vivid representations of sexual love."[76] Where the rabbinical *language-about* empties the text of this erotic imagery, Adler seeks to recover and use it to expose a more engendered vision of sexual relations. We should speak and use a *language-about* to reflect more closely the experiential truth within a *language-of;* but we must also see others within the framework of *language-of.* To see in this way is to ethically affirm the embodied presence of the Other in all his/her sensuality. The Song of Songs cultivates an engendering vision that overcomes a sexualized perspectival gaze. It is the gendered language of visual authenticity.

Adler reads the Song of Songs together with other interpreters, but she largely follows Phyllis Trible's account of the Song as the recovery of a mutual, edifying love to redeem "a love story gone awry." For Trible, the text "speaks from lover to lover with whispers of intimacy, shouts of ecstasy, and silences of consummation."[77] Ilana Pardes also adheres to Trible's account that the Song deviates "from conventional representations of love in the Bible." In the Song we discover two lovers who never consummate their love—it is forever deferred, and the lovers tend to approach and retreat, appear and mysteriously evade the other. But Trible presents a text "with no tensions," for she reads the Song as "out to correct" the patriarchal tradition of Genesis 2–3.[78] Pardes, as Adler notes, reads a more complex text that "both challenges and accepts the authority of patriarchal law over female bodies and female eroticism." Yet even as Adler recognizes this complexity, she nonetheless pursues a less balanced reading, akin to Trible's, in which "carnal love is not an expression of power."[79] In Adler's Song, a polysemous sexuality overcomes a sexualized, objectified body:

> The Song's capacity to give a voice to its female protagonist is directly related to its polymorphous experience of sexuality. Polymorphous eroticism, in which feelings of pleasure are distributed over the entire surface of the body, was regarded by Freud as the most primitive infantile developmental stage (oral-passive). . . . Linking woman's desire to polymorphous eroticism, and to

the entire playground of bodies in relationship, denies this foundational assumption of male sexual dominance.[80]

No longer a body resonate with the "sexual iconography"[81] of genitalia, the feminine figure in the Song enjoys a "polymorphous eroticism" to oppose the objectifying male gaze. This is not Freud's infantile stage, but a more mature exposure of bodily integrity. Where the sexualized perspective recognizes only genitalia, and conceives the entire body as an uncovering of it, here in the Song "feelings of pleasure" overcome sexual stringency, and the entire surface of the body—a "playground of bodies in relationship"—offers a more intense, varied eroticism to the singular focus on sex. This is the "polymorphous experience of sexuality."

Overwhelming the foundational male look, the Song privileges a polymorphous vision of sexual play. The erotic geography is vast and delights all the senses. This eroticism "allows them [the lovers in the Song] to see each other in mountains, and pools, fawns, and doves, and to taste and smell each other in spices, fruit, honey, milk, and wine".[82]

And you, my beloved,
how beautiful you are!
Your eyes are doves.
(Song of Songs 1:15)

And my beloved among the young men
is a branching apricot tree in the wood.
In that shade I have often lingered,
tasting the fruit.
(2:3)

The voice of my love: listen!
bounding over the mountains
toward me, across the hills.
My love is a gazelle, a wild stag.
(2:8–9)

My dove in the clefts of the rock,
in the shadow of the cliff,
let me see you, all of you!
Let me hear your voice,
your delicious song.
I love to look at you.
(2:14)[83]

This poetic language embraces an engendering vision that both situates the gaze within a variegated field of sensual exposure and cultivates a broader canvas of visual pleasure. Adler discovers in the Song an ethics of sexuality to engender a progressive Judaism: "In the Song, genital sexuality is subsumed within an encompassing polymorphous eroticism that makes the lovers equals and connects them to their surroundings." Erotic love turns to the imagination, where it "is its primary erogenous zone." In contrast, a "genitally focused eroticism"—comparable to Adler's account of feminine exposure in *Berakhot* 24a–b—always diminishes the imaginative capacities of embodied selves. It quickly moves to foundations, to stringent and constricting binaries, and speaks a *language-about* far removed from a polymorphous eroticism. The sexualized gaze, Adler claims here, projects a "narrowly focused specificity" to disembody the Other—a form of dis/membering that violates the erotic plentitude of embodied experience.[84]

As a sexualized gaze constricts vision and erotic experience to genitalia, a polymorphous eroticism opens vision to a highly charged metaphorical account of the body. Adler reads the Song of Songs as metaphor, but the rabbis turn it into allegory—they translate the metaphorical *language-of* into a reductive and objectifying allegorical *language-about*. Adler seeks to reclaim this primary metaphorical meaning, one that remains mysteriously but overtly erotic. Recall her discussion of the theological task, in which the theologian negotiates lived experiences with traditional texts to reveal sacred meanings; in the course of this revelatory process, God becomes present. Adler believes the rabbis have dismissed the lived experiences *of* the Song of Songs text in order to turn it into an allegory *about* God's love of Israel. But in Adler's view, the Song poetically exposes sexual human beings, and God's presence confirms this polymorphous eroticism as an authentic human experience. The Song captures a sacred *language-of* to draw us closer to our embodied selves. Rabbinic allegory turns the metaphorical *language-of* into a *language-about* God's love for Israel.

Metaphor and allegory function as rhetorical modes for Adler's reading of vision as either polysemous (metaphor) or sexualized and reductive (allegory). She interprets the Song as metaphor to better speak the *language-of* as both authentic embodied experience and polysemous vision. Yet despite her appeal to "the entire playground of bodies in relationship," or to "an encompassing polymorphous eroticism," or even to the "shit" method, Adler still works with some fundamental binary oppositions: genital/polymorphous eroticism, *language-about/language-of*, allegory/metaphor, sexualized/polysemous vision. And she does not hide her preferential terms nor her texts: the Song of Songs advances a polymorphous, *language-of*, metaphorical, and polysemous vision of engendered Judaism. Indeed, her distinction between metaphor and allegory turns erotic love into the most authentic, because most human of sensual experiences.

Adler's privileging of metaphor over allegory has romantic roots, and she often appropriates common tropes bequeathed by that tradition,[85] distancing metaphor from "literal" readings that "empty language of meaning instead of intensifying its meanings." Yet metaphors can become literal when transformed into "sacred" signification. But this literal "totalization" impoverishes our imagined language of ritual and prayer.[86] Adler enlists Marcia Falk as the most impressive of feminist liturgists who recognize the multivalent character of performative language, even though Adler defends a "spirituality of otherness" to Falk's "unitive spirituality."[87] Falk herself distinguishes metaphor from the literal by appealing to metaphor's imaginative capacity: "the empowering quality of metaphor exists only as long as we remember that it *is* metaphor we are speaking, not literal truth and not fiction. When a metaphor is treated as though it were literal truth, then it becomes a lie." Metaphor "bridges and it leaps," and so lies beyond "literal truth." As a "naming-toward,"[88] metaphor employs more imaginative language of human experience.

Though Falk cautions that metaphor fails as literal truth, Adler believes figural language can still point to it. Yet this truth is neither singular nor uniform, but instead "complex, multivocal, full of resonances, because it is the language of discovery and metamorphosis, the language that points toward the unknown, the language that lights up the darkness." A metaphor, Adler concludes, "has a trajectory, during which it may accumulate meanings unanticipated (or even undesired) by its originators."[89] The multiple and unpredictable meanings of metaphor contrast sharply with the singularity and clarity of allegory:

> Allegorizing the stories or abstracting them flattens all their meanings into a single layer, closes them off to further interpretation, surgically extracts their emotional content, censors all their ambivalences, contradictions, mysteries, and scandals.[90]

The binary is clear: if allegory remains inflexibly singular, metaphor continually yields a diversity of insight; where the one closes off, the other opens to new, imaginative visions; allegory is abstract and so unemotional—it mimics a surgical *language-about*; metaphor is ambivalent and mysterious, and so corresponds to experiential *language-of*. Theological language must be metaphorical, Adler argues, because it speaks to God in the "human language of relationship."[91] In this sense, metaphor is the most human, authentic language of bodily encounter.

The danger lies in replacing metaphor with an allegorical reading that can only reify, and so deaden the metaphorical imagination. The reductive capacity of allegory destroys the multivalent character of expressive language and a polysemous eroticism:

> When a metaphor is reified, frozen into a single category or framework, it is destroyed, first by having its meanings reduced to one, and second, by being perfected. A reified metaphor can no longer be polysemous—literally, many seeded—because its significations have been reduced, its other possible meanings, associations, resonances, winnowed out and discarded.[92]

The Song of Songs redeems metaphor as complex and multivocal, and returns the entire bodily playground to imaginative discoveries. We should not read this text, as Adler claims the rabbis do, as an allegory with "a unidirectional code, cataloguing flat one-to-one correspondences between symbol and abstraction." Instead, we should recognize the Song as a powerful metaphor for erotic relations between men and women, and a new engendering experience of global sensuality:

> Precisely because its eroticism is allusive rather than graphic, globally sensuous rather than reductively genital, the Song can become available once again as a metaphor for relations between man and woman and between God and humanity that are not predicated on differences in power. This richer metaphoric reading strategy frees the imagination, our doorway to the inner worlds of others. . . . The capacity for imaginative eroticism, then, is a potentially redemptive feature of human sexuality.[93]

The Song engenders both God and humanity, drawing them closer to the "inner worlds of others." Its polymorphous eroticism redeems human sexuality, and imaginatively portrays a more authentic relation between men and women. The metaphorical mode, Adler says here, "serves as an erotic common denominator"[94] between human beings, and between human beings and God. This is a sensual playground of whole and authentic bodies.

It is also a visual playground that lays bare the polysemous (rather than genital) character of vision. The Song of Songs can "reverse the rabbis' genitalization of its feminine imagery" and cultivate a polysemous eroticism "as an unspecified territory full of sexual possibilities."[95] Adler wants erotic feelings distributed "over the entire surface of the body" to count as "real sex"—more real, in fact, than genital intercourse. While "penile penetration and ejaculation" count within "holistic eroticism," they are still "not the sole definition of a complete sexual encounter."[96] Here too Adler appeals to a sense of wholeness to capture more authentically the full range of erotic encounters. We must learn to see bodies as more holistic, less concerned with genitalia, and mysteriously open to a range of sensual awareness. So Adler takes Howard Eilberg-Schwartz's work as too singularly focused on the phallus. While she applauds his critique of rabbinic sexual desires, Adler believes Eilberg-Schwartz "does not interrogate the assumption of his rabbinic sources that genital equals sexual." He too easily succumbs to the common perception that "nonphallic eroticism" is "*unreal*" rather than "*hyperreal.*" But Adler's reading of *Berakhot* 24a–b challenges those texts "that systematically reduce women to their genitalia."[97] She enlivens a more diffuse sexuality to expose erotic bodies. This global eroticism presents a new visual optics, for it undermines the sexualized gaze on individual parts of the body and opens a vision of authentic wholeness. When read as imaginative metaphor, the Song of Songs illuminates how to see others as engendered, erotic, and sensual beings.

In one sense Eilberg-Schwartz, and certainly not only him, sexualizes God's body when Adler wants to engender it. God has a body, but one clothed in metaphor rather than allegory. It is also polysemous rather than solely genital, for

God's body remains infinitely mysterious and generative. We tell stories about God, Adler claims, in the rich discourse of ritual performance and prayer. When we get it right, our *language-about* draws us closer to the experiential *language-of*. Adler's engendering vision of the Other highlights a diverse field of erotic wholeness, one that counters a singular and distorted focus on the sexualized body. These radically disparate visions of human authenticity (polysemous and sexualized vision) govern how Adler reads biblical and rabbinic texts, and they ground her provocative reimagining of covenantal marriage at the conclusion to her book. I want to turn, finally, to Adler's reading of the Genesis creation stories as both metaphor and allegory to draw these multiple themes together, and to explore more fully how Adler's reading practices generate claims to visual authenticity.

Embodied Metaphor and Disembodied Allegory: Genesis 1 and 2–3

Adler describes the Genesis creation stories—the "shaping" in Genesis 1 and its "terrible transformation" in Genesis 2–3—as acts of boundary making and maintenance.[98] The sense that something has gone wrong in Genesis 2 has roots in Trible's reading of these stories. Although she criticizes Trible's interpretation here and there, Adler appropriates her basic schema: the first chapter in Genesis reveals a harmonious world that soon becomes estranged in Genesis 2–3, "a love story gone awry."[99] The boundaries created in Genesis 1 out of a formless void "differentiate the primeval wholeness into a multitude of entities." Yet this differentiation retains features of the original harmony. Genesis 1 still maintains "the integrity of entities" flexible enough to accommodate change. To Adler, the boundaries of Genesis 1 sustain and nurture human flourishing:

> Physically, emotionally, ethically, we are best served by boundaries that acknowledge the integrity of both self and other yet are flexible enough to allow for creativity and communion. These are the boundaries advocated by feminist object-relations theorists.

Unlike the male self who, according to these same theorists, violently distances and protects his autonomy from others, Adler's engendered beings negotiate "these delicate calibrations of closeness and distance, interpenetration and distinctness" that characterize fluid boundaries. And origins, in this case, confer authenticity: the fall from flexible to rigid boundaries constitutes a "terrible transformation" from pliant distinctions to unyielding oppositions. "The harmonious world of Genesis 1" becomes a world of "gender polarity" and estrangement in Genesis 2–3.[100]

Still rooted in the fluid balance of the first creation story, human beings enjoy the polymorphous eroticism of engendered persons. Though mindful of textual nuance and language, Adler tends to read the creation stories as ever present possibilities of human encounter. Genesis 1 is less a story about Adam and Eve than it is about human sexuality for us all. Though she does not cite Joseph Soloveitchik's account of the Genesis creation stories in his *Lonely Man of Faith* (1965), she nonetheless adopts his approach to read Genesis 1–3 as existential human encounters. The comparison with Soloveitchik stops here, of course, for he reads these texts in precisely the *opposite* manner in which Adler portrays them in her work. For Soloveitchik, the Adam of Genesis 2 enters into a covenantal community with Eve and God.[101] But to Adler, human sexuality depicted in Genesis 1 offers a glimpse at God's own:

> Something in God seeks to restate itself in flesh and blood. Perhaps it is God's creativity, or delight, or the ingrained yearning for communion with the other that serves as impetus for creation and for covenant. But something in God, in seeking its human mirror, reveals itself as both infinitely varied and utterly whole. That something is, as it were, God's sexuality, which our own sexuality was created to reflect.[102]

Creation in the image and likeness of God (*tselem* and *demut*) engenders a human sexuality as a mirror to God's sexuality. Like Wyschogrod, Adler reads these terms as physical likeness rather than rational relation. And like human polysemous eroticism, God's sexuality is "both infinitely varied and utterly whole." We reflect those nuanced sexual distinctions in our own bodies. And if our own sexuality reflects God's (although Adler's "as it were" suggests the metaphorical play here), then this engendered eroticism is an authentic embodiment of God's image. When we see the Other not as a sexualized body of genitalia but as an erotic one of infinite possibilities, then we more fully reflect that "something in God."

Adler wants to read human sexuality in Genesis 1 as "a metaphor for the infinitude and unity of God." Such a playground of eroticism is at once whole, polysemous, and embodied. The created boundaries are ethically just but flexible, and they cultivate the very kind of engendered vision and practice that Adler seeks in her progressive Judaism. But Genesis 2 closes all of this down, for "the creation of humanity is depicted as a process of opposition and segregation."[103] From a metaphorical world of sexual play, human beings have fallen into an allegorical nightmare. The Adam in Genesis 2 "is both generic human and gendered male. His maleness represents the original human condition, rather than one variety of it." Recall Adler's descriptive imagery for allegorical interpretation: it is abstract, flat, singular, closed, passionless, and lacking in all ambivalence and mystery. An allegorical reading denies the subtlety and imaginative capacities within the text. This Adler does too, but in a way that claims the text *itself* as allegory:

> Genesis 2, then, is a description not of the creation of the universe, but of the creation of the patriarchal perspective, in which the self relates to what

is external to it by subjugating or devouring. Its account of the construction of woman to alleviate man's loneliness, of the process of splitting off and opposing femininity to masculinity, and of the resulting sense of mutilation in patriarchal man resembles the theoretical account offered by feminist object-relations psychology.[104]

This Genesis text, in contrast to its initial chapter, describes a rigid "perspective" representing "the original human condition." Here we find a flat, abstract, "theoretical" and passionless correspondence in which the text and the self signify "to what is external to it." The text functions much like the selves it depicts. The violent oppositions in Genesis 2 estrange selves from their own bodies, and transform the more engendering, harmonious vision in Genesis 1 into a subjugating and devouring one. The "patriarchal perspective" is the sexualized vision of inauthentic creation.

Adler interprets Genesis 1 and Genesis 2–3 as alternative models for reading human sexuality. The metaphorical play in Genesis 1 is the more authentic *language-of* human erotic encounter; the allegorical claims about patriarchy in Genesis 2–3 reveal a *language-about* sexuality that only estranges us from it. The language about sex limits and reifies; but the language drawn from experiential encounter reflects a sexuality in God's image. These two modes of reading mirror Adler's two approaches to vision: the one reductionist and sexualized, the other expansive and engendering. Adler reads texts as she sees them, and I make this linguistic pun in the spirit of Adler's jocular "shit" method. To be attentive, imaginative, and flexible, as this method advocates, means to see the body as polymorphous, erotic, and coherent; and it means to read texts in ways that reveal these sacred meanings. Adler sees this body in Genesis 1, but it is utterly missing in Genesis 2–3. These stories of the patriarchal perspective have no blessings to confer, for they are allegories of a "generic human and gendered male." For Adler, beings are not generic at all, but engendered persons with erotic bodies. We must learn to see these kinds of engendered beings in order to become better readers of the biblical texts, and so more authentic inheritors of our traditions. This is, at its core, the gendered language of visual authenticity.

Adler appeals to coherency, integrity, embodiment, and a polysemous vision as authentic enactments of an engendering Judaism, but these are more than descriptive terms: they are features of a Jewish practice that values personal integrity and just relationships. Adler interweaves these performative values to produce a decidedly provocative text about the meaning and structure of gendered relations. She advances less methodological rigor than heuristic and compelling readings of Jewish texts, and uses well her "shit" method for cultivating an ethically sensitive and multilayered sensual mode of envisioning Judaism. To be sure, there are textual interpretations and ritual practices she wishes to set aside, for they hinder a more just, engendering focus on the *nomic* worlds inhabited by both men and women. This is a call to arms, but it is also a return to a textual tradition open to pluralistic visions, cooperative practices, and erotic bodies. *Engendering Judaism* will fail to convince all its readers, and I too have raised concerns about Adler's interpretive strategies (especially her binary opposition between metaphor and allegory). But Adler develops a larger picture here—a bolder critique of vision in order to engender a different mode of seeing—that I want to pursue, however briefly, in these concluding pages.

Within the discourse of vision and authenticity in modern American Jewish thought, Adler's polysemous vision stands as strong rebuke to the visual embodiment defended by Michael Wyschogrod, discussed in the previous chapter. Recall how Wyschogrod obtained visual certainty of God's presence in the people Israel. His "body of faith" was no metaphor: we could really see God in those Jewish bodies, and this led to some awkward mental gymnastics when he discussed conversion to Judaism. How do converted bodies change into Jewish ones to now expose God's presence? Adler's appeal to metaphor, in strong contrast to Wyschogrod's dismissal of it, takes Marcia Falk's point seriously: "*all* theological naming is really a naming-toward; all honest talk about divinity has an 'as if' embedded in it."[105] Wyschogrod speaks the *language-about* God to reify and so limit God's multifaceted appearance and presence. Both Wyschogrod and Adler seek divine embodiment, but their bodies appear as radically distinct. God inhabits those bodies in some mysterious way for Wyschogrod, and he fears the flight from this physical anthropology to a more conceptual view of God's unity and complete otherness. Adler desires that divine otherness (she even criticizes Falk for drawing God too close to human experience) because she believes only this kind of radical Other can provoke imaginative relations with other physical bodies. She sees God's presence as much as Wyschogrod does, but God arrives to authenticate the sacred work that men and women do together. Wyschogrod's God reveals himself in Jewish bodies; Adler's God confirms what Jews do with their Judaism.

And what they do, in Adler's *Engendering Judaism,* is to make the entire surface of their bodies present before the other. This kind of exposure develops a broader visual landscape, even as it opens to other sensual pleasures. In comparison to this engendered vision, Wyschogrod's focus on God's dwelling in Jewish bodies seems overly constrictive, for one could very well *miss* those bodies for God's presence therein. Adler's work concentrates on Judaism as praxis; Wyschogrod's theology attends to God and God's revelatory appearance. By stretching vision to see more bodily terrain—a polysemous vision rather than a sexualized one—Adler also empowers Jews to do the same. Her *Engendering Judaism* is itself an act of *nomic* creation in the way that Cover has described it: she appeals to stories to cultivate values, and she imagines a future that ties ethical responsibility to the shared work of living together as partners in a sacred order. This is a story, I have argued in this chapter, designed to enrich visual discourse in order to engender a more authentic Jewish practice.

An engendered Judaism is, in Adler's account, a feast for the senses in all the ways that *The Jewish Home Beautiful* and *Kosher by Design* make food a sensual delight. Adler appeals to a polysemous vision, but she also circumscribes its scope within the variegated sensorium of human encounter. Wyschogrod had always been clear about his preferences:

> To some degree, the world reveals itself in smell and touch, hearing and tasting. But a dark world in which odors are smelled, surfaces touched, sounds heard, and flavors tasted but nothing is seen, remains a world that crowds man, that does not open itself but impinges upon him and turns man into a recipient of what the world wishes to deliver to him. Only the seen world, the illuminated world stretches off into the horizon.[106]

I imagine Rachel Adler responding in this way: exactly right, so long as we focus on "a world that crowds man." But this projects a narrow, perhaps even patriarchal vision, dismissing too easily the smells, touches, sounds, and tastes that enliven a "polymorphous eroticism." Wyschogrod should open his eyes to the visual splendors of a polysemous world. He should taste the fruit that Goldberg, Silverman, and Fishbein deliver to their invited guests. This more engendering view, now more alive to *all* the bodily senses, resituates vision within a diverse *nomos* of Jewish practice. We should worry less about how the converted body exposes God's image, Adler might add here, and focus more on the way Jewish praxis draws God's presence into our midst. Adler's progressive Jews see God too, not "in the People Israel," as Wyschogrod's subtitle would have it, but instead in "an Inclusive Theology and Ethics"—Adler's own subtitle for an engendering Judaism. Engendering is an active participle of mutual commitment and trust, and by focusing on what Jews do, Adler sees God's presence in the authentic exposures of men and women stretching themselves into the horizon, together.

6 The Language of Racial Bodies in Melanie Kaye/Kantrowitz's *The Colors of Jews*

> The term "Jew" I associate with white people. I have some conflicting emotions about that. If I say I'm not Jewish because Jewish people are white, it's as if I'm accepting that all Jewish people are white people. Yes, not all Jewish people are white people, I do know that, but at the same time the term "black Jews" doesn't work for me either because it seems to assert that Jewish people are "normally" white. You have these terms, these labels that other people give you, that don't quite work for you, and so you establish your own terms, and those terms are sometimes in reaction to terms that already exist.
>
> —Navonah, in Kaye/Kantrowitz, *The Colors of Jews*

Mrs. i, a married mother of two children, joined Prophet Frank S. Cherry's Church of the Living God in Philadelphia in the late 1930s. She fully participated in Passover observance, accepted two resurrections (the one for good, the other for bad people), and relied on Prophet Cherry as a source of knowledge who could "seal" a person's fate. Conversant in both Yiddish and Hebrew, Prophet Cherry believed he and his congregation of black Jews could trace their lineage within the Hebrew Bible. Like many other black Jewish communities, this one (originally founded at the turn of the twentieth century) appropriated freely from both Jewish and Christian beliefs and practices, and so established a vibrant syncretism of Talmudic lore, baptism by immersion, and Christian hymns together with faith in a black Jesus. When Arthur Huff Fauset introduces Mrs. I in his *Black Gods of the Metropolis*, he notes how his description "closely follows that of the informant," and he offers this telling remark: "Mrs. I. argued with a Jew over a Jewish star she was wearing on her dress. The Jew said that she had no right to it. She upheld her right, and finally she told him that even if he claimed to be white, his damned mammy was a black woman."[1] When Mrs. I and this Jewish white man confront each other, what do they see? How do whiteness and blackness appear to them? Is Jewishness a color, one attached to skin? What claims to authenticity, culture, race, and heritage map onto black and white colors?

Through a reading of Melanie Kaye/Kantrowitz's *The Colors of Jews* (2007), I will explore the language of racial authenticity in the forms that Mrs. I's remarks both manifest and obscure. There is much to disentangle in Mrs. I's charge of mixed inheritance and pure vision, as well as in Fauset's tale of "the Jew" who associates whiteness with Jewish identity, but I will limit my discussion to the rhetorical features of racial discourse, rather than open it up to explore racial identity in Judaism. As in the previous five chapters, I am interested in the visual language of authenticity and in the rhetorical moves that generate and subtend claims to authentic personhood. To begin to understand the language of race as visual discourse, I turn to Kaye/Kantrowitz's highly charged political stance that makes race, vision, and authenticity the critical subjects of her book. Kaye/ Kantrowitz's appeal to a radical diasporism, wherein groups "do not divide along identity lines because they are intrinsically bi- or multi-identified,"[2] is controversial, subtle, and spirited. She interviews a number of prominent religious and political American community leaders, and mobilizes their voices to advance a progressive and tolerant account of Jewish culture. The opening epigraph to this chapter features one of those voices—Navonah, a Hebrew Israelite, who neither accepts that label nor fully relinquishes it—and these interviewees do important work for Kaye/Kantrowitz's politics of disruption, in which "colored" Jews (her term) displace the white–black binary that has produced a vicious form of American racism. In Kaye/Kantrowitz's recovery of Jewish diversity, the colors of Jews emerge as a kaleidoscopic vision of diasporic politics and authentic culture.

The Colors of Jews is a book about visual authenticity and the rhetoric of racial bodies. Kaye/Kantrowitz (b. 1945) positions her radical politics, and the textual voices like Navonah's, as both rhetorical and visual modes of racial discourse. So even as Kaye/Kantrowitz presents her informants as exemplars of a racial politics moving beyond racism, those voices articulate claims about authentic heritage, culture, and religion as visual, racial categories. Like Navonah, Kaye/Kantrowitz continues to talk about race even as she tries to escape it, and in so doing reveals *how* racial labeling invokes claims to visual authenticity. *The Colors of Jews* produces visions of seeing Jewish by constructing racial authenticity as a visual category.

Kaye/Kantrowitz and her interviewees struggle with a language to describe Jews. The term *black Jews,* as Navonah's comments make clear, is a problematic label for groups like the community at Prophet Cherry's Church of God. The phrase reduces the diversity of a Judaism steeped in biblical literacy and black culture to a black–white binary. Even more, the label breaks down because, as Mrs. I recognizes all too well, blackness is rarely conceived as integral to Jewish identity (there are Jews, and then there are black Jews). Many black Jews prefer the name *Black Israelites* or *Black Hebrews,* but even here persons deploy these terms only to classify and assess, rather than to understand the function and scope of religious diversity.[3] Black Judaism is a complex practice, as Jacob S. Dorman makes clear in his recent history of Black Israelite religions. Dorman believes these traditions are "better thought of as ever-evolving, kinetic polycultural assemblages than as reified, bounded 'isms.'"[4] Yet scholars and practitioners alike focus on two competing accounts that do tend to reify this complexity. The one highlights pluralism and the need for white Jews to recognize the diversity and challenges of a vibrant religious culture. The other focuses on black Jews who straddle black and white Jewish cultural traditions. Where the former seeks to open space for black cultural expression within Judaism, the latter exposes the conflicting drama that many black Jews perform in and through their commitments to Judaism and blackness (but here again, the Jewish–black divide often remains in place).

The focus of this chapter is to show *how* these descriptive labels articulate cultural, racial, and historical claims about authenticity, roots, and heritage. I begin with a general account of *The Colors of Jews* to situate my close reading of the interviews within the text. Those interviews expose descriptive, racial labels as claims to visual authenticity. These claims are central to the story I have been tracking in this book, for they position the rhetoric of race at the very center of the modern Jewish narrative about visual authenticity. Kaye/Kantrowitz's interviewees offer a more inclusive yet ever expansive sense of Jewish diasporic identity. But these textual voices, like Navonah's that opened this chapter, struggle to articulate this diasporic position because they too are caught up in racial categories that both challenge and presume the black–white boundary. They struggle for a language to explore racial authenticity that is both visual and uplifting. In her attempt to capture this language, Kaye/Kantrowitz critically examines the longing for home. On the one hand, she privileges the diasporic wandering that Rosenblatt, among others, sought to displace by rooting identity in the soil. But on the other, Kaye/Kantrowitz confers an authentic presence to those who have too often resided outside the visual markings of Jewish identity. Within this fraught dynamic of homecoming and alienation, the rhetoric of race appears as a vexing but ever present exposure of visual authenticity.

The Colors of Jews

The Colors of Jews is a political work designed to interrogate and sabotage common presumptions about Jewish identity. It is also an American text, for much of the racial politics and notions of Diaspora circulate within an American history of racism, slavery, and Jewish immigration. Melanie Kaye/Kantrowitz has worked tirelessly for years to raise social and racial justice issues to the forefront of American Jewish politics. She is of a vanguard that pursues the liberal concept of *tikkun olam* (repairing the world) in the streets, as it were, regarding and fighting inequality against one as an injustice to all. In many ways, her book also pursues a political act of solidarity as she builds alliances among social, cultural, religious, and political institutions. She devotes two of her six chapters to extensive interviews of leaders who work for racial, economic justice (chapter 4) and racial, ethnic diversity (chapter 5), and she admirably initiates coalitions between them. These coalitions tether radical politics to racial justice. In producing a confrontational text in racial politics, Kaye/Kantrowitz asks: "How do we challenge what we have no language to discuss?"[5] *The Colors of Jews* responds to that challenge through a discourse of diasporic identity and ethnic diversity.

Kaye/Kantrowitz deploys the term *Diaspora* carefully and with precision. Diasporic identity is a mode of being-in-the-world that seeks out the stranger, that builds coalitions and solidarity with radical others, that fights for justice "wherever we are," and that values "multicultural complexities."[6] It counters the nationalist focus of Zionist rhetoric and replaces appeals to the center for images of longing, searching, crossing, and wandering. Kaye/Kantrowitz promotes the "intrinsically bi- or multi-identified" Jews in her text as those best situated to fashion this diasporic existence. They already cross borders, yearn for solidarity, and value "motion, fluidity, and multiple vision."[7] Regrettably, Kaye/Kantrowitz directs her text more to converted diasporists like herself than to the unrepentant. She seeks political alliances among those prepared to advance a diasporic existence, but those labeled "fundamentalist" or "right-wing" remain beyond her progressive boundary.[8] Yet even if limited in this way, *The Colors of Jews* advances a vocabulary of racial exposure that expands the diasporic frontier to include Jews often excluded or marginalized because of the color of their skin. Borders must be crossed if Jews are to see themselves as a diasporic community of racial diversity.

For Kaye/Kantrowitz, the term *colored* displaces the bipolar American representations of black and white. To be sure, proposing a third term trades off the other two, so the black/white binary, though dislodged, still remains in force to some extent. This in part explains Kaye/Kantrowitz's desire to move beyond racial language even as she resides firmly within it, and she recognizes this paradox: "It's hard to talk about racial categorization without seeming to accept or even endorse it."[9] For Kaye/Kantrowitz, the category "colored" functions as a buffer between racial perceptions of white and black. This mediating, "colored" term serves as a placeholder for the accused: "colored" Americans are blamed for making money, moving up, competing for jobs, and being sneaky-smart in ways both manipulative and undeserving. But what about the Jews? Where do they fit into this tripartite system? Here Kaye/Kantrowitz's confrontational, sardonic rhetoric is most powerful:

> By now it should be obvious. Mongrels to white supremacists; infidels who continue to refuse the true faith; associated historically with white slavery, prostitution, and syphilis; so good with money you could fairly say Jews ARE money; rootless cosmopolitans tenaciously associated with the impulse to control Christians with Jews' ill-gotten gains and clannish plotting, through

depraved sexual vices, and a sterile degenerate materialistic culture: Jews lodge somewhere between the categories *white* and *colored,* slipping back and forth according to context.[10]

Jews *should* be "colored," Kaye/Kantrowitz seems to imply, but sometimes become white *because* they are so good at being "colored." Jews could pass as white and (so terrifying to supposedly authentic whites) nobody would notice.[11] In marking this buffer zone, Kaye/Kantrowitz describes Jews (like other "colored" groups) as those who undermine the black–white binary, and so advance a "mixed" and more diasporic sense of shifting communities and identities.

Colored Jews—Kaye/Kantrowitz's term for those marginalized and in-between who cross borders in order to build multicultural coalitions—are thereby critical players in her progressive vision of racial and economic justice. Such Jews "can be enormous assets in helping the Jewish world enter a multicultural arena girded appropriately for the struggle against racism and anti-semitism." Coalition building among diverse groups becomes possible, for if one can be "black and Jewish, then the inevitable impossible-to-bridge binary vanishes and we stand on seriously common ground."[12] Not only black and Jewish, but also Latino, Asian, and Egyptian and Jewish—to name only a few diasporic identities— become modalities ripe for border crossings (even if, as I have done here, one still circumscribes identity by geography). Kaye/Kantrowitz asks us to conceive such a world in which boundaries no longer divide outsiders but enable diverse worlds to collide:

> Imagine the possibilities of groups that do not divide along identity lines because they are intrinsically bi- or multi-identified, with all the subtlety and nuances multiple experience can afford. Imagine the possibilities of conversations that include and express the perspectives of those who are both Jewish and black, conversations about economic and social crises, about race relations, even about the Middle Passage / Slavery and the Holocaust.[13]

To jumpstart those conversations, Kaye/Kantrowitz interviews Jews of color and includes their compelling testimony in her book. These voices function as those "enormous assets" that can move readers to a more vibrant, open, and wandering form of diasporic living. Kaye/Kantrowitz positions these voices as testimonial utterances to a "colored" identity in America. Through their words we hear struggles to undermine the white–black binary, and we are called to respond to their desires for new coalitions of racial pluralism. But we also hear claims to visual authenticity, to legitimate heritage, and to genuine culture. These claims articulate a rhetorical mode of seeing Jewish as "colored."

Kaye/Kantrowitz arranges many of her chapters with introductory material followed by lengthy interviews. This format suggests that her interviewees speak on their own terms, in their own voice. But these voices communicate through

Kaye/Kantrowitz. She deploys them to work toward a diasporic community—providing context, building expectations, constructing dialogue, and framing modes of reading—so that her interviewees fit within her diasporic model. Many of Kaye/Kantrowitz's interviewees are well-known outside her book, and some readers might be more aware of their views than other readers. But I explore *how* Kaye/Kantrowitz rhetorically positions their voices *within her text* to construct racial discourse as a mode of authentic racial vision.

Yavilah McCoy and Seeing Race

The interpretive frame in Kaye/Kantrowitz's second chapter, "Black/Jewish Imaginary and Real," is primarily visual. After illustrating the honored memory of the black–Jewish alliance—visually enacted by the photograph of Abraham Joshua Heschel marching along with Dr. Martin Luther King in Alabama—and the equally powerful fantasy that African Americans "are particularly anti-Semitic," Kaye/Kantrowitz takes stock of her imagined communities and offers this insight:

> But look what I've done linguistically, what we do constantly: assume that African Americans and Jews are absolute impenetrable opposites. Assume *black* means *not-Jewish* and *Jewish* means *not-black*. The alacrity with which African American/Jewish opposition is imagined results in a perpetual disappearing act, whereby those who are both black and Jewish become unimaginable. African American Jews in the popular imagination don't exist.[14]

A cultural sensibility (African American/Jewish opposition) has produced an absurd visual image (African American Jews). Such conditionality of the visual authorizes more than the ordinary claim that how we see governs what we see. Visuality—the modes and frames in and through which we see things—goes further back, when cultural value made such visionary frames possible. So here the African American/Jewish opposition already constitutes the visual field for African American Jews. Black Jews cannot be seen because they cannot plausibly exist within this set of social images. Cultural assumptions enable some meanings to be recognizable, and others to be unimaginable and so unseen.

The very term *black Jews* is part of a visual and cultural discourse about race. Historian Matthew Frye Jacobson highlights the visual features of race in America, such that racial distinctions presuppose and articulate perceptual categories as well:

> Like Irishness, Italianness, Greekness, and other probationary whitenesses, visible Jewishness in American culture between the mid-nineteenth and mid-twentieth centuries represented a complex process of social value *become* perception: social and political meanings attached to Jewishness generate a kind of physiognomical surveillance that renders Jewishness itself discernible as a particular pattern of physical traits (skin color, nose shape, hair color and

texture, and the like)—what Blumenbach called "the fundamental configuration of face."

These "visible markers" now register as "outer signs of an essential, immutable, inner moral-intellectual character" that in turn justifies the social value attached to Jewishness: the interpretive circle is firmly closed and self-referential.[15] Racial character has become perceptible in modes that work to confirm racial prejudice. So too in attaching value to *black* and *Jew* in the term *black Jews*: racial character (blackness) becomes perceptible in a category (black Jews) that confirms racial prejudice (Jews, without qualification, are white). Note, however, how Jacobson appeals to a sterile Jewishness polluted only by the assignment of social value. Such Jewishness becomes "discernible"—it only takes visual shape—at the moment those "social and political meanings" attach to it. Without those meanings, Jewishness remains hidden and untraceable. So it is not so much a process of "social value *become* perception" as it is a claim about how social value *constitutes* perception. Coupling race "as a conceptual category" with race "as a perceptual category"[16] allows Jacobson to reveal how social and political meanings enable and so organize visual differences.

Kaye/Kantrowitz wants to reorganize those visual registers. The problem, as she sees it, is that our perceptual categories fail to account for mixed inheritance, "colored" identities, and porous boundaries. We cannot see "colored" Jews but only blacks who are Jewish. And this linguistic "we" is a white "we" now visually impaired from a broader engagement with "the multiracial, multicultural nature of Jewish community."[17] Kaye/Kantrowitz's imagined readers are white Jews who fail to see black Jews because (and this is the force of the prohibition) they ought not to see in these ways. Established notions of an authentic, natural Jewish community inhibit full exposure. The portrait photography that accompanies the three interviews in her second chapter makes these multiracial faces visible to Kaye/Kantrowitz's audience. These photographs create visual truth, and the related texts give voice to this new imaginary. This is an ethics of exposure and an aesthetics of witnessing. The prohibition has been visually annulled. Blindness is overcome by revelation.

That revelation speaks through the image, such that testimony gains a face. But when Yavilah McCoy's image appears on page thirty-seven, the reader has already heard her speak twice. Kaye/Kantrowitz introduces McCoy at the very beginning of her book, and once again some twenty-seven pages later when she inserts a more extensive quotation. In both textual utterances, McCoy discusses Jews of color and her own experience as both "Jewish" and "black." By the time the reader gazes at McCoy's facial image on page thirty-seven, she knows a few things about her: 1) she is, according to Kaye/Kantrowitz, an "African American/Jew"; 2) McCoy calls herself Jewish but others label her black, believing a Jew of color must be a convert or adopted; 3) when McCoy says "of color," she means "having dark skin"; and 4) McCoy wishes she could simply "BE" a Jewish person of color. Later in *The Colors of Jews,* Kaye/Kantrowitz offers a more extensive biography of McCoy as a Jewish-educated writer, editor, and promoter of Jewish diversity. She dedicates another six pages to an interview with McCoy about *Ayecha*—her programs and resources for teaching Jews about diversity. But even if the reader has not skipped ahead to read this background material, she still arrives at McCoy's image with a visual apparatus already at work. Kaye/Kantrowitz positions that image as black and Jewish, as an "African American/Jew" who has "dark skin," but who desires a skin less marked and scarred by American perceptual claims about race. McCoy blames American attitudes about skin color, and appeals to an authentic heritage to oppose them:

> Historically, Jews have been multiple skin colors and it's unfortunate that the passive internalization of color consciousness that happens so easily in American society, helped us to forget the freedom from identifying around color that is a part of our Jewish history.[18]

McCoy's voice articulates claims about authenticity and heritage that resonate throughout *The Colors of Jews.* American perceptions of Jewish racial heritage contradict the historical record. A genuine history should become "our" Jewish history, such that a "colored" heritage reveals a more authentic source of Jewish freedom and identity. Color consciousness has historical roots, and McCoy seeks a time when "identifying around color" will no longer be a live cultural option.

Visual images are both witness and testimony in this book, for readers hear McCoy speak the words on the physical page through the accompanying photograph that Kaye/Kantrowitz positions to the side. This visual and material inscription captures both image and text as material protest. But when McCoy discusses her Hasidic elementary school, do visual readers hear her textual voice through the image of a black, Jewish, and/or "dark skinned" woman? How do persons see this textual image? Like the other facial images that follow, McCoy stares directly at the camera lens and, by extension, at the reader. This gaze confronts, and so taunts the subtitle to these pages: "Am I possible?"[19] Kaye/Kantrowitz employs these visual images with texts in order to dislodge this "I" from the white–black binary: readers, she hopes, will see neither black nor Jewish but "colored." The juxtaposition of photograph with personal commentary on the pages of *The Colors of Jews* offers words and images with sounds and inscriptions. The relational movements of texts and photographs forestall a quick fixing of identity within a visual map or a written word. Kaye/Kantrowitz constructs words to see as personified colors, and images to hear as textual witness. Readers see black ink on white paper, but they also recognize a face that speaks words of diasporic wanderings beyond racial divides.

McCoy recalls the first time she heard the word *shvartse* in school, as the Yiddish term for a black person. She also remembers the racist stereotypes many of her female classmates projected onto black bodies. Like my own grandfather, who often uttered racist comments about others but not about those he knew personally, these girls never saw Yavilah McCoy as a *shvartse*. She did not count as black in that Yiddish sense. Her status was exceptional, even though Yavilah found herself stuck between two cultures. For these (presumably white) elementary-school girls, black means those "monkeys" who go to public schools.[20] *Shvartse* constituted a foreign other, an animalistic body of appetites without intellectual prowess. Yet these girls had no language to account for Yavilah's multiracial identity; their rhetorical powers were limited and confined. They feared that touching her would turn their own skin black. Blackness was a physical disease that could infect others. It was her danger to their purity. In McCoy's telling, only her blackness could pollute and blacken: their touch could not whiten her skin. Blackness could stain and tarnish, but whiteness, when confronted by the black caress, revealed itself less as pigment than as state of being. And yet as physical disease transferred through touch, blackness could radically transform the state of being white. The white skin materially reveals an inward but porous sense of whiteness. Blackness is, to adopt a phrase, a white man's disease: it is to be feared by defenseless whiteness. These racial fears circulate among sexual and gender fantasies of the black male body dominating and contaminating the innocent white female. The elementary school girls *require* protection from those black public school bodies. It is bad enough that Yavilah has infiltrated their sanctuary. Though she is not a *shvartse* like those other black kids, Yavilah is black where it matters most: she can learn and play Jewish, but she does so as black disease.

Kaye/Kantrowitz constructs her interview with Yavilah to counter this racism and black–white binary. In so doing, she reveals a "colored" Jew of mixed heritage who disrupts racial categories. As an example of that third, unruly term "colored," Yavilah struggles to identify with a Jewish community wedded to a binary logic:

> The hardest thing was knowing that racism had become a part of the culture that my parents had so trustingly come to in search of truth, and realizing that the admission of one, eight, or twenty people of dark skin to "the fold" of the community we lived in, had not changed any of the preconceived notions around race, that existed and were upheld by members of the community.[21]

McCoy confronts this culture as multiracial, as both insider and outsider, and this equivocal border status raises visual unrest. This is precisely what Kaye/Kantrowitz believes "colored" Jews can do: they overcome policed boundaries in order to build broader alliances of diasporic communities. But in Yavilah's elementary school, the white kids reside firmly in place, and possess that sense of security that only insiders truly feel. Those from elsewhere must seek admittance to "the fold"—and McCoy's use of this insider language, cited within quotation marks, locates her both within and outside this Jewish community. I want to highlight this insider status of whiteness, together with its intractability, because so much of McCoy's estrangement and disappointment react to it. Add one, eight, or even twenty dark-skinned persons to the fold, and still the "preconceived notions around race" remain unchanged. For these white Jews to see race, indeed to see their own racial bodies, they must recognize an outsider like Yavilah as a true insider. Disclosure comes from without, not from within an insular fold in which "racism had become a part of the culture." This is why Kaye/Kantrowitz believes that "colored" Jews are "enormous assets" in helping white Jews recognize their own racial dispositions.[22] To recognize authentic truth requires touching blackness so that it contaminates and undermines entrenched racial codes. To be authentic, white Jewish culture requires black bodies.[23]

The young Jewish girls in the Hasidic elementary school believed that touching Yavilah's skin might cause their own to darken. McCoy harbors a similar fear about the Jewish community: being a member of the fold might contaminate her own notions of race and culture. But if Jewish culture harbors white inauthenticity, why, then, would McCoy's parents search for truth there? What accounts for their (and her) trust in Judaism? To explain that conviction, McCoy distances Jewish culture from instances of religious practice and faith. In a later interview in *The Colors of Jews,* she describes her parents as "seekers of the truth" who "came to the Orthodox community looking for answers and, in converting, felt that they had made a spiritual link to the past and future of the Jewish people." That link fastens truth to Jewish religion and peoplehood as a spiritual journey— a common trope in contemporary religion, and one that Fishbein employed to great effect in her *Kosher by Design.* McCoy's parents seek truth within a religious journey, but find white racism in culture. This distinction between culture and religion informs McCoy's notion of Jewish identity:

> I was reared in the yeshiva system from age four to seventeen and my growth into my own Jewish identity has been about appreciating the various entry points that there can be for "Jewish" identity and noticing, through the model of my grandparents, that being "Jewish" does not always begin with a ceremony or the trappings of a recognizable Jewish exterior, but on the inside in the choices people make regarding how they will live their lives.[24]

The trappings of a Jewish exterior (without quotation marks) distinguish a public culture from a private Jewish identity. A "Jewish" identity on the inside is always in the making, and so requires quotation marks to indicate its constructed status. But a recognizable Jewish exterior, by contrast, suggests a stubborn, inauthentic culture burdened by racial trappings. Note too, that Kaye/Kantrowitz adds the quotation marks here to highlight McCoy's comments within the ideological boundaries of her text. Perhaps McCoy performed hand signals, as persons often do, to indicate grammatical notes around a phrase. Still, in reading *The Colors of Jews,* we hear McCoy through Kaye/Kantrowitz's text, and that text suggests how authentic Judaism is far less an inherited culture and much more a spiritual journey for those seeking religious truth. This appeal to a rediscovered spirituality is a critical, rhetorical claim of racial authenticity.

Rabbi Angela Warnick Buchdahl,[25] introduced by Kaye/Kantrowitz as "a mixed heritage Korean/Ashkenazi," clarifies why "colored" Jews like McCoy find the language of cultural Judaism so problematic. For many white Ashkenazi Jews, cultural Judaism offers a common heritage often "tied to Jewish immigrant life." Its appeal to Yiddish and Eastern European culture is both popular and effortless as it grounds identity in a common heritage. This is the kind of heritage that Heschel, Schor, Wyschogrod, and even Fishbein trade upon and presume throughout their works. Recall, for example, Fishbein's appeal to Brooklyn and Queens as the geographical and authentic source for her challah napkin rings. These places signify, to adopt Levy's advertisement campaign, real Jewish culture. But for those who neither share nor find meaning in this heritage, their Judaism, according to Buchdahl, "threatens cultural Jews in several ways":

> First it seems to dilute collective Jewish cultural memory—what happens when half the congregation has no relatives from Brooklyn? Secondly, multi-ethnic Jews may seem to taint the purity of Jewish ethnic culture by introducing elements of different traditions into the Jewish community. Lastly, and perhaps most difficult of all, because many multi-ethnic Jews have had to base their Jewish identity on foundations entirely separate from ethnic affiliation, they call into question the very validity of cultural Judaism, because they demonstrate a Jewish identity based solely on actively chosen, religious affiliation.[26]

McCoy's young schoolmates harbored notions of a pure Jewish white culture, and feared its demise through the black touch. Their Yiddish term *shvartse* conveys both racial insensitivity and cultural knowledge, but it also seeks to defend "their" Brooklyn heritage from unknown foreigners. Appeals to cultural Judaism are a form of boundary maintenance and a rhetorical strategy of protection. A Judaism discovered "on the inside in the choices people make" endangers a Judaism grounded in culture or rooted in ethnicity. These cultures and ethnicities, so McCoy and others suggest, are far more mixed, dispersed, and "colored." Seeing Yavilah McCoy incites this borderless anxiety, but it also turns the rhetoric of authenticity into a racial vision.

Rabbi Capers Funnye and Authentic Heritage

The rhetorical appeal to authentic Jewish identity persists in Kaye/Kantrowitz's interview with Rabbi Capers Funnye. While readers might not have heard of Yavilah McCoy before reading *The Colors of Jews,* they may be familiar with Rabbi Funnye (pronounced Fu-NAY), who has become quite well-known outside

Jewish circles. Born in South Carolina in 1952 but raised in Chicago as an African Methodist, Funnye converted to Judaism upon meeting Rabbi Robert Devine in 1971 and hearing his message about calling Africans the true descendants of the biblical Israelites. Devine's House of Israel Congregation had its roots in the Black Judaism of William Saunders Crowdy's Church of God and Saints of Christ community in Lawrence, Kansas, founded in 1896.[27] Crowdy's church is often associated with the beginning of black Jewish practice in America. His syncretic mix of Christian traditions with Jewish observance suggested a "Hebraic-Christian or Judeo-Christian" practice, one that selectively and eclectically appropriated from both traditions. A former Baptist preacher born into slavery, Crowdy could simultaneously venerate Jesus Christ and celebrate Passover, believe Africans were the descendants of the Ten Lost Tribes of Israel, and observe the Sabbath. According to Yvonne Chireau, this pattern of selectively appropriating Jewish and Christian doctrine and practice was typical of early black Jewish communities in America.[28] Indeed, Prophet Frank Cherry's Church of the Living God (where Mrs. I worshiped) followed Crowdy's form of Jewish and Christian practices and beliefs, as did many other black Jewish congregations that surfaced at the turn of the twentieth century—especially in the years 1908–1925 during the Great Migration of southern blacks to northern urban centers.[29] But Funnye found greater appeal in Levi Ben Levy's vision of a Judaism cleansed of Christian notions (as Funnye tells it, "He taught me that real Judaism isn't mixed in with Christianity"), and he received rabbinical ordination within Levy's Hebrew Israelite movement in 1985.[30] Funnye is at the time of this writing the rabbi of Beth Shalom B'nai Zaken Ethiopian Hebrew congregation in Chicago.[31]

Perhaps more than McCoy, Funnye cultivates a presence outside the text as a public, religious figure. But like McCoy, he challenges appeals to cultural Judaism, recuperates a Jewish heritage to replace it, and describes religion as a spiritual quest. In his recovery of an ancient, black heritage, Funnye accentuates Jewish spirituality and soul, but still has much to say about race and notions of authenticity. He seeks a broad alliance and a more inclusive Jewish community that recognizes diverse and competing heritage claims. From the excerpts in *The Colors of Jews*, Funnye presents a thoughtful, balanced, and corrective voice to the often hardened claims by both white and black Jews. Yet his textual voice still reveals how rhetorical claims to visual authenticity are racial exposures of identity.

Kaye/Kantrowitz presents Funnye's vision as both transparent and compelling: by narrowing the influence of cultural inheritance upon Jewish religion, Funnye opens Judaism to a broader coalition of religious searchers. Even more, he can reduce the significant impact of Ashkenazi, European heritage on Jewish practice. This is an important move, for it allows many Jews to engage Judaism without appropriating a cultural legacy as well. Without culture at its center, Judaism now becomes for Funnye a spiritual awakening:

I was drawn to Judaism as a spiritual quest, a lack of spiritual fulfillment I found in other faiths. I tried on Islam for a while. But Judaism just seemed to fit my soul. Judaism is not just something folks are born into. Some, yes. But don't the kabbalists tell us that each human being has a spark and those sparks go into the world. They can go into any soul.[32]

Cultural inheritance, once integral to religious identity, has receded before spiritual traditions now discovered as alternative faiths within the religious marketplace. One cannot try on a culture in quite the same way as a spiritual quest: cultural literacy can take years to acquire, and the sense of being at home often longer. But Judaism, like Islam and other faiths, travels lightly, unburdening itself from this kind of heavy cultural baggage. As a religious quest, Judaism captures a sensibility, a worldview, and a spiritual comportment. One need not enjoy gefilte fish, or even know what it is to feel that "spark" of Jewishness.

Yet a return to religious roots is precisely that: a ground recaptured, a sensibility reawakened, a quest fulfilled. Funnye and others who travel beyond have never really left home: "Many people feel that when some people come to Judaism they were Jews already, they had a Jewish soul, a calling to Judaism."[33] This sense of homecoming, Funnye asserts, belies a reversion to Judaism, rather than a conversion to it.[34] The rhetorical move here is important. A Jewish calling appropriates a spiritual rather than a cultural legacy, but confers recognition in equal measure, thereby legitimating religious reversion as authentic spirituality: "So our return is a return to the worship of our forefathers, not necessarily trying to immolate or imitate Ashkenazi Jewry."[35] An authentic, African heritage of "Hebraic stock"[36] affirms a distinctive culture to counter the mass appeal of Ashkenazi lineage. Funnye's Judaism is both a spiritual quest of the soul and an African heritage of Jewish authenticity.

Spiritual quests overcome racial divides and cultural inheritance—this is part of their rhetorical force, for religion touches the soul directly without cultural mediation. Divine sparks—untainted by history, culture, and tradition—go into any soul. And yet Funnye still appeals to authentic heritage to offset racial assumptions about black conversion. Here he carefully weaves together two competing narratives of Jewish identity: the one rooted in biological descent and cultural inheritance, and the other cultivated in a spiritual calling. He appeases those who still hold to a racial or familial notion of chosenness, even as he expands that category to include anyone with a religious spark recovered. Appealing to this inner sense of "soul," Funnye deflects cultural capital in the form of food ways, habits, and customs—indeed many of the elements that Mordecai Kaplan associated with Judaism as a civilization—and instead situates culture alongside, but not integrally related to, an inner spiritual longing. The focus on the one (culture) often neglects the power of the other (spirituality), and so Funnye seeks to redress the inequality. It is a careful balance and delicate dance to claim both a spiritual and cultural legacy. Funnye often succeeds in finding a compelling middle ground, but he apparently still longs for cultural and familial roots:

> Many years after I converted to Judaism, became very much a practicing Jew, I started digging into my family's history. My mother's mother's name before she was married was Rosella Cohen. Her mother's name was Tamara Cohen. And her husband's name was Cesar Cohen. Is there a connection? I can't prove that definitively but the names suggest it.[37]

What moves Funnye to imply that his forebears held "Jewish" names? Why even appeal to a biological heritage if the spiritual one more than suffices? Here too we can sense that peculiar anxiety of (in)authenticity that haunts rhetorical appeals to origins in order to support innovative practices. Funnye certainly did not revert to Judaism out of loyalty to his Jewish heritage. In fact, he emphasizes that he only learned of this heritage *after* he "became very much a practicing Jew." But the names reaffirm the authenticity of his "reversion"[38] because he had never really left his Jewish heritage. He recovers what had always been his birthright. He appeals to familial heritage to help justify his claim to reverting rather than converting to Judaism (although Funnye describes his turn to Judaism as conversion in the quotation above, he is clear throughout that this describes a return from within). His spiritual quest takes flight upon the bedrock of cultural heritage, and his spiritual journey is no flight of fancy: it is an authentic recovery of lost origins. This too is a critical rhetorical device of authentic heritage production.

Funnye appeals to his Jewish inheritance in order to claim his "reversion" to Judaism as genuine. Associating with names like Rosella, Tamara, and Cesar Cohen, he looks back to a recognizable, familiar inheritance. But he also appeals to an authentic African Jewish heritage: "Jews became a people on the continent of Africa. The Torah was given on the continent of Africa. Sinai is a part of Africa, not Asia."[39] His return to Judaism really is "a return to the worship of our forefathers, not necessarily trying to immolate or imitate Ashkenazi Jewry."[40] Where McCoy's Jewish spirituality lies in the existential freedom of choices made "on the inside," Funnye feels the weight and allure of cultural heritage, and he recognizes that Torah is both a cultural and geographical inheritance. His spiritual quest neither begins in a vacuum nor ends in a bodiless soul.

But it does begin, and here the rhetorical claims to authenticity interweave with racial discourse. Funnye's assertion that Africa remains the home of revealed Torah is more than a geographical claim to ownership; it is a claim about racial origins. The Jews who became a people there were not white Ashkenazi Jews who were somehow transplanted into Africa. The original Jews, in other words, were part of Funnye's familial legacy, sharing his heritage and culture. According to Bernard J. Wolfson, Funnye believes his ancestors were originally Jews before arriving in America as slaves. His Judaism, argues Wolfson, "was thus a reaffirmation and a celebration of his African heritage."[41] So when Funnye discovers ancestors with the name Cohen, he does not recover a white, Ashkenazi lineage but instead defends black Africans as authentically Jewish. Rosella, Tamara, and Cesar Cohen are part of his black ancestry—they are his forebears. Funnye's voice helps to dislodge the insider status often assumed by and for white Jews. Simply, he reverses the racial gaze: there are Jews, and then there are white Jews. The original owners in this story were African Jews, not aunts from Brooklyn. Funnye comes back home to his forebears, and so transforms the visual landscape of Jewish dwellings.

Navonah and Racial Categories

Rediscovering a forgotten home, as Capers Funnye depicts in *The Colors of Jews*, evokes racial claims to authenticity: the original Jews were African people who received the Torah in Africa. But the language of spiritual quest that both Funnye and McCoy adopt tends to work against such appeals to origins, race, and heritage. There are multiple discourses running through these texts, and though many of Kaye/Kantrowitz's interviewees would prefer to move beyond racial language (as even Kaye/Kantrowitz would like to do), they still work with racial imagery, tethering claims to authenticity with perception. Concerns about visual authenticity are front and center in Kaye/Kantrowitz's interview with Navonah, whose insightful words mark the epigraph to this chapter. She recognizes the inadequacy and messiness of her racial terms, and yet continues to employ them. Note how the interview begins:

> I was born into law and I grew up to practice of [sic] the Old Testament observing the law. I would go to the temple and observe Rosh Hashanah, Hanukkah, Yom Kippur, Passover, all the high holy days. I grew up going to temple as part of my life. It's my faith, it's something I maintain and carry with me as a major part of who I am.[42]

Here one reads language often associated with Christianity—born into law, faith, Old Testament—mixed in with Jewish observance days and appeals to an authentic self. Navonah's account of law focuses on specific ritual practices, and she ties her faith to those forms of observance. Her notion of *halakhah* centers on obeying the law rather than adopting a more encompassing comportment toward the world. Her faithful practice marks her identity as religious. Missing in this account, of course, are the terms *Jewish* and *Judaism*. Navonah does not call herself Jewish; as she states it, "the term 'Jew' I associate with white people." She belongs to a self-proclaimed Hebrew Israelite community with lineage to the biblical Jacob (white Jews, she was taught, derive from the line of Esau).[43] This claim to biblical heritage circulates within a racial history that establishes her religious community. She too has biblical ancestors, even if not "Jewish" ones. As one "born into law," Navonah describes not a spiritual rebirth but a racial, ethnic, and cultural adoption of a more complex and weighty religious tradition.

Navonah recognizes this complexity, for she qualifies her claims to heritage and racial ancestry with the passive language of schooling: "I was taught that." As an educator myself, I often witness the peculiar gap between instruction and its appropriation as self-knowledge. This distancing from received wisdom ("I was taught that") situates Navonah at once within the Hebrew Israelite community— "I don't call myself Jewish"—and as estranged from it: "they offer classes, talk about black Americans, especially. But I go to the temple to worship."[44] Navonah tends to reject what she refers to as "a political interpretation of the bible." One senses her frustration at social distinctions that conceal what is truly important: faith and temple worship. She is a victim of religious education that divides, labels, and then channels spiritual practices into identity politics. As she comes to terms with this injustice, she recognizes how the categories she "was taught" no longer function well:

> The term "Jew" I associate with white people. I have some conflicting emotions about that. If I say I'm not Jewish because Jewish people are white, it's as if I'm accepting that all Jewish people are white people. Yes, not all Jewish people are white people, I do know that, but at the same time the term "black Jews" doesn't work for me either because it seems to assert that Jewish people are "normally" white. You have these terms, these labels that other people give you, that don't quite work for you, and so you establish your own terms, and those terms are sometimes in reaction to terms that already exist.[45]

Even as she recognizes how Jews are not white, "normally" or in any other way, Navonah cannot but think in racial terms because no other categories are available to her. The label *black Jews* only magnifies the issue, for it both presumes white normativity and trades off it.[46] One such visual boundary that Kaye/Kantrowitz seeks to undermine is that very term, "black Jews." The discourse on black Jewry establishes identity through categorical description, and so assigns names, and thus fixed limits, to complex cultural activity. Both Kaye/Kantrowitz and Navonah would like to escape that fixity. But what should Navonah call herself? Schooled in the identity politics of her religious education, she recoils from the term *Jew*. The label *Hebrew Israelite* works well for those politically motivated and for other members of Navonah's immediate family, but not for Navonah herself. Navonah was "born into law"—a phrase she employs to escape the racial and social categories of white and black Jews (the labels "other people give you, that don't quite work for you"). But she cannot access another, more appropriate language to reveal an authentic religious sensibility. She just wants to practice her faith, worship in her temple, and live according to the law. As Yavilah McCoy had elsewhere lamented, "it would make it easier to just 'BE' as a Jewish person of color."[47] But the rhetorical claims of race and heritage prevent both McCoy and Navonah from doing so.

As the interview progresses, Navonah often slips back to the accessible language of racial division: white Jews tend to be insular and focused on color, whereas Jews like Navonah understand better the complexity of Jewish ethnicity. She also keenly perceives how her identity can acquire political capital, but still she refuses to play the game:

> Sometimes it's really tough. Part of me says accept that Jewish people are supposed to be white and come to grips with being a Hebrew Israelite. Part of me consistently feels that my faith is too sacred to put into the political realm and debate about. I'm not going to give it to anyone to scrutinize or talk about.[48]

For Navonah, faith belongs to a sacred realm beyond politics, racial categories, and critical inquiry. Religious faith should never devolve into identity politics, so Navonah contends, because politics fails to access the sacred quality of religious belief—a faith that Navonah testifies cannot be revealed in labels that "other people give you." These labels, in turn, produce a warped visual culture: "Like at Passover, when I eat my matzoh I'm so visible."[49] She is visible not as a matzoh-eating Jew, but (like Levy's Rye Bread commercials) as a black person who eats "Jewish food."[50] And Navonah understands how that bifurcating image embodies racial and Jewish assumptions of the very kind she herself struggles against in this interview. She calls on Jews to "diversify the production of images" to define "what it means to be Jewish."[51] But how can Jews do that when the racial and cultural categories they employ fail to account for the diversity and complexity of religious traditions? The rhetorical devices, categories, and languages are too poor to construct a "colored" alternative. Navonah's interview testifies to the troubling dynamic in which Jews seek to displace the visual and racial language that has come to define them. This dynamic is visible when Navonah eats matzoh, or when she enters a synagogue to buy a mezuzah. The racial categories taught by others produce visual images, even as they also blind Jews to other impressions.

Such visual classifications attend to boundary maintenance: defining those who stand outside and inside the authorized limits of community. Jonathan Freedman's recent work on American Jewish culture should alert us to the problems and unstated motivations for such fence building.[52] Like Kaye/Kantrowitz, Freedman challenges us to consider identities that are "mobile, multidimensional, transactional." In his provocative reading of Philip Roth's *The Human Stain* (2000), Freedman suggests how Jewishness complicates the black–white binary, and opens "more complex narratives of racial and ethnic mutability."[53] He recognizes the cultural logic that sustains racial binaries and the entrenched categories that undergird them. But his reading of Roth's *The Human Stain* reveals the inadequacy of those categories to account fully for American diasporic identities. Both Freedman and Kaye/Kantrowitz seek to recover a more nuanced, positional stance toward Jewish identity in America to counter the stringent labeling of insiders and outsiders. Kaye/Kantrowitz's informants also worry about this rhetorical labeling, as Navonah's comments make clear. Navonah seeks to liberate herself from racial markers that define, and so restrict, boundary crossings. But she, like McCoy and Funnye, also appropriates her own form of boundary maintenance. She hides her religious faith within in order to protect it from political debate. To be "born into law" is to claim it as one's natural, biological inheritance; she is not going to give this away to anyone. Seeking to move beyond borders, Navonah inevitably establishes her own.

Navonah recognizes that such cultural labeling no longer works, but she cannot fully escape it herself. She is trapped in the interpretive circle of social value become perception: she glimpses beyond racism within the cultural limits of racial markings. Yet Kaye/Kantrowitz's interview of Navonah witnesses to another visual landscape as well: those categories have produced white and black Jews for visual consumption. Jews of color, any color, do not exist free of social, racial, and visual culture. They may desire to escape visuality altogether ("it would make it easier to just 'BE' as a Jewish person of color"), but only white persons enjoy such neutrality. Navonah wants out from the rhetorical game she inevitably must play. Though a claim to neutral vision is both illusory and racially charged, like Navonah we have all been taught how to see white and black Jews—even if we do not see them at all.

The Rhetoric of Racial Images

Images inform and often cultivate the white–black binary, but they do not control it. Viewers see images in various modes, and transform them into pictures of self-exposure. At times these images reflect what the viewer expects or desires to see. Recall the report from one of Kaye/Kantrowitz's informants—a story I discussed in the introductory chapter—in which Toni Eisendorf views Levy's Rye Bread campaign poster of the black child with the caption, "You don't have to be Jewish to love Levy's!"[54] To Eisendorf, then a young black girl attracted to Jewish culture, Jews look precisely like this image in the poster. As I see it, the image tells an altogether different story: African Americans are not Jewish at all, but they can still enjoy Jewish food (as Navonah experienced herself when eating matzoh during Passover). But to Toni, this advertisement offers the progressive vision of Jewishness decoupled from whiteness. The image registers as an authentic exposure of identity, and so confirms what Toni wishes to see or believe. I discern a more problematic image, one in which black otherness opposes white Jewish culture (*real* Jewish Rye, as the smaller caption reads below the image). The child cannot become what he eats, although he can certainly enjoy the food. That sense of "real" Jewish bread, as the caption indicates, marks the border between authentic (white) Judaism and black otherness. Jewish foods offer delight and comfort to those who ingest its culture, but can never confer authentic belonging to non-whites. The advertisement traffics within the rhetorical claims to visual authenticity, producing both comfortable and painful images of Jewish cultural belonging.

Images certainly register in modes beyond comfort and distaste. They also destabilize or confuse, thereby provoking alternative visions of Jewish authenticity. Reader response theory and notions of spectatorship have taught us that viewers see images in and through multiple registers. Toni and I, for example, do not see the same image in Levy's advertisement. The production and consumption of images move along complicated tracks, and signify in ways both mysterious and local. But Kaye/Kantrowitz wants more than alternative visions; she desires political action. It is one thing to see the world, but quite another to change it. This revolutionary thrust sits uneasily with the textual voices in *The Colors of Jews*. In these interviews, Navonah, Funnye, McCoy, and even Toni Eisendorf are far less the political "colored" radicals Kaye/Kantrowitz would like them to be. Instead, they all struggle to articulate claims to authenticity and heritage beyond a black–white visual discourse that has come to define them. Their struggle reveals the power of visual idioms to inform religious and racial ideology. Even Kaye/Kantrowitz herself falls victim to a binary logic of the black–white divide. When she discusses Katie, who she tells us is "African American, light-skinned enough to pass as white," she goes on to offer this telling remark: "In truth, Katie looks like a light-skinned black, and those who fail to notice this must so presume whiteness that anything else has to smack them in the face."[55] If we take seriously Kaye/Kantrowitz's notion of "colored" as a disruptive category of binary logic, then such language as "light-skinned black" and "in truth" simply reproduces a racial logic that categorizes, binds, and defines. Like her interviewees, Kaye/Kantrowitz too struggles with racial distinctions that fail her. Though she desires to move beyond border maintenance and racial categories, *The Colors of Jews* creates its own. Kaye/Kantrowitz claims a radical diasporism, but the voices in her text reestablish visual boundaries in the very attempt to overcome them. Those racial borders, I contend, do important rhetorical work in the modern Jewish story about visual authenticity.

This tension between radical politics and racial discourse in *The Colors of Jews* produces a fractured text about visual Judaism. Even so, these fissures transform our awareness of how racial categories and claims to authenticity conspire to produce a visual culture. The distinctiveness of Kaye/Kantrowitz's work in this area can be gleaned by comparing it to two other works that maintain similar ambitions: *In Every Tongue: The Racial & Ethnic Diversity of the Jewish People* (2005), and *The Jewish Identity Project: New American Photography* (2005).[56] A book dedicated, as its subtitle articulates, to broadening "the racial and ethnic diversity of the Jewish people," *In Every Tongue* offers a kaleidoscope of Jewish facial images for visual consumption. The editors delimit the meaning of these portraits through captions secured to individual photographs, and through stagings of bundled images. As a whole, these framings of visual identity establish progressive models of being Jewish through new paradigms of seeing Jewish faces. *In Every Tongue* unmasks Jews by exhibiting their various looks, smiles, gazes, and hair. The diversity of Jewish looks confronts the spectator through the inside front and back covers. Different shades of white and black faces appear, with Latino and Mizrachi heritage on display. There are children and adults hugging and playing together, and all gaze at the camera with a smile. This is authentic Jewishness too, these images tell us, here in the faces that challenge Levy's black–white imaginary.

Note, for example, the opening story about Sasha, who while in college searches "for a place to settle her identity." With a white Jewish mother and an African American, Puerto Rican, and Native American Catholic father, Sasha embodies a "mixed" self who fits uneasily within ethnic borders. Members of the African American Student Union claim her mix is welcome, so long as she remains black when she associates with the union—indicating once again the situational and culturally imposed features of racial hierarchies, for Sasha would be seen as black in some contexts but not in others. Sasha rejects that group and many others, she tells us, because "I didn't know what it was like just to choose one thing." But what, precisely, is that "thing" presented as a choice? Does Sasha imagine racial ascription as a buffet from which to choose an identity? Would she prefer a mixed plate rather than a singular entrée? Or is she far more comfortable with a fluid identity than are those who support an identity politics? The authors of *In Every Tongue* summarize Sasha's story with this lament: "To be Jewish and not white is to fall outside the notion of who is a Jew held by most Americans, Jewish or not." Sasha herself seems unsure what lies outside of the white Jew: "If people asked me what I was, I would run down my mix. I wouldn't normally say white. I would usually say Jewish, but to me that was synonymous."[57] Sasha has no vocabulary to define her mix other than to say it's not white. But to her, that means something other than Jewish.

For Diane and Gary Tobin, as well as for Scott Rubin (the three authors of this volume), Sasha too easily identifies Jewish with white, and much of this book seeks to correct that misperception. Judaism, these authors go on to show, is authentically mixed, much like Sasha, and we should all recognize ethnic diversity as an essentially Jewish experience. The point here is not to challenge the category of whiteness so much as to find a place for those like Sasha within normative Judaism. Sasha should not *have to* choose; Judaism is expansive enough to settle her identity there. But she nonetheless does choose by running down her mix. She constitutes her Jewishness through a racial heritage that confronts whiteness with mixed things. Yet even Sasha's mix cannot fully evade racial categories of exclusion. Freedman, we should recall, argues that Jewishness itself explodes the fixed category of whiteness, and one could imagine the Tobins articulating similar claims in this volume. But as Navonah made clear, categories trade off each other, so fixing whiteness also essentializes blackness. More than about finding

Figure 6.1. Kids at Chanukah Celebration. The photo is courtesy of BecholLashon.org.

a home to settle one's identity, Sasha's story is about the cultural assumptions behind the statement "to be Jewish and not white." Those assumptions tacitly circulate within a white–other binary, rather than the "bi- or multi-identified" diasporic community that Kaye/Kantrowitz champions.[58] In short, the Tobins want white Jews to recognize mixed others like Sasha as authentically Jewish; Kaye/Kantrowitz wants those same white Jews to become "bi- or multi-identified" themselves. The one seeks recognition and acceptance; the other desires radical, political change at the core of Jewish identity.

In Every Tongue witnesses to the diversity of every face—all these faces speak an authentic Jewish language. Who looks like a Jew? They all do, for Jewishness registers as diversity, vibrancy, and exotic dress. The captions underwriting the images in the last chapter, "Be'chol Lashon: A Visual Journey" testify to this diversity (the Hebrew *Be'chol Lashon* means "in every tongue"). One takes a journey through children's programs sponsored by Be'chol Lashon—an organizational initiative run by Diane Tobin to highlight ethnic and racial diversity within Jewish communities—and these images sparkle with ethnic and racial mixtures. In a striking image of three children, all with differing ethnic heritage who gaze directly at the camera, the caption reads: "Even the youngest of those who attend *Be'chol Lashon* events have only to glance around them to see that any face can be a Jewish face."[59] More than a claim about these beautiful young children, this caption calls out to the viewer to "glance around" and "see" diversity. These images both witness to the "patches of color"[60] that make up American Jewish communities and demand acceptance of that diversity. One need not focus with a gaze; a quick glance reveals a diverse visual presence. And seeing diversity through this visual journey is the stated intent. As Lewis Gordon notes in the foreword to *In Every Tongue:* "Knowing much about the diversity of Jewish communities worldwide is one thing. Sitting in a room with nearly a hundred representatives of such communities is another matter."[61] Visual representation is empirical knowledge—a mode of experience that confirms and grounds theory. Though readers cannot sit with Gordon at the table, they can still gain a second-hand visual experience of diversity. The images seek visual credibility. Seeing Jewish through these faces is a rhetorical move to establish authentic modes of *being* Jewish in America.

This sense of "sitting in a room" where there is Jewish diversity also captures the production of the Be'chol Lashon Web site, http://www.bechollashon. org. Visually, the site explodes with images: one views the continually running film of faces appearing at the top third of the screen, just above the individual slides describing the organization. These visual snapshots promote the glance—the quick visual register of diversity—rather than the more deliberate, meditative gaze. It is a busy Web page directing viewers to scan the diversity of Jewish faces. The steady appearance of faces seeks to draw one into the site as portal to a world of Jewish ethnic richness. One can watch videos and podcasts, and can view a slideshow of photos to recognize Jews of every tongue, race, and ethnicity. There resides a wealth of information on this site, all engineered to engage the viewer in a global journey through the potpourri of Jewish experience. Be'chol Lashon maintains a presence on Facebook and Twitter, as well as in podcasts on the Apple iTunes store. The point of all this seems clear: Jewish ethnic diversity constitutes a broad, engaged, and critical part of global Judaism. These faces are here to see now and everywhere, and they witness to Jewish diversity as a powerful engine for Jewish renewal. Authentic Judaism is a mixed landscape of diverse faces and lives, this Web site contends, and one can see this authenticity take shape in film, photography, and Internet culture. Be'chol Lashon seeks to transform visual witness into communal acceptance: a journey from curious spectacle to genuine tradition. The rhetoric of seeing Jewish on the site and in the images of *In Every Tongue* exposes a diverse Judaism as resource and authentic heritage.

In Every Tongue reveals and elicits Jewish diversity, but *The Colors of Jews* seeks to transform it. The one uncovers the multiple identities Jews wear and perform, whereas the other takes a political stance toward that diversity. If *In Every Tongue* is a revelatory text of public exhibition, then *The Colors of Jews* is a political text of confrontation seeking to reshape behavior. *The Jewish Identity Project* lies somewhere in-between these notions of public spectacle and political activism. This published catalogue of the museum exhibition is a provocative graphic display of American Jewish diversity. It produces a self-conscious "framing" project in which artists stage their work to provoke anxious response and progressive debate about who looks, acts, and counts as an American Jew. Susan Chevlowe's introductory piece, "Framing Jewishness: Photography and the Boundaries of Community," reviews how Jews have been represented in American media, and suggests that the *Project* reflects "how images reinforce or challenge stereotypes about Jews and Jewish ethnicity." These installations, Chevlowe argues, undermine "easy assumptions about how Jewishness is marked" and unmask stereotypical images.[62] Who and what is Jewish become the content of critical exposure, as do the ways in which artists frame their subjects. Chevlowe closes her essay with this hope: "The photographic projects in *The Jewish Identity Project* may help us to overcome our instinct to privilege unity over multiplicity, and thereby to make room for more fluid, overlapping, and quotidian expressions of Jewishness and Jewish life in the United States."[63] Surely Kaye/Kantrowitz would share this concern, but "to make room for" multiplicity, like sitting in the room with Lewis Gordon, does not yet fight the racist practices that Kaye/Kantrowitz finds everywhere in American culture. *The Colors of Jews* is less a vision than a call to arms. Still, art can function to motivate, to question, and to explore in ways both inspired by, and separate from, the artist's intent. *The Jewish Identity Project* motivates rather than confronts, challenges rather than transforms, and positions rather than demands. Though *In Every Tongue* and *The Jewish Identity Project* expose the vibrancy, richness, and diversity of American Jewish life, only *The Colors of Jews* attacks and criticizes a complacent American public.

Kaye/Kantrowitz's work is a visual politics of confrontational exposure in which she undercuts the white–black binary with a tripartite mix of "colored" Jews. These "bi- or multi-identified" Jews do the vanguard work of revolt: neither Jew nor black, they search for more authentic terms to advance a radical diasporism. This rhetorical stance and political action are critical features of the modern Jewish demand for visual authenticity.

Jewish authenticity appears in *The Colors of Jews*, to adopt Daniel Itzkovitz's provocative account, as "Chameleonic blood": "an absolute fluidity that somehow maintains its mark of difference."[64] The racial discourse of this "somehow" has been the guiding, rhetorical thread weaving throughout this chapter. When diversity becomes the critical, authentic feature of boundary maintenance for modern Jewish existence, as it does in *The Colors of Jews*, how might Jews stake their claim to authentic difference when seeking their place within the American Jewish mosaic? Tracing the language employed by some of Kaye/Kantrowitz's interviewees to find a home for their diverse lives, I have sought to texture Itzkovitz's "somehow" with rhetorical exposures of visual authenticity. To mark a difference, Funnye, McCoy, Navonah and others appeal to a racial vision of presence and heritage. The "somehow," in other words, is both racial and visual, and these discourses sustain claims to authentic Jewish identity.

Reading Kaye/Kantrowitz's *The Colors of Jews* is more than an exercise in racial debunking and political action; it is also a study of authenticity as racial marking. Scholars in whiteness studies—from Karen Brodkin, Jonathan Freedman, and Matthew Frye Jacobson to Michael Rogin—suggest how race covers a problematic, ambiguous terrain of conflicting political, social, and cultural forces. As both Jacobson and Brodkin make clear, many Jews have become white in America by gaining political access and acquiring social goods. But these Jews have rarely given up entirely on that sense of difference analyzed by Itzkovitz. Kaye/Kantrowitz herself appeals to that difference, even if she desires to overcome it. Much of her discourse on "colored" Jews relies on dubious racial categories, and she can be quick to dismiss those less radical than her diasporist colleagues. At one point she even ventures to mark her difference absolutely: "I do not relish this vision of increased separation and alienation among Jews. We are a small community and I'd rather struggle than split. But this kind of conflict is, I believe, preferable to allowing fundamentalist or other right-wing voices to represent the Jewish people."[65] Even "bi- or multi-identified" persons cannot be fully boundless: they too must establish and regulate borders to safeguard a radical politics. This is not a binary, white–black racial difference, but it is identity marking all the same.

Kaye/Kantrowitz interviews Jews who see black, white, "colored," and "mixed" in the idioms of culture, heritage, and visual authenticity. These languages of home and homelessness conspire to produce a fractured but weighty text. They speak to the presence of race in American Jewish thought and culture, and to the rhetorical modes by which racial discourse works with visual appeals to authenticity. Surely communities require boundaries of distinction, and perhaps minority communities require them even more so. Yet those markers of division interact with brilliant visions of diversity, and so challenge the fixed place of boundaries even in the midst of constructing them. *The Colors of Jews* is caught in this intricate dance between constructing authentic borders and dismantling hurtful representations. Its radical diasporism, I submit, lies not in its call to cross every border, but in its demand that those borders become visible and politically unstable. Kaye/Kantrowitz recognizes this all too well: "This theme of Jewish authenticity or visibility resonates from every corner of the room."[66] *The Colors of Jews*, together with its less radical cousins *In Every Tongue* and *The Jewish Identity Project*, attempt to bring the fluctuating hues of Jewish diversity before a gazing public. Yet this is not a story of "authenticity or visibility," but a narrative of the *authentically visible* as radical exposure. Perhaps Jews of every color should travel beyond their recognized borders every so often, if only to see that visual authenticity is somehow far more, if ever, black and white.

Conclusion

Imagining Jewish Authenticity in Every Generation

THIS BOOK HAS presented an extended argument for recognizing visual images and rhetorical discourse as performative utterances. Images do more than refer to or describe things: they produce claims to Jewish authenticity, and so do languages that deploy visual idioms. I have been tracing this narrative thread within American Jewish thought, tethering visual language to articulations of authenticity. In the first section of this book, those expressive claims expose discrete instances of images working with and against textual arguments (as illustrated in Rosenblatt's *Social Zionism*), or images mimicking textual dilemmas (Heschel's *The Sabbath*), and images staging cultural practices (Fishbein's *Kosher by Design*; Greenberg's and Silverman's *The Jewish Home Beautiful*). In the second section I turned to rhetorical modes of persuasion that embody visual authenticity in Jewish (Wyschogrod's *The Body of Faith*), gendered (Adler's *Engendering Judaism*), and racial subjects (Kaye/Kantrowitz's *The Colors of Jews*). All of these texts reveal how, in rhetoric and image, the language of authenticity works as a visual discourse in American Jewish thought. This concern for visual legitimacy also uncovers a parallel discursive thread: the underlying anxiety of inauthenticity. In Heschel's *The Sabbath,* Schor's images might fail as signifiers to the ineffable, or the decorative and elaborate photographs in Fishbein's *Kosher by Design* might witness instead to an ornate façade rather than to hearty substance. The food, we might say, looks too good to eat. Greenberg and Silverman locate their aesthetic tastes within a pageantry of beauty, yet compare their homemaker's designs to God's natural creations—an appeal to continuity that belies the anxiety of new beginnings. This anxiety of (in)authenticity weaves its way into Wyschogrod's concern that while non-Jewish bodies may not convert to Jewish ones, by some miraculous and invisible mutation they become one with Israel. Yet only God can see this. For Wyschogrod, the taint of inauthenticity stains conversion precisely because the converted body lacks visual presence and authority. Adler located the inauthentic gaze in the sexual look that focuses on female genitalia, whereas Yavilah McCoy wanted to deflect the inauthentic entirely, and so live and simply "BE" a Jewish person of color.

By way of concluding this story of American Jewish thought, I want to explore how images work in American Passover Haggadoth—the stories Jews tell of their exodus from Egypt. Again here I do not wish to review the immense and rich history of this literature,[1] but I do want to highlight *how* texts and images work together in this exodus narrative in order to reexamine my analysis in *Imagining Jewish Authenticity*. I will further restrict my reading to one moment in this retelling: the passage that Nathan Englander, in the *New American Haggadah* (2012), translates as "In every generation, a person is obligated to view himself as if he were the one who went out from Egypt."[2] This textual referent to continuity and heritage (*bechol dor ve-dor*) travels with images to inform notions of authenticity, and these visual paradigms draw out the principal concerns of this book. We can revisit, and so reweave the narrative thread traced in *Imagining Jewish Authenticity* by considering the visual language of Passover storytelling.

In 1923 the Central Conference of American Rabbis published a revised version of their *Union Haggadah*, first published in 1892.[3] This was a thoroughly Reform product, and unabashedly so. The *Haggadah* opens left to right as an English text would do, and the translation owes little fidelity to the original Hebrew wording. Indeed, the editors excise troubling Hebrew phrases to befit progressive Jews of this era—the ten plagues and the hope of return to Jerusalem are missing—while adding their own, new variants. And these reform-minded editors confidently assert their practical stance when confronted with outdated customs: "Reform Judaism does not consider these practices [purifying utensils] essential to the proper observance of the Passover."[4] This is a work "modern in spirit," so the editors claim, in its focus on "the moral and spiritual worth" of the seder, but also one attuned to "traditional elements" that claim nostalgic and memorable force.[5] The *Union Haggadah* includes many of the images from the earlier edition, yet adopts as well "the decorative frontispiece, borders and lettering" by Mr. Isadore Lipton. These ornamental additions seek to make "real to our generation the ever fresh story of our deliverance."[6]

The passage beginning "in every generation" (*bechol dor ve-dor*) nicely illustrates both the reformist tendencies of the *Haggadah* and how images complicate textual meaning. The *Union Haggadah* entitles this segment "The Watch-night of the Eternal."[7] It is a phrase meant to explain both the Passover itself and God's vigilance and protection, for the "Watch-Night" describes how God "passed over and spared the houses of Israel."[8] The page draws upon the aesthetic motifs pervading Bernard Rosenblatt's *Social Zionism* (1919), a book published only four years before this *Haggadah*. The classical imagery and bordering appear as mere

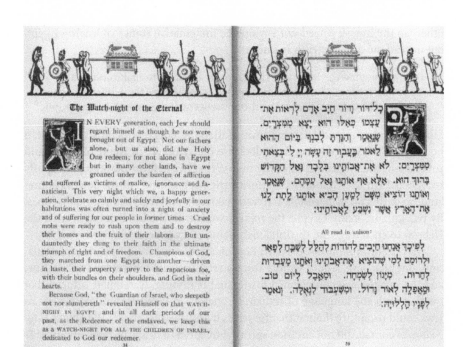

Figure 7.1. The Watch-night of the Eternal. Image from *The Union Haggadah: Home Service for the Passover* © 1923 by the Central Conference of American Rabbis. Used by permission. All rights reserved.

stylistic ornamentation, as they did in the original *Maccabaean* articles from Rosenblatt. Yet the mirroring of the first Hebrew and English letters, with the imperial guard's raised arm smiting the young Egyptian boys, reveal how images work with and against textual inscription. In this *Haggadah*, Lipton's "decorative frontispiece, borders and lettering" engage the English translation, but not the Hebrew text that speaks to the quite different theme of generational continuity. The bordering at the top suggests Egypt's power and Israel's enslavement, while the decorative lettering concerns the killing of Egyptian sons. Yet neither bordering nor lettering communicate how Jews should see themselves as if they too had left Egypt. This is image as mythic adventure, a universal type of historical experience. The Hebrew inscription ties the generations to a particular moment; the English translation universalizes that moment in the style of Lipton's art: "Champions of God, they [Israel] marched from one Egypt into another—driven in haste, their property a prey to the rapacious foe, with their bundles on their shoulders, and God in their hearts."[9] Egyptian bondage and freedom are prototypical moments in Israel's suffering—a people moving from one Egypt to another. So the imagery need not engage the imaginative stance of leaving Egypt, but instead must speak truth to power:

> While enjoying the liberty of this land, let us strive to make secure also our spiritual freedom, that, as the delivered, we may become the deliverer, carrying out Israel's historic task of being the messenger of religion unto all mankind.[10]

Lipton's bordering and lettering universalize the concrete details of Egyptian bondage in the Hebrew text to underscore the symbolic universe of might and suffering in the English. It was only in 1937 that the Reform movement officially recognized (in the Columbus Platform) the "upbuilding" of the Jewish homeland. So in this 1923 *Haggadah,* universal concerns still trumped nationalist ones. By recognizing many Egypts, the images work with the English but against the Hebrew to encourage the spiritual task facing every generation.

In his *Social Zionism,* Bernard Rosenblatt also appealed to a universal mission, one that Jews would export from a rebuilt social laboratory in Palestine, and the images also complicated his textual reasoning. Rosenblatt infused that mission with the language of return: to oneself, to new beginnings. American Jews could recapture their authentic selves by cultivating a land. The *Union Haggadah,* of course, did not envision spiritual freedom in this way. But compare this image from the *Union Haggadah,* one coupled with the historic mission cited above, with the now recognizable sketch from Rosenblatt's text. Where the *Union Haggadah* marches to freedom (note the straight lines demarcating strength and direction, with the historic task "of being the messenger of religion unto all mankind"), Rosenblatt's *Social Zionism* leads to sterile wanderings. These are both exodus stories, but of a very different order. For the *Union Haggadah,* the stylistic lettering and borders convey mythic origins and directed moral purpose. By contrast, the images in Rosenblatt's *Social Zionism* do the very opposite: they picture decrepit beginnings and authentic returns. The editors of the *Union Haggadah* argue that the delivered must become the deliverer for all. Rosenblatt believes the delivered must rediscover their authentic selves, even if this return means expelling inauthentic others. His text did not argue for this expulsion, but his images certainly did so; images persuade when texts remain silent. A textual absence appeals to a visual presence.

Images can appear before the physical eyes or, as Martin Jay makes clear, in the "mind's eye" as well. This is how Descartes saw things, according to Jay.[11] Such an imaginative or speculative viewing underlies the concerns of *The Pesach Haggadah* (1989) published by ArtScroll. This is a *Haggadah* without visual images, but one still immersed in visual discourse. The Passover reading includes commentary "culled from the Classic Baalei Mussar" (the masters of Jewish ethics), and for the "in-every-generation" passage the editors cite musings from Rab-

Figure 7.2. (*top*) Israel on the March. Image from *The Union Haggadah: Home Service for the Passover* © 1923 by the Central Conference of American Rabbis. Used by permission. All rights reserved. Figure 7.3. (*bottom*) Bedouins on the March. Bernard Rosenblatt, *Social Zionism* (1919).

bi Simcha Zissel Ziv (1824–1898, known as the Alter of Kelm).[12] Zissel Ziv ponders the legal requirements for the Jew who regards himself "as though he personally had gone out from Egypt." How does he fulfill such a commandment? According to Zissel Ziv, he does so by employing the power of the mind's eye to picture reality in ways that engage the whole being. This practice works in other contexts as well: one should not think abstractly of death, but instead "picture the pangs of death in all their horrors, as if he is experiencing them now." Even Rabbi Akiba, before his gruesome death, felt pain "by imagining realistic pictures of actually sacrificing himself." Jews should experience enslavement to and freedom from Egypt in the same way:

> He should picture himself as a slave who has been freed. How he would con-
> template the greatness of his Liberator! How he would sacrifice all he pos-
> sessed—and himself—for Him! By imagining such a picture of the mind, he
> will be impressed by the miracles and he will see that the world has a Creator
> and Governor, Whom we should fear and serve.[13]

This is how Jews fulfill their obligation to see themselves "as if" they too had left Egypt. Imagining a "picture of the mind" draws them back to that mythical time and space in which seeing Egypt is a form of physically unseeing the material world.

This imaginative leap of the visual mind nicely captures Abraham Joshua Heschel's appeal to seeing through objects as mirrors to the ineffable. Like Zissel Ziv, Heschel believed in a spiritual sight to elevate Jewish commitment. Seeing things as physical objects could too easily capture selves within the commerce of material consumption, and so blind them to spiritual matters. Rather than looking at objects, American Jews should see through them to their sacred horizons. This spiritual gaze dislodges Jews from the American landscape, and situates them within but not of American culture. Zissel Ziv portrays a similar terrain in which miracles become visible only after forming "a picture of the mind." When Jews see in new ways, a sacred world appears before their eyes. Heschel appropriates an analogous visual technique in which material objects reveal God's sacred presence, but only when seen as icons of spiritual reality rather than idols of selfish consumption. Yet both *The Pesach Haggadah* and Heschel's *The Sabbath* are anxious works: they worry about visual splendor and the allure of the aesthetic object. Ilya Schor's woodcut engravings reproduce Heschel's visual anxiety because his images heighten the charm of material objects. His illustrations might capture the self within material abundance, and so prevent the kind of spiritual insight that Heschel sought to cultivate in his prose. I also imagine Zissel Ziv worried about this reaction to visual splendor. Impressed with a miraculous world of ordered creation, Jews might envision a world full of God's creative possibilities and human freedom. But Zissel Ziv tempers that material joy with stern commitment: "we should fear and serve" the Creator and Governor. This *Pesach Haggadah* from ArtScroll and *The Sabbath* from Heschel construct new vistas for spiritual Judaism. But once enlightened, American Jews might picture very different worlds than even these authors could foresee. How might fear and service, or the quiet serenity of the Sabbath day, prevent the mind's eye from seeing beyond Jewish borders? Both Zissel Ziv and Heschel understand the power of images to reveal spiritual presence. Yet all icons of this nature can become idols of material worship. Seeing Jewish, either through the mind's eye or through material things, inevitably provokes the anxiety of (in)authenticity in Heschel's *The Sabbath* and *The Pesach Haggadah*.

One recently published *Haggadah* that evinces little fear of the material, and even heightens the visual appeal of text as image, is the *New American Haggadah* (2012) edited by Jonathan Safran Foer and translated by Nathan Englander. With commentaries on separate pages, and a timeline running along the top borders, the *New American Haggadah* has garnered both lavish praise and withering criticism.[14] Whatever the work might be, it is visually stunning. The artwork by Oded Ezer is thoughtfully and beautifully rendered, as Ezer sought to engage both text and history in his visual design:

> The notion behind the design of this book was to merge, visually, the history of the Jewish nation with the traditional text of the Haggadah. Toward that end, the letterforms on each page reflect those used in the period reflected in the timeline at the top of the page. In this way, the book is a graphic record of Jewish history.[15]

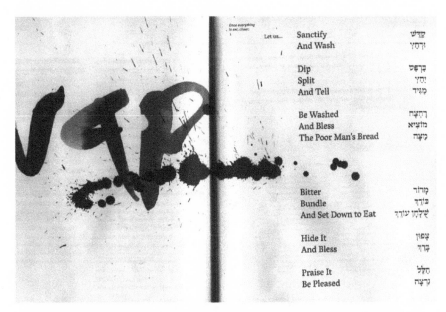

Figure 7.4. The Passover seder. From: NEW AMERICAN HAGGADAH by Jonathan Safran Foer, translated by Nathan Englander. Copyright © 2012 by Jonathan Safran Foer. By permission of Little, Brown and Company. All rights reserved.

This seepage between text and image runs throughout the *New American Haggadah*. We see an example of this on the initial pages reviewing the Passover seder. Note how, on the left side of the page, text becomes image, yet this text–image spills over to the English and Hebrew inscriptions. Art and narrative order intertwine to produce a visual discipline. The timeline running along the top border (not rendered in this facsimile) chronicles the first telling of Jewish slaves in Egypt, but comes full circle by noting that "the papyrus document reporting the escape of the slaves is in the archives of the Jewish Theological Seminary in New York City. Tonight, 3,000 years later, we are here."[16]

If we are "here," then how does the *New American Haggadah* illustrate the obligation to see oneself as if leaving Egypt? The layout of this *Haggadah* invites readers to engage the story as material book: in order to recognize the Hebrew in the text/image, or to follow the timeline running along the top of the page, one must turn the work on its edges, sometimes to the right side, at other times to the left. The *Haggadah* then becomes more than an imaginative recollection, or a collective experience of remembering; the book is a material object to work with, explore, and physically manipulate.[17] This interactive engagement stimulates a more sensual response to the imaginative leap back to Egypt. Ezer's images func-

בְּכָל דּוֹר וָדוֹר חַיָּב אָדָם לִרְאוֹת אֶת
עַצְמוֹ כְּאִלּוּ הוּא יָצָא מִמִּצְרַיִם, שֶׁנֶּאֱמַר: וְהִגַּדְתָּ לְבִנְךָ
בַּיּוֹם הַהוּא לֵאמֹר: בַּעֲבוּר זֶה עָשָׂה יהוה לִי בְּצֵאתִי מִמִּצְרַיִם.
לֹא אֶת אֲבוֹתֵינוּ בִּלְבָד גָּאַל הַקָּדוֹשׁ בָּרוּךְ הוּא, אֶלָּא אַף אוֹתָנוּ
גָּאַל עִמָּהֶם, שֶׁנֶּאֱמַר: וְאוֹתָנוּ הוֹצִיא מִשָּׁם לְמַעַן הָבִיא אֹתָנוּ
לָתֶת לָנוּ אֶת הָאָרֶץ אֲשֶׁר נִשְׁבַּע לַאֲבֹתֵינוּ.

In every generation, a person is obligated to view himself as if he were the one who went out from Egypt, as it is said: *And on that day tell your son, saying, "For this purpose the Lord labored on my behalf, by taking me out of Egypt."* It was not our fathers alone who were delivered by the Holy One, Blessed is He—we were also delivered with them, as it is said: *And He took us out from there in order to bring us—to give us!—the land that He pledged to our fathers.*

Figure 7.5. Text on Left Side of Page. From: NEW AMERICAN HAGGADAH by Jonathan Safran Foer, translated by Nathan Englander. Copyright © 2012 by Jonathan Safran Foer. By permission of Little, Brown and Company. All rights reserved.

tion among multiple registers, seeping back into pages as readers maneuver the book to read the Hebrew calligraphy.

The image facing "in every generation" renders the Hebrew both left-to-right and right-to-left, yet to see this one must turn the book so that the text–image lies either at the top or the bottom (the book must be vertically rendered to read the Hebrew calligraphy, but returned to its horizontal position to read the Hebrew

Figure 7.6. Calligraphy on Right Side of Page. From: NEW AMERICAN HAGGADAH by Jonathan Safran Foer, translated by Nathan Englander. Copyright © 2012 by Jonathan Safran Foer. By permission of Little, Brown and Company. All rights reserved.

and English writings). So "reading" the image (positioning the book vertically) makes the Hebrew/English text unreadable (although, in this vertical position, one can now decipher the timeline). The images reproduced on the previous pages show the book in a horizontal position, with the calligraphy on the right and text on the left side of the page. Imagine the physical gymnastics required to read the Hebrew and English texts together with the artistic calligraphy and timeline. The slight black indentations (they are purple in colored photographs) on the right side of the *Haggadah* text continue Ezer's artwork, and with timeline at the top bordering the Hebrew text in the middle—with characters in large and bold font—distinctions between text and image all but disappear. The Hebrew mirrors the movement of the image on its opposite page: both leap out and recede. "In every generation" includes not only the ones immediately present, but also those in the distant past—in the deeper recesses of the page, as it were. The timeline is thus more than border text; it also reminds us, both textually and visually, that to see oneself "as if" one were a slave in Egypt is to actively cross boundaries—here on the page and among the generations.

With its appeal to continuity and border crossings between text and image, the *New American Haggadah* shares much with Susie Fishbein's *Kosher by Design* and Greenberg's and Silverman's *The Jewish Home Beautiful*. Both cookbooks are self-conscious guides to Jewish practice, and both seek continuity with a past even as they update traditional appeals in a more modern style. They carefully pursue a middle ground between aesthetic beauty and user-friendly interface: Fishbein acts as dependable coach and fashionable hostess, while Greenberg and Silverman choreograph feminine elegance with easy stage direction. And both *Haggadah* and cookbooks stage a visual production: the *New American Haggadah* by physical manipulation, and the cookbooks through aesthetic presentation. *The Jewish Home Beautiful* directs a pageantry of delightful home food rituals in which women take center stage. We see this too in the decorative images, like the Sabbath "S" highlighting female duties (see Figure 3.2): she bakes the challah bread and lights the candles, but the missing kiddush cup marks the absence of male power and position. This is her home beautiful that both continues traditional Jewish motifs and inaugurates new ones in America. The images in *Kosher by Design* are even more striking in their assertive claims to performative authority (see Figure 3.4). This Shabbat table—with the strong visual sensibility of arrangement, serenity, and observance—presents Shabbat as ordered tradition. The superimposed title confers a sense of established regularity with aesthetic appeal to the image: Fishbein's traditional Judaism crosses over to uptown elegance. *Kosher by Design* locates modernity within the contours of traditional observance. Borders might be traversed, but order regulates the movement. This is visual authenticity tied to traditional authority as regulated performance.

The *New American Haggadah* blurs continuous backgrounds to produce a more obscure, even if ever present, sense of movement and belonging. Ezer's images blend, warp, hide, and come in and out of focus. This blurring of the visual register diverges from Fishbein's confident assertions of traditional order, and instead leans toward Michael Wyschogrod's murkier account of light and darkness in *The Body of Faith*. Wyschogrod limits reason's bold assurance by planting darkness in the midst of enlightened vision. He sees through a glass darkly, yet his critical appraisal of Christian enlightenment both honors its influence upon his work and helps to distance his account of "indwelling" from fuller, Christian notions of incarnation. Judaism is for Wyschogrod the most human of religions because it recognizes limited vision, one that follows Ezer's blurred backgrounds into a more obscure world of material darkness. The text/image in the *New American Haggadah* calls attention to the physical, and limits abstract flights by situating images within texts, and texts within images. This continuous border crossing visually enacts Wyschogrod's theological account of perception: we see God's presence in the people Israel. God's indwelling is, like some Christian versions of incarnation, a spiritual crossing into the material that ultimately dissolves the ethereal/corporeal distinction. The *New American Haggadah* and Wyschogrod's *The Body of Faith* enact this visual rhetoric of embodiment.

Wyschogrod grounded continuity in the biological body where God's presence resided. Certainly those "in each generation" who imagine their exodus from Egypt create a historical bridge to the past, and a good many American *Haggadoth* appeal to religious heritage, if not also to biological inheritance. Some, like *The Open Door* (2002),[18] imagine continuity as represented by a wholesome family around the Passover table, where parents, grandparents, and children share their Jewish traditions. We see continuity, and expect it to continue, in the portrayal of joyful gathering. In the image from *The Open Door*, children are at the center of this festival holiday, and this *Haggadah*, like many others, caters to their presence. Indeed, it appears as if this story and its commitments are designed for them.

One such story designed for children is *The Animated Haggadah* (1985, based on the original film).[19] This *Haggadah* portrays continuity and commitment by presenting the same animated characters as ancient Israelites and modern Jewish businessmen. Though the one might carry sackcloth while the other travels with hardened suitcases, they mingle together with ease. This is not a hard-earned inheritance but rather a natural, familial one.

If nothing else, Rachel Adler's *Engendering Judaism* moves us to ask: where are women in these depictions of Jewish continuity? *The Open Door*, published by the Central Conference of American Rabbis, portrays girls and grandmothers, but the father still holds his place at the head of the table. *The Animated Hag-*

Figure 7.7. In Every Generation. Image from: *The Open Door.* Reprinted by permission of Ruth Weisberg.

gadah shows women around the table, but apparently they did not leave Egypt: the images accompanying "when Israel came out of Egypt" and "in every genera-tion" picture only men. Characterizing Israel as male, as these animated images most certainly do, reinforces an exclusionary optics. Women are defaced and defigured, indicating a form of dis/remembering that is also a dis/membering. Rendered invisible, women challenge the easy continuity imagined in *The Ani-mated Haggadah,* for Adler alerts us to the continuous struggle to *see* women in Jewish tradition. Demanding renewed blessings from her texts, Adler engenders the rhetoric of authenticity to better recognize the face of the Other.

The de/facing of the other is both a gendered and a racial politics of exci-sion, and Melanie Kaye/Kantrowitz's *The Colors of Jews* helps us to see this too. Her analysis of "colored" Jews dislodges the kind of sequential narrative that we find in *A Different Night* (2002) published by the Shalom Hartman Institute for an American Jewish audience.[20] This timeline begins and ends in Jerusalem, and travels through a decidedly European and American historical trajectory. True,

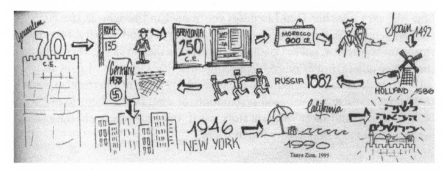

Figure 7.8. Timeline of the Generations. Image from: *A Different Night*. Reprinted by permission of Tanya Zion.

we see Babylonia, Morocco, and Spain, but from 1586 (Holland) onward the work is limited to Russia, Germany, New York, California, and Jerusalem. Where is Sasha's "mix" ("I didn't know what it was like just to choose one thing"),[21] or Funnye's African heritage? Kaye/Kantrowitz presents her "colored" Jews as radical unsettlers; they are diasporic identities who disrupt narratives of closure and settlement. This is a rhetoric of authentic wanderings, where secure homes inhibit new relations of justice. The timeline in *A Different Night* envisions a clear beginning, middle, and end to Jewish historical travel, but it does not open to more unsettling mixtures of inheritance. The voices in *The Colors of Jews* suggest that every generation must face those who do not appear fully exposed, and so are not fully authentic. In the visual discourse of race, seeing Jewish is often too white.

I close where I began: with the image of a young boy eating Levy's Rye Bread in the 1970s commercial posters (Figure 0.1). While not a *Haggadah* depiction of "in every generation," the poster nonetheless exposes those who stand outside the narrative of continuity often required by claims to Jewish heritage. The text accompanying this image delivers the joke that while certain foods can be authentic ("real Jewish Rye"), persons themselves may be seen as inauthentic. The boy can play or eat Jewish, but he cannot become a Jew. My argument throughout this book shows this to reflect a visual anxiety, where bodies and images reveal both the desire for and an unease with authentic exposure. There is surely plenty to see in this text–image: visions of cultural legitimacy, gendered accounts of racial belonging, ethnic food practices, and Jewish continuity. The challenge of the past six chapters has been to discern the rhetoric of authenticity in text and image as a visual discourse in American Jewish thought. This challenge persists in a commercial image for Levy's Rye Bread, as it does for the many other images and texts in this book. My hope is that readers detect how this image of the "little Black boy," the very one that Toni Eisendorf confronted in the subway station,[22] asserts authenticity within and alongside the anxiety of inauthenticity. Texts make rhetorical arguments, but so do images. Sometimes they work together, yet other times they reflect similar or even opposing anxieties. But they all show us what authenticity looks like—whether in the blossoming fields of Palestine, in Schor's *shtetl* imaginary, in festival food preparation, or even in the rhetoric of Jewish bodies, gender, and race. This is a story worth telling in every generation; but perhaps, even more, it is a story worth seeing.

Notes

Introduction

1. Reena Bernards, "An Ethiopian GILGUL Come to Life: An Interview with Toni Eisendorf," *Bridges* 9, no. 1 (Summer 2001): 21–25. Quotation from page 22.

2. Melanie Kaye/Kantrowitz, *The Colors of Jews: Racial Politics and Radical Diasporism* (Bloomington: Indiana University Press, 2007), 40.

3. Whitey Ruben, owner of Levy's Jewish Rye Bread, selected DDB for its advertisement campaign that turned Levy's into the largest seller of rye bread in New York. Howard Zieff (1927–2009), the photographer for the posters, in an interview in 2001 had this to say about the ethnic images: "We wanted normal-looking people, not blond, perfectly proportioned models. . . . I saw the Indian on the street; he was an engineer for the New York Central. . . . The Chinese guy worked in a restaurant near my Midtown Manhattan office. And the kid we found in Harlem. They all had great faces, interesting faces, expressive faces." See Bernard Weinraub, "Arts in America: From Ordinary Faces, Extraordinary Ads," *New York Times* (February 21, 2002), http://www.nytimes.com/2002/02/21/arts/arts-in-america-from-ordinary-faces-extraordinary-ads.html. Accessed November 4, 2013.

4. Charles Lindholm, *Culture and Authenticity* (Oxford: Blackwell Publishing, 2008), 1 and 2.

5. Charles Taylor, *The Ethics of Authenticity* (Cambridge, Mass.: Harvard University Press, 1991).

6. Lionel Trilling, *Sincerity and Authenticity* (Cambridge, Mass.: Harvard University Press, 1972).

7. Ibid., 52 and 99; see also Lindholm, 3–4.

8. Trilling, 124.

9. Ibid., 5.

10. Taylor, 16 and 17.

11. Ibid., 26.

12. Corey Anton, *Selfhood and Authenticity* (Albany: State University of New York Press, 2001), 8.

13. Taylor, 11; also see Anton, 4.

14. Adam B. Seligman, Robert Weller, Michael Puett, and Bennett Simon, *Ritual and Its Consequences: An Essay on the Limits of Sincerity* (New York: Oxford University Press, 2008), 24.

15. Ibid., 6, 20, 31, and 8.

16. Ibid., 122.

17. Ibid., 181 and 112.

18. Ibid., 24.

19. Ibid., 181: "What we usually call the 'modern' period, therefore, should instead be understood in part as a period in which sincerity claims have been given a rare institutional and cultural emphasis."

20. Taylor, 61.

21. Bernards, 21–22.

22. David Freedberg, *The Power of Images: Studies in the History and Theory of Response* (Chicago: University of Chicago Press, 1989), xxii.

23. David Morgan, *The Sacred Gaze: Religious Visual Culture in Theory and Practice* (Berkeley: University of California Press, 2005), 3.

24. Rachel Neis, *The Sense of Sight in Rabbinic Culture: Jewish Ways of Seeing in Late Antiquity* (Cambridge: Cambridge University Press, 2013), 3–4.

25. There is practically a cottage industry of work in this burgeoning field, but I have found the following particularly helpful: Michael Berkowitz, "Art in Zionist Popular Culture and Jewish National Self-Consciousness, 1897–1914," in *Art and Its Uses: The Visual Image and Modern Jewish Society,* ed. Ezra Mendelsohn, Studies in Contemporary Jewry VI (New York: Oxford University Press, 1990), 9–42; Richard Cohen, *Jewish Icons: Art and Society in Modern Europe* (Berkeley: University of California Press, 1998); James Elkins, *The Object Stares Back: On the Nature of Seeing* (New York: Simon & Schuster, 1996); Elkins, *Visual Studies: A Skeptical Introduction* (New York: Routledge, 2003); Martin Jay, *Downcast Eyes: The Denigration of Vision in Twentieth-Century French Thought* (Berkeley: University of California Press, 1993); Marshall McLuhan, *The Medium is the Massage* (Corte Madera, Calif.: Gingko Press, 2001); Nicholas Mirzoeff, ed., *The Visual Culture Reader* (London: Routledge, 1998); David Morgan and Sally Promey, eds., *The Visual Culture of American Religions* (Berkeley: University of California Press, 2001); Marita Sturken and Lisa Cartwright, *Practices of Looking: An Introduction to Visual Culture* (New York: Oxford University Press, 2001); and John A. Walker and Sarah Chaplin, *Visual Culture: An Introduction* (Manchester: Manchester University Press, 1997).

26. See W. J. T. Mitchell, *Iconology: Image, Text, Ideology* (Chicago: University of Chicago Press, 1986); Mitchell, *Picture Theory* (Chicago: University of Chicago Press, 1994); and Mitchell, *What Do Pictures Want? The Lives and Loves of Images* (Chicago: University of Chicago Press, 2005).

27. Neis makes a compelling argument to broaden visual studies to include more than pictorial images. She refers to these materials that "come into view" as visual objects. See Neis, 18–19.

28. Morgan, 52–53.

29. Ibid., 2.

30. Ibid., 29.

31. Ibid., 93–94.

32. Ibid., 3.

33. Neis, 18.

34. Morgan, 30–31.

35. Ibid., 55.

36. Morgan, 94.

37. See Willi Goetschel, *The Discipline of Philosophy and the Invention of Modern Jewish Thought* (New York: Fordham University Press, 2013), 3.

38. See Naomi W. Cohen, *The Americanization of Zionism, 1897–1948* (Hanover, N.H.: Brandeis University Press, 2003); Mark Raider, *The Emergence of American Zionism* (New York: New York University Press, 1998).

39. Rachel Adler, *Engendering Judaism* (Philadelphia: The Jewish Publication Society, 1998), 138.

40. Jonathan Safran Foer, *New American Haggadah,* trans. Nathan Englander (New York: Little, Brown and Company, 2012), 77.

41. Shalom M. Wallach, *Pesach Haggadah with a Commentary Culled from the Classic Baalei Mussar* (New York: Mesorah, 1989), 103.

1. Seeing Israel in Bernard Rosenblatt's *Social Zionism*

1. See Arthur A. Goren, "'Anu banu artza' in America: The Americanization of the *Halutz* Ideal," in *Envisioning Israel: The Changing Ideals and Images of North American Jews*, ed. Allon Gal (Detroit: Wayne State University Press, 1996), 81–113, reprinted in Arthur A. Goren, *The Politics and Public Culture of American Jews* (Bloomington: Indiana University Press, 1999), 165–185; and Raider, *The Emergence of American Zionism*, 69–124. Jeffrey Shandler and Beth S. Wenger describe the *halutzim* in this very helpful description: "*Halutzim* provided American Zionists with compelling role models of the 'new' Jewish man and woman—proud, athletic, activist, visionary, and committed to modern, collectivist ideals. Yet these were exemplars for American Jews to admire and support, rather than imitate." See Jeffrey Shandler and Beth S. Wenger, "'The Site of Paradise': The Holy Land in American Jewish Imagination," in *Encounters with the "Holy Land": Place, Past and Future in American Jewish Culture*, ed. Jeffrey Shandler and Beth S. Wenger (Hanover, N.H.: Brandeis University Press, 1998), 11–40, especially page 34.

2. Walter Ackerman, "Israel in American Jewish Education," in *Envisioning Israel: The Changing Ideals and Images of North American Jews*, 173–190, especially pages 173 and 189.

3. Rafael Medoff, *Zionism and the Arabs: An American Jewish Dilemma, 1898–1948* (Westport, Conn.: Praeger, 1997), 24; See Bernard Rosenblatt, *Two Generations of Zionism* (New York: Shengold, 1967), 44; and Melvin Urofsky, *American Zionism from Herzl to the Holocaust* (Lincoln: University of Nebraska Press, 1995), 117.

4. For the notion of "upbuilding" the land, see Raider, 74. On the close relation between American Zionism and the progressive tradition, see Urofsky, 133.

5. See Jonathan Sarna, "'The Greatest Jew in the World since Jesus Christ': The Jewish Legacy of Louis D. Brandeis," *American Jewish History* 81, no. 3–4 (1994): 346–364; Sarna, "A Projection of America as It Ought to Be: Zion in the Mind's Eye of American Jews," in *Envisioning Israel*, 41–59, especially pages 51–57; and Urofsky, 255–256. According to Urofsky, "Brandeis, although consulting with his colleagues, wrote the so-called Pittsburgh Platform mainly by himself" (255). Sarna offers the more modest view that "Horace Kallen drafted and Brandeis refined" the platform ("'The Greatest Jew in the World since Jesus Christ,'" 360).

6. Bernard Rosenblatt, *Social Zionism* (New York: The Public Publishing Company, Inc., 1919), 12. Rosenblatt reproduced the six planks in the Pittsburgh Program on pages 10–11, but he added an additional principle that, according to Jonathan Sarna, "was deleted from the text [the Pittsburgh Program] at the last minute." In Kallen's original draft it is listed as the fifth principle, and Rosenblatt reproduces it in this way: "The fiscal policy shall be framed so as to protect the people from the evils of land speculation and from every other form of financial oppression" (11). See Sarna, "Projection of America as It Ought to Be," 53.

7. Shandler and Wenger, 34.

8. See Rosenblatt, *Social Zionism*, 13; Goren, "'Anu banu artza' in America," 82; and Raider, 76.

9. Anita Shapira, *Land and Power: The Zionist Resort to Force, 1881–1948* (Stanford, Calif.: Stanford University Press, 1999), 117.

10. Sarna, "Projection of America as It Ought to Be," 55.

11. See Asher Biemann, "Aesthetics and Art," in *The Cambridge History of Jewish Philosophy: The Modern Era*, ed. Martin Kavka, Zachary Braiterman, and David Novak, vol. 2 (Cambridge: Cambridge University Press, 2012), 759–779, especially pages 767 and 775.

12. See Yael Zerubavel, *Recovered Roots: Collective Memory and the Making of Israeli National Tradition* (Chicago: University of Chicago Press, 1995), 215: "Zionist memory portrayed the land as empty and desolate, yearning for the return of its ancient Hebrew inhabitants."

13. David Morgan, *The Sacred Gaze: Religious Visual Culture in Theory and Practice* (Berkeley: University of California Press, 2005), 46.

14. Raider, 96.

15. Ibid., 95.

16. Ibid., 97.

17. Mitchell Hart's excellent work on the Zionist use of social scientific "evidence" reveals how scientists employed images as "proof" for their racial and environmental claims. Hart recognizes that such images "supplemented arguments adduced from statistics" and are "bound up with particular ideological commitments and goals." But Hart's scientists view pictures through more restricted lenses: "the visual narrative offers further proof." It is this sense of "further proof"—evidence that arrives after the written claims have left their mark—that I intend to problematize in this chapter. See Mitchell Hart, *Social Science and the Politics of Modern Jewish Identity* (Stanford, Calif.: Stanford University Press, 2000), 170, 24, 192.

18. W. J. T. Mitchell has devoted much of his scholarly career to explore these features of textual production, and has made us aware of the interplay between text and image in ways that complicate this deceptive binary. See Mitchell, *Iconology: Image, Text, Ideology* (Chicago: University of Chicago Press, 1986); Mitchell, *Picture Theory* (Chicago: University of Chicago Press, 1994), 11–82; and Mitchell, *What Do Pictures Want? The Lives and Loves of Images* (Chicago: University of Chicago Press, 2005).

19. Eric Zakim, *To Build and Be Built: Landscape, Literature, and the Construction of Zionist Identity* (Philadelphia: University of Pennsylvania Press, 2006), 12.

20. Three of the four images appear more than once in *The Maccabaean* as ornamental appendages to published articles in the journal; the fourth sketch is part of the title page for the recurring section, "The Zionist Movement: A Review of Zionist Events." See *The Maccabaean* 31 (May and July, 1918): 126 (May) and 188 (July); *The Maccabaean* 31 (July, September, and October, 1918): 210 (July), 282 (September), and 310 (October); *The Maccabaean* 31 (December, 1918; July and September, 1919): 344 (December), 199 (July), and 292 (September); and *The Maccabaean* 31 (December, 1918): 360. My research assistant at Haverford College, Aaron Madow, worked tirelessly to check volumes of *The Maccabaean* in search of similar sketches, and he deserves much of the credit and praise for this original research.

21. It is likely that either Rosenblatt himself or the publisher of *Social Zionism* commissioned these sketches for the book from a staff artist at *The Maccabaean*. Despite extensive inquiries, we could not track down the name of this artist, nor discover how these images made their way into Rosenblatt's *Social Zionism*. Indeed, it is even unclear whether Rosenblatt himself oversaw this project.

22. Rosenblatt, *Social Zionism*, 9.

23. For Horace Kallen's own sense of the Pittsburgh Program that he originally drafted, see Horace Meyer Kallen, *Zionism and World Politics: A Study in History and Social Psychology* (Garden City, N.Y.: Doubleday, Page & Company, 1921), 192–193.

24. See Derek J. Penslar, *Zionism and Technocracy: The Engineering of Jewish Settlement in Palestine, 1870–1918* (Bloomington: Indiana University Press, 1991), 41 and 59 for his account of this relation between political and practical Zionists: "After Herzl's death, it became the task of practical Zionists to attempt to realize, at least in part, Herzl's dream of an ideal society in a Jewish state" (59).

25. Rosenblatt, *Social Zionism*, 110.

26. Ibid., 9–10.

27. See Naomi W. Cohen, *The Americanization of Zionism, 1897–1948* (Hanover, N.H.: Brandeis University Press, 2003), 7; Allon Gal, "Overview: Envisioning Israel—The American Jewish Tradition," in *Envisioning Israel*, 13–37, especially pages 22–23; and Rosenblatt, *Two Generations of Zionism*, 53 and 267.

28. Sarna, "Projection of America as It Ought to Be," 56. Also see Sarna, "'The Greatest Jew In the World since Jesus Christ,'" 358–360: "The Jewish homeland represented American liberal intellectuals' fondest and most romantic visions of a better world, a world influenced by the postwar dreams of Woodrow Wilson and made only more attractive, in Brandeis's case, by his first (and only) visit to the Holy Land in 1919" (360).

29. See Shapira, 40–52, especially pages 41–42. Shapira claims this slogan "was common among Zionists at the end of the nineteenth, and the beginning of the twentieth, century" (42), even though the concept, if not parts of the slogan, may have roots in eighteenth-century Christian restorationists.

30. Michael Berkowitz, *Zionist Culture and West European Jewry before the First World War* (Chapel Hill: University of North Carolina Press, 1993), 150. Note too Berkowitz's account of Jewish landscape: "Arabs were, by and large, made to appear as less than vital elements of the Palestinian society. This was achieved through photography and narratives that relegated them to marginality in a Jewish native landscape. The Zionist view of Palestine showed Jews to be operating in a cultural void, that is, in a space where the indigenous population had not created a society with a unique character, discernible to European eyes. Predictably it was often reported the Jews of Palestine were at a higher stage of morality, culture, and education than the Arabs" (147).

31. See Amos Elon, *Herzl* (New York: Holt, Rinehart and Winston, 1975), 312; and Daniel Boyarin, *Unheroic Conduct: The Rise of Heterosexuality and the Invention of the Jewish Man* (Berkeley: University of California Press, 1997), 310.

32. See Lila Corwin Berman, *Speaking of Jews: Rabbis, Intellectuals, and the Creation of an American Public Identity* (Berkeley: University of California Press, 2009), for her account of social scientific discourse in twentieth-century American Jewish thought.

33. See Shandler and Wenger, 23.

34. Medoff, 10 and 11; also see Urofsky, 241: "The Jews, for their part, really had given very little thought to the Palestinian Arabs."

35. Yael Zerubavel, "Desert and Settlement: Space Metaphors and Symbolic Landscapes in the Yishuv and Early Israeli Culture," in *Jewish Topographies: Visions of Space, Traditions of Place*, ed. Julia Brauch, Anna Lipphardt and Alexandra Nocke (Aldershot: Ashgate, 2008), 201–222, especially page 208.

36. Zakim, 9 and 150.

37. See Shapira, 30; and Zerubavel, "Desert and Settlement," 209. As Berkowitz has it: "The notion of barrenness—a lack of distinguishing natural characteristics, of trees, of cities, of people—was presented as a divinely ordained precondition for the Jewish national regeneration." Berkowitz, *Zionist Culture and West European Jewry*, 163.

38. See Shandler and Wenger, 31.

39. Zerubavel, "Desert and Settlement," 209.

40. Rosenblatt, *Social Zionism*, 111. Rosenblatt echoes Arthur Ruppin, who as a member of Brit Shalom recognized in the 1920s that Arabs inhabited Palestine, but still could only see a vast emptiness: "it will not be necessary to destroy before one can build." Quoted in Shapira, 165.

41. Rosenblatt, *Social Zionism*, 91.

42. See Todd Samuel Presner, *Muscular Judaism: The Jewish Body and the Politics of Regeneration* (New York: Routledge, 2007), 156; and S. Ilan Troen, *Imagining Zion: Dreams, Designs, and Realities in a Century of Jewish Settlement* (New Haven, Conn.: Yale University Press, 2003), xiv. For an account of early *Yishuv* colonization, and the perceived difference between colonization and colonialism, see Ran Aaronsohn, "Settlement in Eretz Israel—A Colonialist Enterprise? 'Critical' Scholarship and Historical Geography," *Israel Studies* 1, no. 2 (Fall 1996): 214–229.

43. Rosenblatt, *Social Zionism,* 44–45. For this distinction between colonization and colonialism, see Troen, *Imagining Zion,* 57. Also note Shapira's account of Jewish conquest: "The concept *kibbush* (conquest) is frequent in the literature of the period; but it has a connotation of settlement, not militant action. In the terms employed before World War I, 'conquering the land' generally meant one thing: settling in Palestine." See Shapira, 41.

44. W. J. T. Mitchell, "Holy Landscapes: Israel, Palestine, and the American Wilderness," *Critical Inquiry* 26, no. 2 (Winter 2000): 193–223, especially page 198.

45. See Shapira, 214.

46. Edward Said, "Invention, Memory, and Place," *Critical Inquiry* 26, no. 2 (Winter 2000): 175–192, especially page 188.

47. Mitchell, "Holy Landscapes," 198.

48. Presner, 167–168; see too George L. Mosse, *The Image of Man: The Creation of Modern Masculinity* (New York: Oxford University Press, 1996), 57–58.

49. Zerubavel, "Desert and Settlement," 210.

50. Rosenblatt, *Social Zionism,* 13.

51. See Presner, 155–186.

52. Rosenblatt, *Social Zionism,* 17 and 16.

53. Presner, 168.

54. Hannan Hever, "We Have Not Arrived from the Sea: A Mizrahi Literary Geography," *Social Identities* 10, no. 1 (2004): 31–51, especially page 34; also see Presner, 185–186, for his appreciation and critique of Hever's account of the sea.

55. Rachel Arbel, *Blue and White in Colors: Zionism's Visual Images, 1897–1947* (Hebrew) (Tel Aviv: The Diaspora Museum and Am Oved, 1997), 29, 49, and 53.

56. Berkowitz, *Zionist Culture and West European Jewry,* 149.

57. See Troen, *Imagining Zion,* 57.

58. Rosenblatt, *Social Zionism,* 17.

59. Ibid.

60. Shandler and Wenger, 23.

61. Rosenblatt, *Social Zionism,* 17.

62. See Presner, 63.

63. Rosenblatt, *Social Zionism,* 10.

64. Ibid., 17.

65. Ibid., 14.

66. Boyarin, *Unheroic Conduct,* 303.

67. See Medoff, 23 and 10–11, for the popular American sense that the Holy Land was virtually unpopulated and Bedouins only roam and never settle in one place very long.

68. Rosenblatt, *Social Zionism,* 19–20.

69. Ibid. 40.

70. See Scott McCloud, *Understanding Comics: The Invisible Art* (New York: HarperCollins, 1993), 60–93.

71. Zerubavel, "Desert and Settlement," 211.

72. Rosenblatt, *Social Zionism,* 10.

73. Ibid., 10–11.

74. Goren, "'Anu banu artza' in America," 93; also see Claudia Prestel, "Arabs and Women: Constructing Zionist Images of the 'Other' in Pre-State Israeli Films," *Nashim* 1 (Winter 1998): 95–105.

75. See Presner, 87–105, especially page 89; Raider, 95–97; Michael Berkowitz, "Art in Zionist Popular Culture and Jewish National Self-Consciousness, 1897–1914," in *Art and Its Uses: The Visual Image and Modern Jewish Society,* ed. Ezra Mendelsohn, Studies in Contemporary Jewry VI (New York: Oxford University Press, 1990), 17–19; Arbel, especially the images on

pages 1, 17, 53, and 92; and the cover of *The Maccabaean* 31 (August, 1918) dedicated to the Pittsburgh Program.

76. Rosenblatt, *Social Zionism*, 10.

77. Berkowitz, "Art in Zionist Popular Culture," 12.

78. Rosenblatt, *Social Zionism*, 13.

79. Quotation from Arthur Hertzberg, *The Zionist Idea: A Historical Analysis and Reader* (Philadelphia: Jewish Publication Society of America, 1959), 381. Also see Zakim, 54–57; and Gideon Shimoni, *The Zionist Ideology* (Hanover, N.H.: Brandeis University Press, 1995), 208–216, 305–309.

80. See Presner, 138–139; and Boyarin, *Unheroic Conduct*, 271–312.

81. See Rosenblatt, *Social Zionism*, 13.

82. Goren, "'Anu banu artza' in America," 81.

83. Zakim, 186.

84. S. Ilan Troen, "Frontier Myths and their Applications in America and Israel: A Transnational Perspective," *Israel Studies* 5, no. 1 (2000): 301–329, especially page 305; also see Troen, *Imagining Zion*, 10.

85. Rosenblatt, *Social Zionism*, 13.

86. Troen, "Frontier Myths and their Applications," 303.

87. See Asher Biemann, "'Thus Rome shows us our True Place': Reflections on the German Jewish Love for Italy," in *German-Jewish Thought between Religion and Politics: Festschrift in Honor of Paul Mendes-Flohr on the Occasion of his Seventieth Birthday,* ed. Christian Wiese and Martina Urban (Berlin and Boston: Walter deGruyter, 2012), 241–261, especially page 254.

88. Brandeis and others often leveled this critique on collective farming initiatives in Palestine. See Troen, *Imagining Zion,* 22–34; Michael Berkowitz, *Western Jewry and the Zionist Project, 1914–1933* (Cambridge: Cambridge University Press, 1997), 56–63; and Penslar, 153.

89. Rosenblatt, *Social Zionism,* 14.

90. Ibid., 33.

91. Ibid., 35.

92. Zerubavel, "Desert and Settlement," 210. See also *Die Neuen Hebräer: 100 Jahre Kunst in Israel,* ed. by Doreet Levitte Harten and Yigal Zalmona (Berlin: Nicolaische Verlagsbuchhandlung, 2005); and Troen, *Imagining Zion,* 17.

93. Rosenblatt, *Social Zionism,* 15.

94. Zerubavel, "Desert and Settlement," 210.

95. See Rosenblatt, *Social Zionism,* 34.

96. See *The Maccabaean* 32 (August, 1919), 216.

97. See Michael Banton, *Racial Theories* (Cambridge: Cambridge University Press, 1987), especially pages 38–43; and Harriet Washington, *Medical Apartheid: The Dark History of Medical Experimentation on Black Americans from Colonial Times to the Present* (New York: Anchor Books, 2006), especially pages 38–39.

98. Rosenblatt, *Social Zionism,* 21.

99. Ibid., 24.

100. Ibid., 22.

101. See *Die Neuen Hebräer: 100 Jahre Kunst in Israel.*

102. Rosenblatt, *Social Zionism,* 23.

103. Ibid., 26.

104. Presner, 161.

105. Rosenblatt, *Social Zionism,* 26.

106. Ibid., 30–31.

107. Ibid., 32.

108. Bernard Rosenblatt, "Zionism as a Progrom [*sic*] of Social Reform," *The Maccabaean* 22 (August, 1912): 50–56, especially page 54.

109. Rosenblatt, *Social Zionism*, 123.

110. Daniel Kevles, *In the Name of Eugenics: Genetics and the Uses of Human Heredity* (Berkeley: University of California Press, 1985), 56–59; and Hart, 169. Also see Wendy Chun's illuminating discussion of the scientific debates surrounding genetics, eugenics, and programmability in early twentieth-century Europe and America in Wendy Chun, *Programmed Visions: Software and Memory* (Cambridge, Mass.: MIT Press, 2013), 120–131.

111. John M. Efron, *Defenders of the Race: Jewish Doctors and Race Science in Fin-de-Siècle Europe* (New Haven, Conn.: Yale University Press, 1994), 148.

112. Rosenblatt, *Social Zionism*, 124.

113. Ibid., 55.

114. Ibid., 56.

115. Hart, 101.

116. Presner, 152.

117. Rosenblatt, *Social Zionism*, 55–56. To hear how this language echoes race science of the early twentieth century, see Efron, 123–174; and Presner, 139–154.

118. Rosenblatt, *Social Zionism*, 56–57.

119. Ibid., 60.

120. Zerubavel, "Desert and Settlement," 202.

2. Seeing Things in Abraham Joshua Heschel's *The Sabbath*

1. Abraham Joshua Heschel, *The Sabbath: Its Meaning for Modern Man* (New York: Farrar, Straus and Giroux, 1951).

2. J. Hoberman and Jeffrey Shandler, eds., *Entertaining America: Jews, Movies, and Broadcasting* (Princeton, N.J.: Princeton University Press, 2003), 113–127.

3. Heschel, *The Sabbath*, 6.

4. Elliot Wolfson, *Through a Speculum that Shines: Vision and Imagination in Medieval Jewish Mysticism* (Princeton, N.J.: Princeton University Press, 1994), 5 and 195.

5. See Martin Jay, *Downcast Eyes: The Denigration of Vision in Twentieth-Century French Thought* (Berkeley: University of California Press, 1993); Asher Biemann, "Aesthetics and Art," in *The Cambridge History of Jewish Philosophy: The Modern Era*, ed. Martin Kavka, Zachary Braiterman, and David Novak, vol. 2 (Cambridge: Cambridge University Press, 2012), 759–770; and Rachel Neis, *The Sense of Sight in Rabbinic Culture: Jewish Ways of Seeing in Late Antiquity* (Cambridge: Cambridge University Press, 2013), 1–10.

6. See Jean-Luc Marion, *The Crossing of the Visible*, trans. James K. A. Smith (Stanford, Calif.: Stanford University Press, 2004), 20. Also note Neis's perceptive analysis of being seen in rabbinic texts. See Neis, 41–81.

7. Abraham Joshua Heschel, *God in Search of Man: A Philosophy of Judaism* (New York: The Noonday Press, 1955), 416.

8. Heschel, *The Sabbath*, 28.

9. Ibid., 10.

10. Elliot Wolfson, *Alef, Mem, Tau: Kabbalistic Musings on Time, Truth, and Death* (Berkeley: University of California Press, 2006), 204 fn. 361.

11. Heschel, *The Sabbath*, 4.

12. See Einat Ramon, "Idolatry and the Dazzle of the Enlightenment in Abraham Joshua Heschel's Thought," (Hebrew) *Daat* 71 (2011): 105–131. Note, however, Shai Held's claim that

"Heschel wants to avoid a modern paganism which deifies mystery, or which worships a God who is perpetually shrouded in absolute mystery." See Shai Held, *Abraham Joshua Heschel: The Call of Transcendence* (Bloomington: Indiana University Press, 2013), 35.

13. See Biemann, 764.

14. Heschel, *The Sabbath,* 3–4.

15. Richard Lanham also employs this distinction between looking at and looking through, but in a slightly different modality of visual awareness. Still, Lanham's "looking through" registers an immediacy that Heschel seeks to recover as well. See Richard Lanham, *The Electronic Word: Democracy, Technology, and the Arts* (Chicago: University of Chicago Press, 1993), 3–52, especially pages 5 and 43–50; also see Jay David Bolter and Richard Grusin, *Remediation: Understanding New Media* (Cambridge, Mass.: MIT Press, 2000), 41.

16. Heschel, *The Sabbath,* 4.

17. Ibid.

18. Jay, 14.

19. Heschel, *The Sabbath,* 5.

20. Ibid., 3.

21. Ibid., 97.

22. Ibid., 5.

23. Ibid., 6.

24. Ibid., 5 and 6.

25. For a provocative notion of the hybrid and its place in the "modern constitution," see Bruno Latour, *We Have Never Been Modern* (Cambridge, Mass.: Harvard University Press, 1993).

26. Wolfson, *Through a Speculum that Shines,* 66.

27. David Morgan, *The Sacred Gaze: Religious Visual Culture in Theory and Practice* (Berkeley: University of California Press, 2005), 130.

28. Jean-Luc Marion, *God without Being,* trans. Thomas A. Carlson (Chicago: University of Chicago Press, 1991), 9.

29. Ibid., 10, 11, and 12.

30. Ibid., 17.

31. Ibid., 19.

32. Marion, *Crossing of the Visible,* 51.

33. Ibid., 57.

34. Neis, 59.

35. Robyn Horner, *Jean-Luc Marion: A Theo-Logical Introduction* (Burlington, Vt.: Ashgate, 2005), 63 and 64.

36. See Heschel, *The Sabbath,* 35–41, 47–48. Heschel appropriates this story from Talmudic tractate *Shabbat 33b.*

37. I take this descriptive account of Heschel's retelling from my own work in which I discuss Heschel's reading of time and space. See Ken Koltun-Fromm, *Material Culture and Jewish Thought in America* (Bloomington: Indiana University Press, 2010), 168–169.

38. Heschel, *The Sabbath,* 35.

39. Ibid., 36.

40. Ibid., 37.

41. Ibid., 39.

42. Neis, 63–64: "The motif of rabbis killing, incinerating, or injuring with their gazes is found in Palestinian and Babylonian sources; this capacity is attributed to both Palestinian and Babylonian sages. This kind of harmful gaze seems to reflect Greco-Roman theories of 'extramissive' vision, which explained the power of vision, sometimes understood as a fiery ray, as a force that emanated from the eye."

43. Heschel, *The Sabbath*, 52.

44. Ibid., 59.

45. Ibid.

46. Ibid., 54.

47. Ibid., 51.

48. Ibid.

49. See Jacques Lacan, *The Four Fundamental Concepts of Psychoanalysis* (New York: W. W. Norton, 1981), especially page 92; and Jay, 329–370, especially page 364.

50. Heschel, *The Sabbath*, 53.

51. Ibid., 59.

52. Neis, 81.

53. Heschel, *The Sabbath*, 59 and 60.

54. Edward Kaplan, *Holiness in Words: Abraham Joshua Heschel's Poetics of Piety* (Albany: State University of New York Press, 1996), 86.

55. Heschel, *The Sabbath*, 59–60.

56. Jay, 80.

57. Heschel, *The Sabbath*, 21.

58. Ibid., 76 and 28.

59. Ibid., 13 and 67.

60. Ibid., 29 and 28.

61. Jonathan Crary, *Techniques of the Observer* (Cambridge, Mass.: MIT Press, 1992), 10.

62. Heschel, *The Sabbath*, 10.

63. Ibid., 27.

64. See Abraham Joshua Heschel, *Heavenly Torah as Refracted through the Generations*, trans. Gordon Tucker (New York: Continuum, 2005), 708–710, where Heschel discusses "the path of vision" and "the path of reason," together with the relative blindness within each mode of apprehension.

65. See Wolfson, *Through a Speculum that Shines*, 331, 377–392.

66. Heschel, *The Sabbath*, 12.

67. Ira Eisenstein, "Of Time and the Sabbath," *The Reconstructionist* 22 (February 1952): 23–24, especially page 24.

68. Nahum Glatzer, "Review of *The Sabbath*," *Judaism: A Quarterly Journal of Jewish Life and Thought* 1, no. 3 (1952): 283–286, especially pages 285–286. Edward Kaplan misreads Glatzer's critique, for he claims that, "for Glatzer, Schor's combination of folkloric and abstract conceptions fitly symbolized Heschel's attempt to insert a sense of eternal holiness into contemporary thinking." But Glatzer is clear that the engravings "only partly" fit the volume, and they could very well "distract" the reader from the "immense actuality of the text." See Edward Kaplan, *Spiritual Radical: Abraham Joshua Heschel in America, 1940–1972* (New Haven, Conn.: Yale University Press, 2007), 412 fn. 37.

69. See Abraham Joshua Heschel, *The Earth Is the Lord's*; and *The Sabbath* (Cleveland: World Publishing Company, 1963).

70. See Jeffrey Shandler, "Heschel and Yiddish: A Struggle with Signification," *Journal of Jewish Thought and Philosophy* 2 (1993): 245–299, especially page 284; Barbara Kirshenblatt-Gimblett, "Imagining Europe: The Popular Arts of American Jewish Ethnography," in *Divergent Jewish Cultures: Israel & America*, ed. Deborah Dash Moore and S. Ilan Troen (New Haven, Conn.: Yale University Press, 2001), 155–191, especially page 175; and the various essays in Steven T. Katz, ed., *The Shtetl: New Evaluations* (New York: New York University Press, 2007).

71. Kaplan, *Spiritual Radical*, 103.

72. Ilya Schor, "A Working Definition of Jewish Art," *Conservative Judaism* 16, no. 1 (1961): 28–33.

73. Ibid., 28.

74. Ibid., 29.

75. Ibid.

76. See Biemann, 765–769.

77. For a thoughtful account of the relation between sight and touch, see Neis, 27–31.

78. Schor, 30 and 31.

79. Abraham Joshua Heschel, "Ilya Schor," *Conservative Judaism* 16, no. 1 (1961): 20–21; and see Kaplan, *Spiritual Radical,* 204.

80. Heschel, "Ilya Schor," 20–21.

81. See Kaplan, *Spiritual Radical,* especially pages 176–177 and 201. I want to thank Steven Zipperstein for alerting me to Heschel's self-image.

82. Heschel, *The Sabbath,* 28.

83. Ibid., 13.

84. Wolfson, *Through a Speculum that Shines,* 392.

85. Heschel, *God in Search of Man,* 116.

86. See Emil Fackenheim, "Review of *God in Search of Man,*" *Conservative Judaism* 15 (1960): 50–53; Eliezer Berkovits, *Major Themes in Modern Philosophies of Judaism* (New York: Ktav Publishing House, Inc., 1974), 192–224; and Arnold Eisen, "Re-Reading Heschel on the Commandments," *Modern Judaism* 9, no. 1 (1989): 1–33, especially pages 1–2 for his review of this type of literature.

87. Heschel, *God in Search of Man,* 117. On the issue of wonder in Heschel's works, see Held, 28–71.

88. Heschel, *The Sabbath,* 20.

89. Ibid., 30.

90. The term *visual piety* comes from David Morgan, *Visual Piety: A History and Theory of Popular Religious Images* (Berkeley: University of California Press, 1998).

91. Heschel, *The Sabbath,* 91.

3. Seeing Food in *The Jewish Home Beautiful* and *Kosher by Design*

1. Betty Greenberg and Althea Silverman, *The Jewish Home Beautiful* (New York: National Women's League of the United Synagogue of America, 1941); Susie Fishbein, *Kosher by Design: Picture Perfect Food for the Holidays & Every Day* (New York: Mesorah, 2003).

2. For two very different but revealing ways to approach cookbooks as sources for Jewish culture, see Barbara Kirshenblatt-Gimblett, "Kitchen Judaism," in *Getting Comfortable in New York: The American Jewish Home, 1880–1950,* ed. Susan Braunstein and Jenna Weissman Joselit (New York: The Jewish Museum, 1990), 77–105; and Marcie Cohen Ferris, *Matzoh Ball Gumbo: Culinary Tales of the Jewish South* (Chapel Hill: University of North Carolina Press, 2005).

3. Jeremy Stolow, *Orthodox by Design: Judaism, Print Politics, and the ArtScroll Revolution* (Berkeley: University of California Press, 2010), 121.

4. Jenna Weissman Joselit, *The Wonders of America: Reinventing Jewish Culture, 1880–1950* (New York: Henry Holt and Company, 1994), 238.

5. Ann Mason and Marian Meyers, "Living with Martha Stewart Media: Chosen Domesticity in the Experience of Fans," *Journal of Communication* 51 (2001): 801–823, especially pages 815 and 820.

6. Fishbein, 3.

7. Shuly Rubin Schwartz, *The Rabbi's Wife: The Rebbetzin in American Jewish Life* (New York: New York University Press, 2006), 143.

8. Norma Baumel Joseph, "Introduction: Feeding an Identity—Gender, Food, and Survival," *Nashim* 5 (Fall 2002): 7–13, especially page 8.

9. Stolow, *Orthodox by Design*, 131.

10. The flap jacket to *Kosher by Design* reads: "Feast your eyes on **Kosher by Design**—an engaging and elegant cookbook that delights the senses as it feeds your soul!"

11. See Barbara Kirshenblatt-Gimblett, "Playing to the Senses: Food as a Performance Medium," *Performance Research* 4, no. 1 (1999): 1–30; and Kirshenblatt-Gimblett, "The Kosher Gourmet in the Nineteenth-Century Kitchen: Three Jewish Cookbooks in Historical Perspective," *Journal of Gastronomy* 2, no. 4 (Winter 1986/87): 51–89.

12. Greenberg and Silverman, 58.

13. Fishbein, 16.

14. Note Stolow's insightful comment: "This scene of domestic conviviality and maternal aura, supplemented by the benefits of modern technology (cooks are free to choose between the convenience of a bread machine and the social benefits accrued from enlisting family members in collective labor), underscores the links between religious obligation and traditions of practice that stand at the heart of challah baking." See Stolow, *Orthodox by Design*, 127.

15. For the multiple relations between performance and food, see Kirshenblatt-Gimblett, "Playing to the Senses," 1–2.

16. Jenna Weissman Joselit, "'A Set Table': Jewish Domestic Culture in the New World, 1880–1950," in *Getting Comfortable in New York*, 21–76, especially pages 29, 48–49.

17. Greenberg and Silverman, 14.

18. Shaul Magid, *American Post-Judaism: Identity and Renewal in a Postethnic Society* (Bloomington: Indiana University Press, 2013), 167–168.

19. Jeremy Stolow, "Communicating Authority, Consuming Tradition: Jewish Orthodox Outreach Literature and Its Reading Public," in *Religion, Media, and the Public Sphere*, ed. Birgit Meyer and Annelies Moors (Bloomington: Indiana University Press, 2006), 73–90, especially page 74.

20. Fishbein, front cover.

21. Stolow, *Orthodox by Design*, 52–53, 178–179.

22. Magid, 173.

23. Stolow, "Communicating Authority," 75.

24. Greenberg and Silverman, 13.

25. Ibid., 11.

26. The narrative and dramatic versions almost mirror each other in order of holiday discussions: they each begin with the Jewish New Year (Rosh Hashanah), but where the dramatic version then stages Yom Kippur, Greenberg's narrative (for reasons I do not fully understand) skips this festival. Both then move, in parallel order, to Sukkot, Hanukkah, Purim, Pesach, Shavuot (spelled *Shabuot* in the text), and each concludes with Shabbat. Fishbein's *Kosher by Design* follows this same list but adds Tu B'shvat and Simchat Torah—perhaps a sign of their growing popularity for American Jews.

27. Greenberg and Silverman, 35.

28. Ibid.

29. See Joselit, "'A Set Table,'" 52; and Kirshenblatt-Gimblett, "Kitchen Judaism," 102.

30. Greenberg and Silverman, 13.

31. Ibid.

32. Ibid.

33. Rachel Gross, "Draydel Salad: The Serious Business of Jewish Food and Fun in the 1950s," in *Religion, Food, and Eating in North America,* ed. Benjamin E. Zeller et al. (New York: Columbia University Press, 2014), 91–113, especially page 97.

34. Greenberg and Silverman, 13.

35. Ibid., 13–14.

36. See Joselit, "'A Set Table,'" 23: "Whatever the physical setting . . . the home played host to changing notions of Jewish domestic culture. As the intimate site of acculturation, home served a symbolic purpose as well. 'The function of the home,' explained the author of a 1930s guidebook to Jewish parenting, 'must therefore be to transmit a civilization, to provide for the continuity of a cultural inheritance as well as an ethnological one.'"

37. Ibid., 59.

38. Greenberg and Silverman, 35. Fishbein is a bit more stringent and precise about the time for lighting of the candles: "Lighting the Shabbat candles is a *mitzvah* performed by the wife/mother of the household eighteen minutes before sundown." See Fishbein, 10.

39. Greenberg and Silverman, 78.

40. Ibid., 78 and 79.

41. Ibid., 78.

42. Ibid., 65 and 66.

43. Ibid., 65.

44. Ibid., 65–66.

45. See Joselit, "'A Set Table,'" 45–49.

46. Greenberg and Silverman, 41.

47. Ibid., 67.

48. Ibid., 73.

49. Ibid., 13.

50. Ibid., 87 and 88.

51. Ibid., 88.

52. Elliott Weiss, "Packaging Jewishness: Novelty and Tradition in Kosher Food Packaging," *Design Issues* 20, no. 1 (Winter 2004): 48–61, especially pages 53 and 55.

53. Greenberg and Silverman, 121. I wish to thank my student, Paige Winokur, for bringing this evocative text to my attention.

54. Ibid., 41.

55. Fishbein, 3.

56. Ibid.

57. See Steven Cohen and Arnold Eisen, *The Jew Within: Self, Family, and Community in America* (Bloomington: Indiana University Press, 2000).

58. Fishbein, 3 and 8.

59. Ibid.

60. Greenberg and Silverman, 87.

61. Fishbein, 3.

62. Stolow, *Orthodox by Design,* 131.

63. Fishbein, 3.

64. Kirshenblatt-Gimblett, "Playing to the Senses," 2.

65. Stolow, *Orthodox by Design,* 154.

66. Elaine Durbach, "Dining by Design," *New Jersey Jewish News,* October 30, 2003, http://njjewishnews.com/njjn.com/103003/ltdiningbydesign.html. Accessed August 20, 2014.

67. Fishbein, 3.

68. See Stolow, *Orthodox by Design,* 173: "Even the most mundane accessory item, it seems, has the power to contribute to the manifestation of sacred aura."

69. Stolow also recognizes the confluence of Fishbein's discussion of food display (what he calls here "bourgeois self-representation") and traditional language for Shabbat. See Stolow, *Orthodox by Design*, 125.

70. Gavriel Aryeh Sanders, "Kosher Diva Outdoes Herself with Latest Offering," *Jewish World Review*, March 14, 2005, http://jewishworldreview.com/kosher/fishbein.php3. Accessed August 20, 2014.

71. Stolow, *Orthodox by Design*, 153 and 154.

72. Stolow, "Communicating Authority," 86.

73. Fishbein, 17. Stolow calls this the "artful combination of 'cute' and 'classical' modes of food preparation and presentation." See Stolow, *Orthodox by Design*, 127.

74. http://www.isjl.org/traveling-exhibits.html. Accessed May 14, 2014.

75. Ferris, 24.

76. Stolow understands the power of these images to draw readers "into contact with an authentic presence," and he recognizes how the written instructions serve visual goals. But he also harnesses this visual awareness within his more general argument about scripturalism, "the production of text-centrism," and "the authority invested in books." Still, it is not that the image "carries with it a more radical promise of perfect mimesis," as Stolow would have it, but rather that readers, as Kirshenblatt-Gimblett suggests, "can 'play' the recipe in their mind's eye," and as Fishbein believes, "people eat with their eyes." See Stolow, *Orthodox by Design*, 155 and 157; Kirshenblatt-Gimblett, "Playing to the Senses," 3; and Suzi Brozman, "Not your Bubbe's Cooking," *Texas Jewish Post*, March 10, 2005, http://texashistory.unt.edu/ark:/67531 /metapth188070/m1/19/. Accessed August 20, 2014.

77. Stolow, *Orthodox by Design*, 155.

78. Fishbein, 10.

79. Stolow, *Orthodox by Design*, 155.

80. See Etan Diamond, "The Kosher Lifestyle: Religious Consumerism and Suburban Orthodox Jews," *Journal of Urban History* 28, no. 4 (May 2002): 488–505, especially page 489: "The expansion of a consumerist culture, far from being even loosely incompatible with Orthodox Judaism, actually made it easier to maintain traditional Jewish practice. . . . Thus, rather than shed their religious traditionalism on contact with secular suburban commercial culture, Orthodox Jews used that commercial culture to facilitate, strengthen, and even expand their traditionalist religious behaviors." Also see Jack Kugelmass, "Green Bagels: An Essay on Food, Nostalgia, and the Carnivalesque," in *Yivo Annual,* ed. Deborah Dash Moore, vol. 19 (Evanston, Ill.: Northwestern University Press, 1990), 57–80.

81. Fishbein, 10–11.

82. Greenberg and Silverman, 35.

83. Ibid., 65.

84. Fishbein, 3 and 13.

85. Sanders, "Kosher Diva Outdoes Herself with Latest Offering," http://jewishworldreview .com/kosher/fishbein.php3.

86. Mason and Meyers, 820.

87. http://www.amazon.com/Kosher-Design-Picture-Perfect-Holidays/product-reviews /1578197074/ref=cm_cr_pr_btm_link_4?ie=UTF8&pageNumber=4&showViewpoints=0. Accessed July 29, 2013.

88. http://www.amazon.com/Kosher-Design-Picture-Perfect-Holidays/product-reviews /1578197074/ref=cm_cr_pr_btm_link_1?ie=UTF8&showViewpoints=0. Accessed July 29, 2013.

89. Fishbein, 13.

90. See Diamond, "The Kosher Lifestyle," 496.

91. Fishbein, 14.

92. Greenberg and Silverman, 88.

93. Fishbein, 26.

94. See Brozman.

95. Greenberg and Silverman, 27.

96. Ibid., 54–57.

97. Ibid., 57.

98. Ibid., 71.

99. Ibid., 71 and 54.

100. Ibid., 27.

101. Fishbein, 192.

102. Ibid., 192–193.

103. Ibid., 193 and 195.

104. Ibid., 195.

105. Ibid.

106. Ibid.

107. Ibid., 17.

108. Jonathan Z. Smith, *To Take Place: Toward Theory in Ritual* (Chicago: University of Chicago Press, 1987), 46.

109. Greenberg and Silverman, 88.

110. Fishbein, 231.

4. The Language of Jewish Bodies in Michael Wyschogrod's *The Body of Faith*

1. Michael Wyschogrod, *The Body of Faith: God in the People Israel* (Northvale, N.J.: Jason Aronson Inc., 1996), xiii.

2. Ibid., xxxv.

3. See the collected essays in Michael Wyschogrod and R. Kendall Soulen, *Abraham's Promise: Judaism and Jewish-Christian Relations* (Grand Rapids, Mich.: Wm. B. Eerdmans Publishing Company, 2004); and note as well the essays on Wyschogrod in the special issue of *Modern Theology* 22, no. 4 (October 2006).

4. See Wyschogrod, "Why Was and Is the Theology of Karl Barth of Interest to a Jewish Theologian?" in Wyschogrod and Soulen, *Abraham's Promise: Judaism and Jewish-Christian Relations,* 211–224; Wyschogrod, *Body of Faith,* 75–79; and Shai Held, "The Promise and Peril of Jewish Barthianism: The Theology of Michael Wyschogrod," *Modern Judaism* 25, no. 3 (2005): 316–326.

5. Wyschogrod, *Body of Faith,* 64.

6. Ibid., 59.

7. Ibid., 185–190, 241.

8. David Novak, *The Election of Israel: The Idea of the Chosen People* (Cambridge: Cambridge University Press, 1995).

9. Wyschogrod, *Body of Faith,* 92.

10. Ibid., 65.

11. Ibid., 1.

12. Ibid.

13. See Martin Jay, *The Denigration of Vision in Twentieth-Century French Thought* (Berkeley: University of California Press, 1993).

14. Wyschogrod, *Body of Faith,* 1.

15. Ibid., 2.

16. Ibid., 3.

17. See Jean-Luc Marion, *God without Being* (Chicago: University of Chicago Press, 1991), 9–12.

18. Wyschogrod, *Body of Faith*, 3.

19. See Rachel Neis, *The Sense of Sight in Rabbinic Culture: Jewish Ways of Seeing in Late Antiquity* (Cambridge: Cambridge University Press, 2013), 27–31, 130.

20. Wyschogrod, *Body of Faith*, 3.

21. Ibid., 4.

22. Ibid., 203.

23. Ibid., 205.

24. Ibid., 104–108.

25. Ibid., 4 and 5.

26. Ibid., 7.

27. Ibid.

28. See Joseph Soloveitchik, *The Lonely Man of Faith* (New York: Doubleday, 1965).

29. Wyschogrod, *Body of Faith*, 9.

30. Ibid.

31. Ibid., 10.

32. Ibid., 17.

33. Ibid., 18.

34. Ibid.

35. Ibid., 18 and 19.

36. Ibid.

37. Ibid., 20–23.

38. Ibid., 23.

39. Ibid., 43–45.

40. Ibid., 42.

41. Ibid., 46 and 47.

42. Ibid., 47 and 48.

43. Wyschogrod draws heavily from the interpretive tradition that reads Marx as a modern humanist. See the influential work from Shlomo Avineri, *The Social and Political Thought of Karl Marx* (Cambridge: Cambridge University Press, 1968).

44. Wyschogrod, *Body of Faith*, 45.

45. Ibid., 49.

46. Ibid., 248 and 249. See Clement Greenberg, "Avant-Garde and Kitsch," in *Art and Culture: Critical Essays* (Boston: Beacon, 1961), 3–21.

47. Wyschogrod, *Body of Faith*, 248 and 249.

48. Ibid., 249.

49. Ibid., 10.

50. Ibid., 60.

51. Ibid., 10.

52. Ibid., 10 and 11.

53. Ibid., 57–58.

54. Ibid., 9.

55. Novak, 246.

56. Wyschogrod, *Body of Faith*, 64.

57. Wyschogrod and Soulen, *Abraham's Promise*, 171.

58. Wyschogrod, *Body of Faith*, 115.

59. Ibid., 115–116.

60. Ibid., 96 and 1.

61. Ibid., 96.

62. Even Wyschogrod admits to the arduous nature of this section: "This chapter is somewhat more difficult than the others, though it should not be beyond the attentive, nontechnically trained reader" (*Body of Faith,* xxxv). On philosophical approaches to nonbeing, see the helpful analysis by Martin Kavka, *Jewish Messianism and the History of Philosophy* (Cambridge: Cambridge University Press, 2004).

63. Michael Wyschogrod, *Kierkegaard and Heidegger: The Ontology of Existence* (London: Routledge & Paul, 1954).

64. R. Kendall Soulen, "The Achievement of Michael Wyschogrod," *Modern Theology* 22, no. 4 (October 2006): 677–685, especially page 681.

65. Wyschogrod, *Body of Faith,* 159.

66. Ibid., 171 and 163.

67. Ibid., 171–172.

68. Ibid., xxxiii–xxxv.

69. Ibid., 10 and 212–213.

70. Walter James Lowe, "The Intensification of Time: Michael Wyschogrod and the Task of Christian Theology," *Modern Theology* 22, no. 4 (October 2006): 693–699.

71. Michael Wyschogrod, "A Jewish Perspective on Incarnation," *Modern Theology* 12, no. 2 (April 1996): 195–209, especially page 208.

72. Wyschogrod, *Body of Faith,* xvi–xix.

73. Ibid., xxi.

74. Ibid.

5. The Language of Gendered Bodies in Rachel Adler's *Engendering Judaism*

1. Rachel Adler, *Engendering Judaism* (Philadelphia: Jewish Publication Society, 1998), 2.

2. Ibid., xiv.

3. Ibid., xxiv.

4. Ibid., xiv.

5. Rochelle Millen, "'Her Mouth Is Full of Wisdom': Reflections on Jewish Feminist Theology," in *Women Remaking American Judaism,* ed. Riv-Ellen Prell (Detroit: Wayne State University Press, 2007), 27–49.

6. Personal correspondence with Rachel Adler, March 19, 2012.

7. Tamar Ross, *Expanding the Palace of Torah: Orthodoxy and Feminism* (Waltham, Mass.: Brandeis University Press, 2004), 197 and 161. Ross offers trenchant critique of Adler's *Engendering Judaism,* and I include some of it later in this chapter. For a helpful review of Ross's text, though to my mind not sufficiently critical, see Elizabeth Shanks Alexander, "Review of Tamar Ross, *Expanding the Palace of Torah: Feminism and Orthodoxy*," *Nashim* 10 (Fall 2005): 243–249.

8. Susannah Heschel, ed., *On Being a Jewish Feminist* (New York: Schocken Books, 1983).

9. Cynthia Ozick, "Notes toward Finding the Right Question," in *On Being a Jewish Feminist,* 120–151, especially pages 126 and 149.

10. Tikva Frymer-Kensky, "The Bible and Women's Studies," in *Feminist Perspectives on Jewish Studies,* ed. Lynn Davidman and Shelly Tenenbaum (New Haven, Conn.: Yale University Press, 1994), 16–39, especially page 26.

11. Ibid., 24.

12. Judith Plaskow, "The Right Question Is Theological," in *On Being a Jewish Feminist,* 223–233.

13. Judith Plaskow, "Jewish Theology in Feminist Perspective," in *Feminist Perspectives on Jewish Studies,* 62–84, especially page 77.

14. Plaskow, "The Right Question Is Theological," 231 and 226.

15. Plaskow, "Jewish Theology in Feminist Perspective," 78.

16. Ilana Pardes, *Countertraditions in the Bible: A Feminist Approach* (Cambridge, Mass.: Harvard University Press, 1992).

17. Adler, 170.

18. Here I appropriate her own use of the term *polysemous* for multiple and "many-seeded" significations. See Adler, 87.

19. Adler, 212.

20. Ibid., xix.

21. Ross, 159.

22. Adler, xxv.

23. Note Tamar Ross's rhetorical question to Adler's description of the theological task: "But why would anyone be drawn to wrestle with and draw sacred meanings from a text that does not uphold the metaphysical grounding upon which this activity is usually based?" To my mind, Ross reveals less about Adler's views than her own failure to imagine other modes of religious wrestling that do not require "metaphysical grounding." See Ross, 160.

24. Adler, xiv.

25. Ibid., 1.

26. Ibid., 11.

27. Judith Plaskow, *Standing Again at Sinai: Judaism from a Feminist Perspective* (New York: Harper Collins, 1990), 32–36, especially page 34.

28. Adler, 1.

29. Ibid., 3.

30. Ibid., 63.

31. Ibid., 4.

32. Plaskow, *Standing Again at Sinai,* 34.

33. Ross, 193 and 197.

34. Pardes, 51.

35. Adler, 6 and 4.

36. Ibid., 67.

37. See Bernard Wolfson, "African American Jews: Dispelling Myths, Bridging the Divide," in *Black Zion: African American Religious Encounters with Judaism,* ed. Yvonne Chireau and Nathaniel Deutsch (New York: Oxford University Press, 2000), 33–54, especially page 44.

38. Adler, 34.

39. See Ross, 149–156.

40. Adler, 25 and 26.

41. Ibid., 225.

42. Ibid., 25.

43. Ibid., 26.

44. Ross, 178.

45. Adler, 26.

46. Ibid., 34.

47. Ibid., 30. Also see Ross, 60–70.

48. Adler, 34.

49. Robert Cover, "Nomos and Narrative," *Harvard Law Review* 97, no. 1 (November 1983): 4–68, especially pages 4 and 5.

50. Ibid., 10.

51. Ibid., 9 and 27.

52. Adler, 35.

53. Cover, 31.

54. Adler, 35.

55. Ibid., 37.

56. See Adler, 48–50 for Adler's discussion of McIntyre and other virtue theorists.

57. Ibid., 36, 57, and 51.

58. Rachel Neis, *The Sense of Sight in Rabbinic Culture: Jewish Ways of Seeing in Late Antiquity* (Cambridge: Cambridge University Press, 2013), 121.

59. Ibid., 139–146.

60. Adler, 12 and 13.

61. Ibid., 4 and 5.

62. Ibid., 13.

63. Ibid., 123.

64. Ibid., 12–13.

65. Ibid., 54 and 55.

66. For a thorough analysis of this rabbinic passage, see Neis, 117–124.

67. Adler, 141.

68. Ibid., 145.

69. Ibid., 36.

70. Ibid., xxiv.

71. Ibid., 76.

72. Adam B. Seligman et al., *Ritual and Its Consequences: An Essay on the Limits of Sincerity* (New York: Oxford University Press), 4.

73. Adler, 78.

74. Ibid., 106 and 107.

75. Ibid., 108 and 109.

76. Ibid., 134 and 133.

77. Phyllis Trible, *God and the Rhetoric of Sexuality* (Philadelphia: Fortress Press, 1978), 144.

78. Pardes, 118–119.

79. Adler, 137.

80. Ibid., 138.

81. Ibid., 146.

82. Ibid., 138.

83. Translation taken from Ariel Bloch and Chana Bloch, *The Song of Songs: A New Translation with an Introduction and Commentary* (New York: Random House, 1995), 53–61. Adler uses this translation in her *Engendering Judaism*.

84. Adler, 138.

85. For a helpful survey of the metaphor–allegory dualism, one that has ancient roots, see John David Dawson, *Christian Figural Reading and the Fashioning of Identity* (Berkeley: University of California Press, 2001); and Susan Handelman, *Fragments of Redemption* (Bloomington: Indiana University Press, 1991), 105–107.

86. Adler, 65 and 66.

87. Ibid., 90 and 92.

88. Marcia Falk, "Notes on Composing New Blessings," in *Weaving the Visions: New Patterns in Feminist Spirituality,* ed. Judith Plaskow and Carol P. Christ (New York: Harper & Row, 1989), 128–138, especially pages 132 and 131.

89. Adler, 85 and 86.

90. Ibid., 96.
91. Ibid.
92. Ibid., 87.
93. Ibid., 147.
94. Ibid.
95. Ibid., 146 and 147.
96. Ibid., 138–139.
97. Ibid., 140.
98. Ibid., 114 and 116.
99. Trible, 72.
100. Adler, 114, 115, 116 and 121.
101. See Joseph Soloveitchik, *The Lonely Man of Faith* (New York: Doubleday, 1965), 34–46.
102. Adler, 118.
103. Ibid., 118 and 121.
104. Ibid., 121–122, 123.
105. Falk, 131. Seligman and his contributors speak of ritual in this subjunctive mode as well, for ritual is "the creation of an order *as if* it were truly the case." See Seligman et al., 20.
106. Wyschogrod, *The Body of Faith*, 1.

6. The Language of Racial Bodies in Melanie Kaye/Kantrowitz's *The Colors of Jews*

1. See Arthur Huff Fauset, *Black Gods of the Metropolis* (Philadelphia: University of Pennsylvania Press, 1944), 31–32; Yvonne Chireau, "Black Culture and Black Zion: African American Religious Encounters with Judaism, 1790–1930, an Overview," in *Black Zion: African American Religious Encounters with Judaism,* ed. Yvonne Chireau and Nathaniel Deutsch (New York: Oxford University Press, 2000),15–32, especially page 21; and James Tinney, "Black Jews: A House Divided," *Christianity Today* (December 7, 1973): 52–53.
2. Melanie Kaye/Kantrowitz, *The Colors of Jews: Racial Politics and Radical Diasporism* (Bloomington: Indiana University Press, 2007), 58.
3. See Tinney, 52. For a more nuanced account that locates Black Judaism within African American struggles for religious legitimacy and power, see James Landing, *Black Judaism: Story of an American Movement* (Durham, N.C.: Carolina Academic Press, 2002), 12: "This sense of established legitimacy, a need to place blacks in some meaningful divine plan, regardless of the nature of their contemporary plight, became one of the most distinctive features of Black Judaism." Also see Marla Brettschneider, *The Family Flamboyant: Race Politics, Queer Families, Jewish Lives* (Albany: State University of New York Press, 2006), 17–36.
4. Jacob S. Dorman, *Chosen People: The Rise of American Black Israelite Religions* (New York: Oxford University Press, 2013), 4.
5. Kaye/Kantrowitz, 30.
6. Ibid., 198 and 199.
7. Ibid., xii.
8. Ibid., 212. For insightful discussions of Diaspora and border maintenance, see Allan Arkush, "From Diaspora Nationalism to Radical Diasporism," *Modern Judaism* 29, no. 3 (October 2009): 326–350; Daniel Boyarin and Jonathan Boyarin, *Powers of Diaspora: Two Essays on the Relevance of Jewish Culture* (Minneapolis: University of Minnesota Press, 2002); Boyarin and Boyarin, "Diaspora: Generation and the Ground of Jewish Identity," *Critical Inquiry* 19, no. 4 (Summer 1993): 693–725; James Clifford, "Diasporas," *Cultural Anthropology* 9, no. 3

(August 1994): 302–338; Shaul Magid, "In Search of a Critical Voice in the Jewish Diaspora: Homelessness and Home in Edward Said and Shalom Noah Barzofsky's Netivot Shalom," *Jewish Social Studies* 12, no. 3 (2006): 193–227; and Derek Penslar, "Normalization and Its Discontents: Israel as a Diaspora Jewish Community," in *Critical Issues in Israeli Society,* ed. Alan Dowty (Westport, Conn.: Praeger, 2004), 223–249.

9. Kaye/Kantrowitz, 19.

10. Ibid., 24.

11. For an astute account of these tropes of American Jewry see Daniel Itzkovitz, "Passing Like Me: Jewish Chameleonism and the Politics of Race," in *Passing: Identity and Interpretation in Sexuality, Race, and Religion,* ed. María Carla Sánchez and Linda Schlossberg (New York: New York University Press, 2001), 38–63; and Daniel Itzkovitz, "Secret Temples," in *Jews and Other Differences: The New Jewish Cultural Studies,* ed. Jonathan Boyarin and Daniel Boyarin (Minneapolis: University of Minnesota Press, 1997), 176–202.

12. Kaye/Kantrowitz, 91 and 98.

13. Ibid., 58.

14. Ibid., 35 and 36.

15. Matthew Frye Jacobson, *Whiteness of a Different Color: European Immigrants and the Alchemy of Race* (Cambridge, Mass.: Harvard University Press, 1998), 174.

16. Ibid., 173.

17. Kaye/Kantrowitz, 37.

18. Ibid., 27.

19. Ibid., 37.

20. Ibid.

21. Ibid., 38.

22. Ibid. 91.

23. For the notion of the objectified Other displacing the controlling gaze of the subject, see Homi Bhabha, *The Location of Culture* (London: Routledge, 1994), especially page 127: "I want to turn to this process by which the look of surveillance returns as the displacing gaze of the disciplined, where the observer becomes the observed and 'partial' representation rearticulates the whole notion of *identity* and alienates it from essence."

24. Kaye/Kantrowitz, 72.

25. Kaye/Kantrowitz misspells Buchdahl's last name as Buchdale. See Kaye/Kantrowitz, 70.

26. Ibid., 70 and 71.

27. See Dorman, 23–55.

28. Chireau, 21. Also see Zev Chafets, "Obama's Rabbi," *New York Times Magazine* (April 2, 2009), together with the online version: http://www.nytimes.com/2009/04/05/magazine /05rabbi-t.html?pagewanted=2&%2359&_r=0&%2339%E2%80%A619056-czMx1vvgZ4cТl /hLEr31QQ. Accessed August 1, 2013.

29. Chireau, 22; Landing, 340–347.

30. See Chafets. For Funnye's relation to the Hebrew Israelite movement, see Bernard Wolfson, "African American Jews: Dispelling Myths, Bridging the Divide," in Chireau and Deutsch, *Black Zion,* 44–49; also visit the Web site http://blackjews.org. Historian James Tinney has classified these congregations into three distinct groups: Black Jews, Black Hebrews, and Black Israelites. According to Tinney, both Crowdy's and Cherry's communities belong to the Black Jews, "who believe that Negroes are truly Jews but who accept Christ as a prophet." The Black Hebrews include those like Rabbi W. A. Matthew's Ethiopian Hebrew Congregation in New York City, and Robert Devine's in Chicago. These communities recognize themselves as the original Hebrews, practice the art of conjuring, yet still follow an Orthodox form of Judaism. The third group, the Black Israelites, is perhaps best known for founding communities in Israel, yet Tinney calls this group "the farthest from traditional Judaism in beliefs and

practices." All three groups should be distinguished from the Ethiopian Falashas who claim King Solomon and the Queen of Sheba as their ancestors, and who "observe all Jewish rites, sacrifices, and festivals except Hanukkah." See Tinney, 52 and 53; Chireau, 29, fn. 2; Landing, 137–140; Merrill Singer, "Symbolic Identity Formation in an African American Religious Sect: The Black Hebrew Israelites," in Chireau and Deutsch, *Black Zion*, 55–72; and Ethan Michaeli, "Another Exodus: The Hebrew Israelites from Chicago to Dimona," in Chireau and Deutsch, *Black Zion*, 73–90.

31. For this brief biographical sketch, see Chafets; and Wolfson, "African American Jews," 33–54.

32. Kaye/Kantrowitz, 38.

33. Ibid.

34. See Wolfson, "African American Jews," 44.

35. Kaye/Kantrowitz, 39.

36. Ibid.

37. Ibid., 38–39.

38. See Wolfson, "African American Jews," 44.

39. Kaye/Kantrowitz, 159.

40. Ibid., 39.

41. Wolfson, "African American Jews," 34.

42. Kaye/Kantrowitz, 40.

43. Ibid., 41.

44. Ibid., 40 and 41.

45. Ibid.

46. For a helpful discussion of the ways "blackness" plays off normative visions of "whiteness," see Victor Anderson, *Beyond Ontological Blackness: An Essay on African American Religious and Cultural Criticism* (New York: Continuum, 1995).

47. Kaye/Kantrowitz, 27.

48. Ibid., 42.

49. Ibid., 43.

50. Frantz Fanon describes this uncanny experience in this way: "What I am asserting is that the European has a fixed concept of the Negro, and there is nothing more exasperating than to be asked: 'How long have you been in France? You speak French so well.'" See Frantz Fanon, *Black Skin, White Masks* (New York: Grove Press, 1967), 35.

51. Kaye/Kantrowitz, 43.

52. Jonathan Freedman, *Klezmer America: Jewishness, Ethnicity, Modernity* (New York: Columbia University Press, 2008).

53. Ibid., 194 and 197.

54. Kaye/Kantrowitz, 40. Kaye/Kantrowitz takes this from Reena Bernards's interview with Eisendorf. See Bernards, "An Ethiopian GILGUL Come to Life: An Interview with Toni Eisendorf," 22. Also see Brettschneider, *Family Flamboyant*, 40–43.

55. Kaye/Kantrowitz, 220.

56. Diane Kaufmann Tobin, Gary A. Tobin, and Scott Rubin, *In Every Tongue: The Racial & Ethnic Diversity of the Jewish People* (San Francisco: Institute for Jewish & Community Research, 2005); Susan Chevlowe, *The Jewish Identity Project: New American Photography* (New York and New Haven, Conn.: Jewish Museum and Yale University Press, 2005).

57. Tobin, Tobin, and Rubin, 17 and 18.

58. There is a veritable cottage industry of ethnic (and particularly white) studies and modern Judaism. The most important works in the field, and ones that have had the greatest influence on my own thinking in this area, are Karen Brodkin, *How Jews Became White Folks* (New Brunswick: Rutgers University Press, 2002); Eric Goldstein, *The Price of Whiteness: Jews, Race,*

and American Identity (Princeton, N.J.: Princeton University Press, 2006); Matthew Frye Jacobson, *Roots Too: White Ethnic Revival in Post-Civil Rights America* (Cambridge, Mass.: Harvard University Press, 2006); Eric Lott, *Love and Theft: Blackface Minstrelsy and the American Working Class* (New York: Oxford University Press, 1993); Jeffrey Melnick, *A Right to Sing the Blues: African Americans, Jews, and American Popular Song* (Cambridge, Mass.: Harvard University Press, 1999); Michael Rogin, *Blackface, White Noise: Jewish Immigrants in the Hollywood Melting Pot* (Berkeley: University of California Press, 1996); and Daniel Sack, *Whitebread Protestants: Food and Religion in American Culture* (New York: St. Martin's Press, 2000).

59. Tobin, Tobin, and Rubin, 181.
60. Ibid., 141.
61. Ibid., 13.
62. Chevlowe, 7 and 9.
63. Ibid., 25.
64. Itzkovitz, "Passing Like Me," 50.
65. Kaye/Kantrowitz, 212.
66. Ibid., 185.

Conclusion

1. See Marc Michael Epstein, *The Medieval Haggadah: Art, Narrative, and Religious Imagination* (New Haven, Conn.: Yale University Press, 2011); Stephan O. Parnes, Bonni-Dara Michaels, and Gabriel M. Goldstein, eds., *The Art of Passover* (New York: Hugh Lauter Levin Associates, 1994); Yosef Hayim Yerushalmi, *Haggadah and History: A Panorama in Facsimile of Five Centuries of the Printed Haggadah* (Philadelphia: The Jewish Publication Society of America, 1975).

2. Jonathan Safran Foer, *New American Haggadah*, trans. Nathan Englander (New York: Little, Brown and Company, 2012), 77.

3. *The Union Haggadah: Home Service for the Passover* (United States of America: The Central Conference of American Rabbis, 1923).

4. Ibid., 142.
5. Ibid., viii.
6. Ibid., 162.
7. Ibid., 38.
8. Ibid., 34.
9. Ibid., 38.
10. Ibid., 40.

11. Martin Jay, *Downcast Eyes: The Denigration of Vision in Twentieth-Century French Thought* (Berkeley: University of California Press, 1973), 76 and 80.

12. ArtScroll appropriated the European Mussar movement within its publication series, and according to Shaul Magid, helped to facilitate the ready acceptance by American Jews for an approach focused on personal development as a form of self-formation. See Shaul Magid, *American Post-Judaism: Identity and Renewal in a Postethnic Society* (Bloomington: Indiana University Press, 2013), 174–175.

13. Shalom M. Wallach, *Pesach Haggadah with a Commentary Culled from the Classic Baalei Mussar* (New York: Mesorah, 1989), 102 and 103.

14. See Leon Wieseltier, "Comes the Comer," *Jewish Review of Books*, no. 9 (Spring 2012): 5–9, together with comments and reactions to his stinging appraisal.

15. Foer, 149.

16. Ibid., 6–7.

17. For a discussion of book as material object, see Ari Y. Kelman, "Reading a Book like an Object: The Case of *The Jewish Catalog*," in *Thinking Jewish Culture in America*, ed. Ken Koltun-Fromm (Lanham, Md.: Lexington Books, 2014), 109–128.

18. Sue Levi Elwell, *The Open Door: A Passover Haggadah* (New York: Central Conference of American Rabbis, 2002).

19. Rony Oren, *The Animated Haggadah* (London: Scopus Films, 1985).

20. Noam Zion and David Dishon, *A Different Night* (Jerusalem: Shalom Hartman Institute, 2002).

21. Diane Kaufmann Tobin, Gary A. Tobin, and Scott Rubin, *In Every Tongue: The Racial & Ethnic Diversity of the Jewish People* (San Francisco: Institute for Jewish & Community Research, 2005), 17.

22. Reena Bernards, "An Ethiopian GILGUL Come to Life: An Interview with Toni Eisendorf," *Bridges* 9, no 1 (Summer 2001): 22.

Bibliography

Aaronsohn, Ran. "Settlement in Eretz Israel—A Colonialist Enterprise? 'Critical' Scholarship and Historical Geography." *Israel Studies* 1, no. 2 (Fall 1996): 214–229.

Ackerman, Walter. "Israel in American Jewish Education." In *Envisioning Israel: The Changing Ideals and Images of North American Jews,* edited by Allon Gal, 173–190. Detroit: Wayne State University Press, 1996.

Adelman, Penina V. *Miriam's Well: Rituals for Jewish Women Around the Year.* New York: Biblio Press, 1986.

Adler, Rachel. *Engendering Judaism.* Philadelphia: Jewish Publication Society, 1998.

Alexander, Elizabeth Shanks. "Review of Tamar Ross, *Expanding the Palace of Torah: Feminism and Orthodoxy.*" *Nashim* 10 (Fall 2005): 243–249.

Anderson, Victor. *Beyond Ontological Blackness: An Essay on African American Religious and Cultural Criticism.* New York: Continuum, 1995.

Anton, Corey. *Selfhood and Authenticity.* Albany: State University of New York Press, 2001.

Arbel, Rachel. *Blue and White in Color: Visual Images of Zionism, 1897–1947* (Hebrew). Tel Aviv: Beth Hatefutsoth, the Nahum Goldmann Museum of the Jewish Diaspora, 1997.

Arkush, Allan. "From Diaspora Nationalism to Radical Diasporism." *Modern Judaism* 29, no. 3 (October 2009): 326–350.

Avineri, Shlomo. *The Social and Political Thought of Karl Marx.* Cambridge: Cambridge University Press, 1968.

Banton, Michael. *Racial Theories.* Cambridge: Cambridge University Press, 1987.

Berger, David. "Introducing Michael Wyschogrod." *Modern Theology* 22, no. 4 (October 1, 2006): 673–675.

Berkovits, Eliezer. *Major Themes in Modern Philosophies of Judaism.* New York: Ktav, 1974.

Berkowitz, Michael. "Art in Zionist Popular Culture and Jewish National Self-Consciousness, 1897–1914." In *Art and Its Uses: The Visual Image and Modern Jewish Society,* edited by Ezra Mendelsohn, 9–42. New York: Oxford University Press, 1990.

———. *Western Jewry and the Zionist Project, 1914–1933.* Cambridge: Cambridge University Press, 1997.

———. *Zionist Culture and West European Jewry before the First World War.* Chapel Hill: University of North Carolina Press, 1993.

Berman, Lila Corwin. *Speaking of Jews: Rabbis, Intellectuals, and the Creation of an American Public Identity.* Berkeley: University of California Press, 2009.

Bernards, Reena. "An Ethiopian GILGUL Come to Life: An Interview with Toni Eisendorf." *Bridges* 9, no. 1 (Summer 2001): 21–25.

Bhabha, Homi K. *The Location of Culture.* London: Routledge, 1994.

Biemann, Asher. "Aesthetics and Art." In *The Cambridge History of Jewish Philosophy: The Modern Era,* edited by Martin Kavka, Zachary Braiterman, and David Novak, 759–779. Cambridge: Cambridge University Press, 2012.

———. "'Thus Rome Shows Us Our True Place': Reflections on the German Jewish Love for Italy." In *German-Jewish Thought between Religion and Politics: Festschrift in Honor of Paul Mendes-Flohr on the Occasion of his Seventieth Birthday,* edited by Christian Wiese and Martina Urban, 241–261. Berlin and Boston: Walter deGruyter, 2012.

Bloch, Ariel, and Chana Bloch. *The Song of Songs: A New Translation with an Introduction and Commentary.* New York: Random House, 1995.

Bolter, Jay David, and Richard Grusin. *Remediation: Understanding New Media.* Cambridge, Mass.: MIT Press, 2000.

Boyarin, Daniel. *Unheroic Conduct: The Rise of Heterosexuality and the Invention of the Jewish Man.* Berkeley: University of California Press, 1997.

Boyarin, Daniel, and Jonathan Boyarin. "Diaspora: Generation and the Ground of Jewish Identity." *Critical Inquiry* 19, no. 4 (Summer 1993): 693–725.

———. *Powers of Diaspora: Two Essays on the Relevance of Jewish Culture.* Minneapolis: University of Minnesota Press, 2002.

Braunstein, Susan, and Jenna Weissman Joselit, eds. *Getting Comfortable in New York: The American Jewish Home, 1880–1950.* New York: The Jewish Museum, 1990.

Brettschneider, Marla. *The Family Flamboyant: Race Politics, Queer Families, Jewish Lives.* Albany: State University of New York Press, 2006.

Brodkin, Karen. *How Jews Became White Folks.* New Brunswick, N.J.: Rutgers University Press, 2002.

Bronstein, Herbert, ed. *A Passover Haggadah: The New Union Haggadah.* New York: Central Conference of American Rabbis, 1974.

Brozman, Suzi. "Not Your Bubbe's Cooking." *Texas Jewish Post,* March 10, 2005. http://texashistory.unt.edu/ark:/67531/metapth188070/m1/19/.

Burrell, David B. "Talking with Christians: Musings of a Jewish Theologian." *Modern Theology* 22, no. 4 (October 2006): 705–709.

Chafets, Zev. "Obama's Rabbi." *New York Times Magazine,* April 5, 2009. http://www.nytimes.com/2009/04/05/magazine/05rabbi-t.html?#59=&_r=1&adxnnl=1'...19056-czMx1vvgZ4cTl/hLEr31QQ=&pagewanted=1&adxnnlx=1400137365-5GLVJXyX4HiHmFmhdLZD4A.

Chevlowe, Susan. *The Jewish Identity Project: New American Photography.* New York and New Haven, Conn.: Jewish Museum and Yale University Press, 2005.

Chireau, Yvonne. "Black Culture and Black Zion: African American Religious Encounters with Judaism, 1790–1930, an Overview." In *Black Zion: African American Religious Encounters with Judaism,* edited by Yvonne Chireau and Nathaniel Deutsch, 15–32. New York: Oxford University Press, 2000.

Chireau, Yvonne, and Nathaniel Deutsch, eds. *Black Zion: African American Religious Encounters with Judaism.* New York: Oxford University Press, 2000.

Christ, Carol P., Ellen M. Umansky, and Anne E. Carr. "Roundtable Discussion: What Are the Sources of My Theology?" *Journal of Feminist Studies in Religion* 1, no. 1 (April 1, 1985): 119–131.

Chun, Wendy. *Programmed Visions: Software and Memory.* Cambridge, Mass.: MIT Press, 2013.

Clifford, James. "Diasporas." *Cultural Anthropology* 9, no. 3 (August 1994): 302–338.

Cohen, Naomi W. *The Americanization of Zionism, 1897–1948.* Hanover, N.H.: Brandeis University Press, 2003.

Cohen, Richard. *Jewish Icons: Art and Society in Modern Europe.* Berkeley: University of California Press, 1998.

Cohen, Steven, and Arnold Eisen. *The Jew Within: Self, Family, and Community in America.* Bloomington: Indiana University Press, 2000.

Cover, Robert. "Nomos and Narrative." *Harvard Law Review* 97, no. 1 (November 1983): 4–68.

Crary, Jonathan. *Techniques of the Observer: On Vision and Modernity in the 19th Century.* Cambridge, Mass.: MIT Press, 1992.

Davidman, Lynn, and Shelly Tenenbaum, eds. *Feminist Perspectives on Jewish Studies.* New Haven, Conn.: Yale University Press, 1994.

Dawson, John David. *Christian Figural Reading and the Fashioning of Identity.* Berkeley: University of California Press, 2001.

Diamond, Etan. "The Kosher Lifestyle: Religious Consumerism and Suburban Orthodox Jews." *Journal of Urban History* 28, no. 4 (May 2002): 488–505.

Dorman, Jacob S. *Chosen People: The Rise of American Black Israelite Religions.* New York: Oxford University Press, 2013.

Durbach, Elaine. "Dining by Design." *New Jersey Jewish News,* October 30, 2003. http://njjewishnews.com/njjn.com/103003/ltdiningbydesign.html.

Efron, John M. *Defenders of the Race: Jewish Doctors and Race Science in Fin-de-Siècle Europe.* New Haven, Conn.: Yale University Press, 1994.

Eisen, Arnold. "Re-Reading Heschel on the Commandments." *Modern Judaism* 9, no. 1 (1989): 1–33.

Eisenstein, Ira. "Of Time and the Sabbath." *The Reconstructionist* 22 (February 1952): 23–24.

Elkins, James. *The Object Stares Back: On the Nature of Seeing.* New York: Simon & Schuster, 1996.

———. *Visual Studies: A Skeptical Introduction.* New York: Routledge, 2003.

Elon, Amos. *Herzl.* New York: Holt, Rinehart and Winston, 1975.

Elwell, Sue Levi. *The Open Door: A Passover Haggadah.* New York: Central Conference of American Rabbis, 2002.

Epstein, Marc Michael. *The Medieval Haggadah: Art, Narrative, and Religious Imagination.* New Haven, Conn.: Yale University Press, 2011.

Fackenheim, Emil. "Review of God in Search of Man." *Conservative Judaism* 15 (1960): 50–53.

Falk, Marcia. "Notes on Composing New Blessings." In *Weaving the Visions: New Patterns in Feminist Spirituality,* edited by Judith Plaskow and Carol P. Christ, 128–138. New York: Harper & Row, 1989.

———. *The Song of Songs: Love Lyrics from the Bible.* Lebanon, N.H.: Brandeis University Press, 2004.

Fanon, Frantz. *Black Skin, White Masks.* Translated by Richard Philcox. New York: Grove Press, 1967.

Fauset, Arthur Huff. *Black Gods of the Metropolis.* Philadelphia: University of Pennsylvania Press, 1944.

Ferris, Marcie Cohen. *Matzoh Ball Gumbo: Culinary Tales of the Jewish South.* Chapel Hill: University of North Carolina Press, 2005.

Fishbein, Susie. *Kosher by Design: Picture Perfect Food for the Holidays & Every Day.* New York: Mesorah, 2003.

Foer, Jonathan Safran. *New American Haggadah.* Translated by Nathan Englander. New York: Little, Brown and Company, 2012.

Freedberg, David. *The Power of Images: Studies in the History and Theory of Response.* Chicago: University of Chicago Press, 1989.

Freedman, Jonathan. *Klezmer America: Jewishness, Ethnicity, Modernity.* New York: Columbia University Press, 2008.

Frymer-Kensky, Tikva. "The Bible and Women's Studies." In *Feminist Perspectives on Jewish Studies,* edited by Lynn Davidman and Shelly Tenenbaum, 16–39. New Haven, Conn.: Yale University Press, 1994.

Gal, Allon. *Envisioning Israel: The Changing Ideals and Images of North American Jews.* Detroit: Wayne State University Press, 1996.

———. "Overview: Envisioning Israel—The American Jewish Tradition." In *Envisioning Israel: The Changing Ideals and Images of North American Jews,* edited by Allon Gal, 13–37. Detroit: Wayne State University Press, 1996.

Glatzer, Nahum. "Review of The Sabbath." *Judaism* 1, no. 3 (July 1952): 283–286.

Goetschel, Willi. *The Discipline of Philosophy and the Invention of Modern Jewish Thought.* New York: Fordham University Press, 2013.

Goldstein, Eric. *The Price of Whiteness: Jews, Race, and American Identity.* Princeton, N.J.: Princeton University Press, 2006.

Goren, Arthur A. "'Anu Banu Artza' in America: The Americanization of the Halutz Ideal." In *Envisioning Israel: The Changing Ideals and Images of North American Jews,* edited by Allon Gal, 81–113. Detroit: Wayne State University Press, 1996.

———. *The Politics and Public Culture of American Jews.* Bloomington: Indiana University Press, 1999.

Greenberg, Betty, and Althea Silverman. *The Jewish Home Beautiful.* New York: National Women's League of the United Synagogue of America, 1941.

Greenberg, Blu. *On Women and Judaism: A View from Tradition.* Philadelphia: Jewish Publication Society of America, 1998.

Greenberg, Clement. "Avant-Garde and Kitsch." In Greenberg, *Art and Culture: Critical Essays,* 3–21. Boston: Beacon Press, 1961.

Gross, Rachel. "Draydel Salad: The Serious Business of Jewish Food and Fun in the 1950s." In *Religion, Food, and Eating in North America,* edited by Benjamin E. Zeller, Marie W. Dallam, Reid L. Neilson, and Nora L. Rubel, 91–113. New York: Columbia University Press, 2014.

Handelman, Susan A. *Fragments of Redemption: Jewish Thought and Literary Theory in Benjamin, Scholem, and Levinas.* Bloomington: Indiana University Press, 1991.

Hart, Mitchell. *Social Science and the Politics of Modern Jewish Identity.* Stanford, Calif.: Stanford University Press, 2000.

Harten, Doreet Levitte, and Yigal Zalmona, eds. *Die Neuen Hebräer: 100 Jahre Kunst in Israel.* Berlin: Nicolaische Verlagsbuchhandlung, 2005.

Held, Shai. *Abraham Joshua Heschel: The Call of Transcendence.* Bloomington: Indiana University Press, 2013.

———. "The Promise and Peril of Jewish Barthianism: The Theology of Michael Wyschogrod." *Modern Judaism* 25, no. 3 (2005): 316–326.

Hertzberg, Arthur. *The Zionist Idea: A Historical Analysis and Reader.* Philadelphia: Jewish Publication Society of America, 1997.

Heschel, Abraham Joshua. *The Earth Is the Lord's; and The Sabbath.* Cleveland: World Publishing Company, 1963.

——. *God in Search of Man: A Philosophy of Judaism.* New York: The Noonday Press, 1955.

——. *Heavenly Torah as Refracted through the Generations.* Translated by Gordon Tucker. New York: Continuum, 2005.

——. "Ilya Schor." *Conservative Judaism* 16, no. 1 (1961): 20–21.

——. *The Sabbath: Its Meaning for Modern Man.* New York: Farrar, Straus and Giroux, 1951.

Heschel, Susannah, ed. *On Being a Jewish Feminist.* New York: Schocken Books, 1983.

Hever, Hannan. "We Have Not Arrived from the Sea: A Mizrahi Literary Geography." *Social Identities* 10, no. 1 (2004): 31–51.

Hoberman, J., and Jeffrey Shandler, eds. *Entertaining America: Jews, Movies, and Broadcasting.* Princeton, N.J.: Princeton University Press, 2003.

Horner, Robyn. *Jean-Luc Marion: A Theo-logical Introduction.* Burlington, Vt.: Ashgate, 2005.

Itzkovitz, Daniel. "Passing Like Me: Jewish Chameleonism and the Politics of Race." In *Passing: Identity and Interpretation in Sexuality, Race, and Religion,* edited by María Carla Sánchez and Linda Schlossberg, 38–63. New York: New York University Press, 2001.

——. "Secret Temples." In *Jews and Other Differences: The New Jewish Cultural Studies,* edited by Jonathan Boyarin and Daniel Boyarin, 176–202. Minneapolis: University of Minnesota Press, 1997.

Jacobson, Matthew Frye. *Roots Too: White Ethnic Revival in Post-Civil Rights America.* Cambridge, Mass.: Harvard University Press, 2006.

——. *Whiteness of a Different Color: European Immigrants and the Alchemy of Race.* Cambridge, Mass.: Harvard University Press, 1998.

Jay, Martin. *Downcast Eyes: The Denigration of Vision in Twentieth-Century French Thought.* Berkeley: University of California Press, 1993.

Joselit, Jenna Weissman. "Culture on a Plate: What Our Dietary Choices Tell Us about Ourselves." *Reform Judaism* 27 (Winter 1998): 28–32.

——. "The Jewish Home Beautiful." In *The American Jewish Experience,* edited by Jonathan Sarna, 236–242. New York: Holmes & Meier, 1997.

——. "'A Set Table': Jewish Domestic Culture in the New World, 1880–1950." In *Getting Comfortable in New York: The American Jewish Home, 1880–1950,* edited by Susan Braunstein and Jenna Weissman Joselit, 21–76. New York: The Jewish Museum, 1990.

——. *The Wonders of America: Reinventing Jewish Culture, 1880–1950.* New York: Henry Holt and Company, 1994.

Joseph, Norma Baumel. "Introduction: Feeding an Identity—Gender, Food, and Survival." *Nashim* 5 (Fall 2002): 7–13.

Kallen, Horace Meyer. *Zionism and World Politics: A Study in History and Social Psychology.* Garden City, N.Y.: Doubleday, Page & Company, 1921.

Kaplan, Edward. *Holiness in Words: Abraham Joshua Heschel's Poetics of Piety.* Albany: State University of New York Press, 1996.

——. *Spiritual Radical: Abraham Joshua Heschel in America, 1940–1972.* New Haven, Conn.: Yale University Press, 2007.

Katz, Steven, ed. *The Shtetl: New Evaluations.* New York: New York University Press, 2007.

Kavka, Martin. *Jewish Messianism and the History of Philosophy.* Cambridge: Cambridge University Press, 2004.

Kaye/Kantrowitz, Melanie. *The Colors of Jews: Racial Politics and Radical Diasporism.* Bloomington: Indiana University Press, 2007.

Kelman, Ari Y. "Reading a Book like an Object: The Case of *The Jewish Catalog.*" In *Thinking Jewish Culture in America,* edited by Ken Koltun-Fromm, 109–128. Lanham, Md.: Lexington Books, 2014.

Kevles, Daniel. *In the Name of Eugenics: Genetics and the Uses of Human Heredity.* Berkeley: University of California Press, 1985.

Kirshenblatt-Gimblett, Barbara. "Imagining Europe: The Popular Arts of American Jewish Ethnography." In *Divergent Jewish Cultures: Israel and America,* edited by Deborah Dash Moore and S. Ilan Troen, 155–191. New Haven, Conn.: Yale University Press, 2001.

———. "Kitchen Judaism." In *Getting Comfortable in New York: The American Jewish Home, 1880–1950,* edited by Susan Braunstein and Jenna Weissman Joselit, 77–105. New York: The Jewish Museum, 1990.

———. "The Kosher Gourmet in the Nineteenth-Century Kitchen: Three Jewish Cookbooks in Historical Perspective." *Journal of Gastronomy* 2, no. 4 (Winter 1986/87): 51–89.

———. "Playing to the Senses: Food as a Performance Medium." *Performance Research* 4, no. 1 (1999): 1–30.

———. "Recipes for Creating Community: The Jewish Charity Cookbook in America." *Jewish Folklore and Ethnology* 9 (1987): 8–12.

Koltun-Fromm, Ken. *Material Culture and Jewish Thought in America.* Bloomington: Indiana University Press, 2010.

———, ed. *Thinking Jewish Culture in America.* Lanham, Md.: Lexington Books, 2014.

Kugelmass, Jack. "Green Bagels: An Essay on Food, Nostalgia, and the Carnivalesque." In *YIVO Annual* 19, edited by Deborah Dash Moore, 57–80. Evanston, Ill.: Northwestern University Press, 1990.

Lacan, Jacques. *The Four Fundamental Concepts of Psychoanalysis.* New York: W.W. Norton & Company, 1981.

Landing, James. *Black Judaism: Story of an American Movement.* Durham, N.C.: Carolina Academic Press, 2002.

Lanham, Richard A. *The Electronic Word: Democracy, Technology, and the Arts.* Chicago: University of Chicago Press, 1993.

Latour, Bruno. *We Have Never Been Modern.* Cambridge, Mass.: Harvard University Press, 1993.

Lindholm, Charles. *Culture and Authenticity.* Oxford: Blackwell Publishing, 2008.

Lott, Eric. *Love & Theft: Blackface Minstrelsy and the American Working Class.* New York: Oxford University Press, 1993.

Lowe, Walter James. "The Intensification of Time: Michael Wyschogrod and the Task of Christian Theology." *Modern Theology* 22, no. 4 (October 2006): 693–699.

The Maccabaean 31 (1918).

Magid, Shaul. *American Post-Judaism: Identity and Renewal in a Postethnic Society.* Bloomington: Indiana University Press, 2013.

———. "In Search of a Critical Voice in the Jewish Diaspora: Homelessness and Home in Edward Said and Shalom Noah Barzofsky's Netivot Shalom." *Jewish Social Studies* 12, no. 3 (2006): 193–227.

Marion, Jean-Luc. *The Crossing of the Visible.* Stanford, Calif.: Stanford University Press, 2004.

———. *God without Being.* Chicago: University of Chicago Press, 1991.

Mason, Ann, and Marian Meyers. "Living with Martha Stewart Media: Chosen Domesticity in the Experience of Fans." *Journal of Communication* 51 (2001): 801–823.

McCloud, Scott. *Understanding Comics: The Invisible Art.* New York: HarperCollins, 1993.

McLuhan, Marshall. *The Medium Is the Massage.* Corte Madera, Calif.: Gingko Press, 2001.

Medoff, Rafael. *Zionism and the Arabs: An American Jewish Dilemma, 1898–1948.* Westport, Conn.: Praeger, 1997.

Melnick, Jeffrey. *A Right to Sing the Blues: African Americans, Jews, and American Popular Song.* Cambridge, Mass.: Harvard University Press, 1999.

Michaeli, Ethan. "Another Exodus: The Hebrew Israelites from Chicago to Dimona." In *Black Zion: African American Religious Encounters with Judaism,* edited by Yvonne Chireau and Nathaniel Deutsch, 73–90. New York: Oxford University Press, 2000.

Millen, Rochelle. "'Her Mouth Is Full of Wisdom': Reflections on Jewish Feminist Theology." In *Women Rethinking American Judaism,* edited by Riv-Ellen Prell, 27–49. Detroit: Wayne State University Press, 2007.

Mirzoeff, Nicholas, ed. *The Visual Culture Reader.* London: Routledge, 1998.

Mitchell, W. J. T. "Holy Landscapes: Israel, Palestine, and the American Wilderness." *Critical Inquiry* 26, no. 2 (Winter 2000): 193–223.

———. *Iconology: Image, Text, Ideology.* Chicago: University of Chicago Press, 1986.

———. *Picture Theory.* Chicago: University of Chicago Press, 1994.

———. *What Do Pictures Want? The Lives and Loves of Images.* Chicago: University of Chicago Press, 2005.

Morgan, David. *The Sacred Gaze: Religious Visual Culture in Theory and Practice.* Berkeley: University of California Press, 2005.

———. *Visual Piety: A History and Theory of Popular Religious Images.* Berkeley: University of California Press, 1998.

Morgan, David, and Sally Promey, eds. *The Visual Culture of American Religions.* Berkeley: University of California Press, 2001.

Mosse, George L. *The Image of Man: The Creation of Modern Masculinity.* New York: Oxford University Press, 1996.

Neis, Rachel. *The Sense of Sight in Rabbinic Culture: Jewish Ways of Seeing in Late Antiquity.* Cambridge: Cambridge University Press, 2013.

Novak, David. *The Election of Israel: The Idea of the Chosen People.* Cambridge: Cambridge University Press, 1995.

———. *Natural Law in Judaism.* Cambridge: Cambridge University Press, 1998.

———. "Response to Michael Wyschogrod." *Modern Theology* 11, no. 2 (April 1995): 211–218.

Ochs, Vanessa L. *Inventing Jewish Ritual.* Philadelphia: Jewish Publication Society of America, 2007.

Oren, Rony. *The Animated Haggadah*. London: Scopus Films, 1985.

Ozick, Cynthia. "Notes toward Finding the Right Question." In *On Being a Jewish Feminist*, edited by Susannah Heschel, 120–151. New York: Schocken Books, 1983.

Pardes, Ilana. *Countertraditions in the Bible: A Feminist Approach*. Cambridge, Mass.: Harvard University Press, 1992.

Parnes, Stephan O., Bonni-Dara Michaels, and Gabriel M Goldstein, eds. *The Art of Passover*. New York: Hugh Lauter Levin Associates, 1994.

Penslar, Derek. "Normalization and Its Discontents: Israel as a Diaspora Jewish Community." In *Critical Issues in Israeli Society*, edited by Alan Dowty, 223–249. Westport, Conn.: Praeger, 2004.

———. *Zionism and Technocracy: The Engineering of Jewish Settlement in Palestine, 1870–1918*. Bloomington: Indiana University Press, 1991.

Plaskow, Judith. "Jewish Theology in Feminist Perspective." In *Feminist Perspectives on Jewish Studies*, edited by Lynn Davidman and Shelly Tenenbaum, 62–84. New Haven, Conn.: Yale University Press, 1994.

———. "The Right Question Is Theological." In *On Being a Jewish Feminist*, edited by Susannah Heschel, 223–233. New York: Schocken Books, 1983.

———. *Standing Again at Sinai: Judaism from a Feminist Perspective*. New York: Harper Collins, 1990.

Plaskow, Judith, and Carol P. Christ. *Weaving the Visions: New Patterns in Feminist Spirituality*. New York: Harper & Row, 1989.

Prell, Riv-Ellen. "The Vision of Woman in Classical Reform Judaism." *Journal of the American Academy of Religion* 50, no. 4 (December 1982): 575–589.

Presner, Todd Samuel. "'Clear Heads, Solid Stomachs, and Hard Muscles': Max Nordau and the Aesthetics of Jewish Regeneration." *Modernism/Modernity* 10, no. 2 (2003): 269–296.

———. *Muscular Judaism: The Jewish Body and the Politics of Regeneration*. New York: Routledge, 2007.

Prestel, Claudia. "Arabs and Women: Constructing Zionist Images of the 'Other' in Pre-State Israeli Films." *Nashim* 1 (Winter 1998): 95–105.

Raider, Mark. *The Emergence of American Zionism*. New York: New York University Press, 1998.

Ramon, Einat. "Idolatry and the Dazzle of the Enlightenment in Abraham Joshua Heschel's Thought" (Hebrew). *Daat* 71 (2011): 105–131.

Rashkover, Randi L., and Martin Kavka. *Tradition in the Public Square: A David Novak Reader*. Grand Rapids, Mich.: Wm. B. Eerdmans Publishing Company, 2008.

Rogin, Michael. *Blackface, White Noise: Jewish Immigrants in the Hollywood Melting Pot*. Berkeley: University of California Press, 1996.

Rosenblatt, Bernard. *Social Zionism*. New York: Sinai Press, 1919.

———. *Two Generations of Zionism*. New York: Shengold Publishers, Inc., 1967.

Ross, Tamar. *Expanding the Palace of Torah: Orthodoxy and Feminism*. Waltham, Mass.: Brandeis University Press, 2004.

Sack, Daniel. *Whitebread Protestants: Food and Religion in American Culture*. New York: St. Martin's Press, 2000.

Said, Edward. "Invention, Memory, and Place." *Critical Inquiry* 26, no. 2 (Winter 2000): 175–192.

Sanders, Gavriel Aryeh. "Kosher Diva Outdoes Herself with Latest Offering." *Jewish World Review,* March 14, 2005. http://jewishworldreview.com/kosher/fishbein .php3.

Sarna, Jonathan. "'The Greatest Jew in the World since Jesus Christ': The Jewish Legacy of Louis D. Brandeis." *American Jewish History* 81, no. 3–4 (1994): 346–364.

———. "A Projection of America as It Ought to Be: Zion in the Mind's Eye of American Jews." In *Envisioning Israel: The Changing Ideals and Images of North American Jews,* edited by Allon Gal, 41–59. Detroit: Wayne State University Press, 1996.

Schor, Ilya. "A Working Definition of Jewish Art." *Conservative Judaism* 16, no. 1 (1961): 28–33.

Schwartz, Shuly Rubin. *The Rabbi's Wife: The Rebbetzin in American Jewish Life.* New York: New York University Press, 2006.

Seligman, Adam B., Robert P. Weller, Michael J. Puett, and Bennett Simon. *Ritual and Its Consequences: An Essay on the Limits of Sincerity.* New York: Oxford University Press, 2008.

Shandler, Jeffrey. "Heschel and Yiddish: A Struggle with Signification." *Journal of Jewish Thought and Philosophy* 2 (1993): 245–299.

Shandler, Jeffrey, and Beth S. Wenger. "'The Site of Paradise': The Holy Land in American Jewish Imagination." In *Encounters with the "Holy Land": Place, Past and Future in American Jewish Culture,* edited by Jeffrey Shandler and Beth S. Wenger, 11–40. Hanover, N.H.: Brandeis University Press, 1998.

Shapira, Anita. *Land and Power: The Zionist Resort to Force, 1881–1948.* Stanford, Calif.: Stanford University Press, 1999.

Shimoni, Gideon. *The Zionist Ideology.* Hanover, N.H.: Brandeis University Press, 1995.

Singer, David. "The New Orthodox Theology." *Modern Judaism* 9, no. 1 (February 1989): 35–54.

Singer, Merrill. "Symbolic Identity Formation in an African American Religious Sect: The Black Hebrew Israelites." In *Black Zion: African American Religious Encounters with Judaism,* edited by Yvonne Chireau and Nathaniel Deutsch, 55–72. New York: Oxford University Press, 2000.

Smith, Jonathan Z. *To Take Place: Toward Theory in Ritual.* Chicago: University of Chicago Press, 1987.

Soloveitchik, Joseph. *The Lonely Man of Faith.* New York: Doubleday, 1965.

Sommer, Benjamin D. *The Bodies of God and the World of Ancient Israel.* Cambridge: Cambridge University Press, 2009.

Soulen, R. Kendall. "The Achievement of Michael Wyschogrod." *Modern Theology* 22, no. 4 (October 2006): 677–685.

Stolow, Jeremy. "Communicating Authority, Consuming Tradition: Jewish Orthodox Outreach Literature and Its Reading Public." In *Religion, Media, and the Public Sphere,* edited by Birgit Meyer and Annelies Moors, 73–90. Bloomington: Indiana University Press, 2006.

———. *Orthodox by Design: Judaism, Print Politics, and the ArtScroll Revolution.* Berkeley: University of California Press, 2010.

Sturken, Marita, and Lisa Cartwright. *Practices of Looking: An Introduction to Visual Culture.* New York: Oxford University Press, 2001.

Taylor, Charles. *The Ethics of Authenticity.* Cambridge, Mass.: Harvard University Press, 1991.

Tinney, James. "Black Jews: A House Divided." *Christianity Today* (December 7, 1973): 52–53.

Tobin, Diane Kaufmann, Gary A. Tobin, and Scott Rubin. *In Every Tongue: The Racial & Ethnic Diversity of the Jewish People*. San Francisco: Institute for Jewish & Community Research, 2005.

Trible, Phyllis. *God and the Rhetoric of Sexuality*. Philadelphia: Fortress, 1978.

Trilling, Lionel. *Sincerity and Authenticity*. Cambridge, Mass.: Harvard University Press, 1972.

Troen, S. Ilan. "Frontier Myths and Their Applications in America and Israel: A Transnational Perspective." *Israel Studies* 5, no. 1 (2000): 301–329.

———. *Imagining Zion: Dreams, Designs, and Realities in a Century of Jewish Settlement*. New Haven, Conn.: Yale University Press, 2003.

The Union Haggadah: Home Service for the Passover. United States of America: The Central Conference of American Rabbis, 1923.

Urofsky, Melvin I. *American Zionism from Herzl to the Holocaust*. Lincoln: University of Nebraska Press, 1995.

Walker, John A., and Sarah Chaplin. *Visual Culture: An Introduction*. Manchester: Manchester University Press, 1997.

Wallach, Shalom M. *Pesach Haggadah with a Commentary Culled from the Classic Baalei Mussar*. New York: Mesorah, 1989.

Walzer, Michael. "Morality and Politics in the Work of Michael Wyschogrod." *Modern Theology* 22, no. 4 (October 2006): 687–692.

Washington, Harriet A. *Medical Apartheid: The Dark History of Medical Experimentation on Black Americans from Colonial Times to the Present*. New York: Anchor, 2006.

Weinraub, Bernard. "Arts in America: From Ordinary Faces, Extraordinary Ads." *New York Times*, February 21, 2002. http://www.nytimes.com/2002/02/21/arts/arts-in-america-from-ordinary-faces-extraordinary-ads.html.

Weiss, Elliott. "Packaging Jewishness: Novelty and Tradition in Kosher Food Packaging." *Design Issues* 20, no. 1 (Winter 2004): 48–61.

Wieseltier, Leon. "Comes the Comer." *Jewish Review of Books*, no. 9 (Spring 2012): 5–9.

Wolfson, Bernard. "African American Jews: Dispelling Myths, Bridging the Divide." In *Black Zion: African American Religious Encounters with Judaism*, edited by Yvonne Chireau and Nathaniel Deutsch, 33–54. New York: Oxford University Press, 2000.

Wolfson, Elliot. *Alef, Mem, Tau: Kabbalistic Musings on Time, Truth, and Death*. Berkeley: University of California Press, 2006.

———. *Through a Speculum that Shines: Vision and Imagination in Medieval Jewish Mysticism*. Princeton, N.J.: Princeton University Press, 1994.

Wyschogrod, Michael. *The Body of Faith: God in the People Israel*. Northvale, N.J.: Jason Aronson Inc., 1996.

———. "The Election of Israel: The Idea of the Chosen People." *Modern Theology* 12, no. 4 (October 1996): 491–493.

———. "A Jewish Perspective on Incarnation." *Modern Theology* 12, no. 2 (April 1996): 195–209.

———. *Kierkegaard and Heidegger: The Ontology of Existence*. London: Routledge & Paul, 1954.

———. "Responses to Friends." *Modern Theology* 22, no. 4 (October 2006): 701–704.

Wyschogrod, Michael, and R. Kendall Soulen. *Abraham's Promise: Judaism and Jewish–Christian Relations.* Grand Rapids, Mich.: Wm. B. Eerdmans Publishing Company, 2004.

Yerushalmi, Yosef Hayim. *Haggadah and History: A Panorama in Facsimile of Five Centuries of the Printed Haggadah.* Philadelphia: Jewish Publication Society of America, 1975.

Zakim, Eric. *To Build and Be Built: Landscape, Literature, and the Construction of Zionist Identity.* Philadelphia: University of Pennsylvania Press, 2006.

Zerubavel, Yael. "Desert and Settlement: Space Metaphors and Symbolic Landscapes in the Yishuv and Early Israeli Culture." In *Jewish Topographies: Visions of Space, Traditions of Place,* edited by Julia Brauch, Anna Lipphardt, and Alexandra Nocke, 201–222. Aldershot: Ashgate, 2008.

———. *Recovered Roots: Collective Memory and the Making of Israeli National Tradition.* Chicago: University of Chicago Press, 1995.

Zion, Noam, and David Dishon. *A Different Night.* Jerusalem: Shalom Hartman Institute, 2002.

Index

KEN KOLTUN-FROMM is Professor of Religion at Haverford College and author of *Moses Hess and Modern Jewish Identity* (IUP, 2001), which won the Koret Jewish Book Award for Philosophy and Thought; *Abraham Geiger's Liberal Judaism* (IUP, 2006); and *Material Culture and Jewish Thought in America* (IUP, 2010). He is also the editor of *Thinking Jewish Culture in America* (2014).